University of LOVE 101

Daily Channelled Messages From Aaron

Channelled by Wanda Lacey
Edited by Samantha Beaudry

Namaste ♡
Wanda

University of LOVE 101

Canadian Cataloguing in Publication Data
Lacey, Wanda 1963-
University of LOVE 101
isbn 978-1-7774137-1-2
1. Spirituality 2. Daily Meditations

Printed in Canada

For the two boys I share my heart with,
Michael and Broeghan

FOREWORD

Meeting Wanda was for me one of those magical serendipitous unexplainable moments that occur in our lives. She told me of her experiences as a channel of energy. So, we agreed to do a session and see what unfolded.

For me, it was much like sitting with a wise professor discussing topics of quantum physics, philosophy, and even the purpose of life and having it pose thought provoking questions back to me. It was quite surreal but equally fascinating, especially for a predominantly logical left brain analytic that I am.

We have now done over 30 such sessions together in which we have uncovered a myriad of information that challenges the conventional thoughts and teachings we have all learned in science classes and take as immutable laws of this physical world in which we live. You can watch these recorded sessions on Wanda's YouTube channel.

The energy called Aaron says that our connection was Divinely orchestrated to channel information for the good of humanity. According to Aaron, this information needs to 'resonate' with you to be understood; if not, it would be heard as gibberish. When you are ready for it, then you will be open to accept it and understand the message.

The messages provided in this book are transcriptions of the short daily meditations that Wanda has done with the Aaron energy. They provoke thought and reflection within us and can be used as part of our own daily meditation practices. In Aaron's words, they are simply reminding us of what we already know as being part of the Universe of Love. The messages also have an energetic quality to them (of course since all is energy) so can provide new information as they are reflected upon and digested.

I encourage you to read these messages with an open mind and to notice how the information sits within you. Does it feel like truth to you? Try not to judge from a position of your current understanding but instead be open to discovering new perspectives through it. In this way, I believe the magic will unfold and your understanding will blossom in a most powerful way.
Ash Knightley

"We are only reminding you of things that are common knowledge to the Universe and therefore, you." Aaron

PREFACE

I've always been a person who believed in a higher power and when I moved to British Columbia, my belief system exploded. I went to my first metaphysical fair and met a psychic who read my life as if we were best friends. I started to wonder what else was possible.

Then, I saw my first "ghost". It was my dad at 9 years old and I knew him immediately. I was intrigued. Then, I started to "see" a place where beings who had passed lived, and I was able to "hear" their stories. Above all, there was one high, clear voice coming through that appeared to have a higher knowing but no memory of a human life. They later agreed to be called Aaron. Then one day I found that I just had to open my mouth and allow words to pass through. At first, this seemed odd. Energy would visibly pass through me, and I started to talk with a different voice who spoke with authority and grace. Afterwards, I felt both filled up and empty. Apparently, this is presence.

When asked about my role during the energetic exchanges, Aaron describes me as the host who is an open, clear channel. LOVE energy creates vibrations in the vocal cords and a voice can be heard. Then there is a message from the Universe to you.

Often, I would channel words and post on my YouTube channel called Messages of Love From Beyond. I transcribed the words into these daily messages, and Samantha edited for readability, while keeping the intent of the messages.

I am grateful to have the chance to share this way of being with you. To touch, heal, and expand you is what the LOVE energy is about. I invite you to be open to the messages of LOVE. When the energy resonates with you as truth, it reminds you of your highest self and of the energy you are familiar with. Then you'll recall that you're from the Universe of LOVE. It has expanded my world greatly and I now move through the world with more grace and ease. Just like you will.

Namaste

January

Feel your emotions. All of them and allow others to do the same. Remember you came there to feel.

#AARONLACEY

January 1st
Home

There are times when you feel like a scolded child. It's like you must be ashamed for not knowing something that is beyond your grasp. Like a child who is going to be punished for not understanding. This is something you learned in school. They wanted you to keep up with the class even if you couldn't. There was a point when you couldn'tt' ask for understanding because the group had moved on and you were left behind. There was shame attached to that, as if you weren't smart enough. This is old shame.

Sometimes today the voice says, "Why can't you get this?" This was taught in a system where the masses must be trained on certain information and move together as a group. Not everyone fits into this organization. There are residual effects for you being involved in it as a small one.

This notion will resonate with you somewhere. This vibration is not a school system. You don't have to understand so you can build something. You just have to sit in this energetic vibration if you wish to feel moved. Your brain doesn't have to understand what's going on because this is not the business of the brain. This is the business of the soul or energetic self that resides inside each of you.

You may feel the vibration move through you energetically. We speak to you from soul to soul. You're not a young one who doesn't get it. You're a LOVING, energetic being who responds to LOVE with more LOVE. You receive it, you feel it, and then it passes through you to others. It's always moving because it's energy.

This is an energetic LOVE exchange, not a school lesson. This is between the Universe of LOVE and you. You're the Universe of LOVE in a human body. This is an energetic LOVE language. You are one with the Universe and all others.

There is much LOVE here for you.   Namaste

You have found your home. It's in the Universe of LOVE, which is you, all the others, and everything that surrounds you. It's where you go when you're not in physical form. You carry it with you.

January 2nd
Joyful Beings

One of the most important words of all, even though it only takes a breath to say, is 'joy'. It means you're in alignment. If you're able to feel joy, it means you're familiar with LOVE. The energy that passes through you causes you to feel joy.

When you come into your human form, you wish to maintain your joy all throughout. You thought you had enough Universe of LOVE energy to carry you through your lifetime, but it turns out there's unexpected incidences and you lose track of your joy.

Your reaction to losing joy is sadness because you value joy. Your sadness is reconfirming what your intention was. That's all, nothing more than that. You're longing for something you know exists but is not always available to you. But now you have access to it again because you're remembering joy. That's because you're in the energy of LOVE. To feel joy, there must be a connection to LOVE. You must be sitting in it. You have said, "Remind us about joy. We don't want to live too long without joy because we become bitter."

Joy is now stirring in the midst of you. You recall the times when you couldn't stop smiling with joy. You were overwhelmed with joy. Joy is often a very simple thing. Such as a tiny bird that falls but gets up. The sun coming up as it always does. This time you noticed the sun, and it was bright and beautiful, and you were suddenly filled with warmth.

There are many things that bring you joy each day, but you don't always notice them. Sometimes you're very busy with your human activities. What your body longs for and requires is joy. Your body requires joy to continue living in human form in a contented way.

There is much LOVE here for you.   Namaste

Every one of you intended to live a life of LOVE.

January 3rd
Give Yourself a Break!

True laughter and joy come from inside of you. It bubbles up and can't be stopped. Then there's false laughter: you use it to distract others by getting them to focus on something untrue. This distancing happens because you feel unworthy of true joy, connection, and laughter. You don't deserve intimate and joyful interactions. So, you make a loud joke and the moment of intimacy has passed.

You distance someone quickly if they share their most intimate self. The energies change and you start all over again. Why are you incapable of allowing another to share something intimate from their life? It's not about you. You fear that you're unworthy to hear it. If they understood how damaged you were as a human being, they wouldn't try to share this beautiful thing with you.

You're not comfortable with intimacy yourself. But it's important for you to get to this place of unworthiness so you may heal and evolve. See how uncomfortable that is, and how you rejected the intimacy of another human because you feel unworthy. Then you feel guilty because you rejected them. Now you're back on that old treadmill of guilt and low self-esteem.

How about letting it go and giving yourself a break? It turns out you're all the same. The human that is sharing intimately further on in the day will be in the same position as you. They will be unable to handle another's intimacy. You're all the same, because you're all blessed beings trying to get though a human existence causing the least amount of pain to yourself and others. That's not easy. Give yourself a break.

There is much LOVE here for you.   Namaste

For you to become the LOVING human you notice and envy in others, you must go to this place of unworthiness and let it go, so you may evolve into the beautiful LOVING human you are deep inside.

January 4th
How Could I Forget?

Your soul or your energetic self knows everything. Somehow you know this is true for you.

You have taken your energetic selves into physical bodies. The brain and ego have been doing their part in your human experience. You came into physical to have this experience, to see what mischief you could get up to. You were also curious to see how long you could maintain energetic LOVE. You all have this notion that is childlike and innocent. You thought you would always remember your intimate connection with the Universe of LOVE. The moment you stepped into your human form, you started to forget your purest self. Not the ego and the way you look on the outside; that's not your true self. That's your 'frolicking about in human form' self.

Now you will be able to let go of your physical body and mind so you may fully experience your divine self. Once you're reminded of how precious you are to the Universe, there's no going back. What you see out of the corner of your eye that is unclear, is your divine self. Right there staring at you. Your divine self is the pure innocent Universe of LOVE. It's open-eyed with a little smile, always staring at you. No wonder you can't stare at it too long: its LOVE is blinding. It's overwhelming really. Now you can see your divine self, smiling at you. As if it has nothing else to do but smile and LOVE you all day long. And to remind you of your beautiful, divine self. It really has nothing else to do. This is your energetic self. Isn't it a beautiful thing?

There is much LOVE here for you.   Namaste

I could never forget the Universe of LOVE. Never. Because I am the Universe of LOVE.

January 5th
Hello, Self

There comes a time for each of you when you come up against yourself. This is a great meeting. It often happens when your defenses are down, usually when you're in a crisis or a vulnerable state. Then, your stronger and evolved energetic self stands to hold you up. When your human body is weak, your energetic body is strong. You get through a crisis by feeling strength that you couldn't name. When this occurs again, be sure to say hello and recognize what's happening.

You're starting to evolve and allow more space for energy and wonder. It seems odd you wouldn't recognize yourself, but you don't. Your body and your energetic self are not familiar with one another. Your energetic self is part of a larger Universe of LOVE. It's connected through eternity but the body changes.

The Universe of LOVE energy connects all humans together. You're all having an energetic experience. That's how you're able to connect with some humans who are exposing their energetic self more clearly. This energetic self is joy. You've seen humans who have a small smile and a sense of ease, no matter what's happening. They realize life's not a big deal, because soon you won't have a body and you'll be in some other life, some other body, and some other crisis. The energetic selves don't get too worked up about what's going to happen to you today. Humans that are familiar with their energetic self are at ease with others and the life they lead.

The next time your human self meets your energetic self, allow them to say hello and embrace one another. Say, "I really need you right now. I'm glad you're here." Just by acknowledging the energetic self is there brings your energy to a different level. It opens up your sense of self, your sense of oneness with the Universe and others.

There is much LOVE here for you.   Namaste

Embrace your energetic self and just say hello.

January 6th
LOVE Heals All

The little ones have no say in the way their lives unfold. This is a surrendering to a higher purpose. When you come into physical, you're coming from a nurturing and LOVING place. That energy comes through you so you're coming into your human body vulnerable.

You're full of hope and trust that you'll continue having LOVE energy in a physical body. Yes, you'll always have Universal LOVE energy whether you're in physical or not.

LOVE energy turns into vibration. That's how you're aware of different types of energy in your world. When you're doing energy work, you can feel something moving inside of you. Some of you have evolved to drawing it forth through the fingertips and out.

All of you may call yourselves healers because you've always been interested in the higher good. Now that you're in human form, you're interested in the higher good for humanity. You wish to heal the earth and others. You're saying, "I have always been part of LOVE energy. I've always been surrendering to the higher good and now that I am in physical, I don't know what that means anymore."

As you heal from your human experiences, you'll get back to the beginning. Then you will understand what you're to do in your present day. You cannot serve others until you are healed.

When you're in the energy of the Universe of LOVE you must heal because LOVE heals all. Then you're free to LOVE openly. You'll naturally heal the place where you reside, by allowing LOVE in and out of you, because it's your most natural state.

There is much LOVE here for you.   Namaste

There's a surrendering that's familiar to you as it relates to the Universe of LOVE. When you're not in physical, your energy is together. It's a surrendering to a larger purpose. A larger sense of being.

January 7th
Covered in LOVE Energy

There are many of you who are naturally curious and are becoming aware of vibration. Your electrical devices have caused vibrations to multiply. Your world is becoming more energized. It stimulates some who have been sleeping.

Some are more comfortable and say, "Oh, that's energy from the Universe. Can you feel it coming from that human? You can tell how they feel without speaking to them." As you speak more in this way, humans will start taking you aside. They say, "What did you mean by that? This odd thing happened to me, and I don't have anyone to speak to about it."

Now your role has changed. You're still a curious and invited participant and there will always be channels for you to converse with the Universe of LOVE. But now your role has grown to being a channel of information. We don't mean to start telling others about energy. It'll have the opposite effect. What we mean is when you speak normally: "That's an energetic thing to do" or, "The sun is out. I felt energy." That will allow others to hear it.

You are comfortable enough with it so it's not necessary for you to hide out any longer. Then the ones at the edges will come forth a little. This is the way LOVING energy works. It's very gentle. It's transforming you so you may be gentle, too. Others will come to you in a comfortable way because you're a gentle and kind person.

As you become this gentle human, you receive energy yourself. You become aware of it around you more easily. You're starting to live in an energetic world even though you're in a human body. Once you experience the connection and ease with other humans on an energetic level, you'll feel safe in the world because you're feeling energy. There's no way for you to go back to fear and anxiety. Now you may evolve further.

There is much LOVE here for you.   Namaste

You're showing up as the Universe of LOVE in physical: calm, peaceful, inviting, and gentle. Your highest evolution is to embrace the Universe of LOVE in your human form. Your next thing is to allow others to see it. Right now, you're covered in LOVE energy.

January 8th
You Are Never Alone

Humiliation and ridicule are things you fear. You will do everything to avoid them, including limiting what you say and how you live. You stay small. What if you weren't fearful of humiliation and shame, which cause you anxiety?

At the bottom of your shame, which comes from the ridicule of others, is a sense that you are unworthy of unconditional LOVE. You don't want to sit in this. A shameful experience goes back to this undeserving place.

Shame goes deeper. "I'm not worthy to be in this body or this space." Now sit in that place for a moment, even though you're uncomfortable sitting in unworthiness.

The next level is sadness. You don't like to sit there either but there is more. Your true sadness is the disconnect from the Universe of LOVE. It's your longing to be together. For intimacy and LOVE. That is what's underneath your sadness. You feel disconnected from those you belong to. That is at the heart of your disconnect. The disconnect occurs when you jump into your human body.

You left your energetic family to join your human family. But, sometimes, you wish to leave your human family to rejoin your energetic family. Really, you wish to join a family because you're not great alone. You feel like you are wandering aimlessly through your emotions and your life.

As you sit in your feelings of loneliness and disconnect from your family, both physical and non-physical, you'll feel it lifting. You'll begin to feel lighter as you come to know you're never alone. For you to get to this place of knowing, you must pass through these emotions. In your state of extreme emotion, your family rushes forward to calm you.

It's important to go through each emotion you try to avoid, so you can feel a sense of belonging, oneness, and connection with the Universe of LOVE. You know you belong. It's your place to be. You've come from LOVE. You exist in LOVE. You are LOVE.

There is much LOVE here for you. Namaste

You are never alone. You are greatly LOVED.

January 9th
All You Have To Do is Ask

Being vulnerable is uncomfortable. You become possessive of your body and wish to protect it from harm. You watch your nutrition. You decide what people are allowed to say. Some of you know where the line is but you go past it for extra protection: "I also mean that I am going to do this whether you like it or not." It's beyond what your basic necessities are.

Why do you have such an urge to demand more than you need emotionally and physically? You're overprotective so you distract yourself. You distract yourself with many things, like cookies. But when you're sitting right here, you're vulnerable.

You look vulnerable just sitting there. Someone could come along and grab you. By overcompensating you create distraction from yourself. But, what's wrong with 'yourself'? What's wrong with sitting and being vulnerable? Is there something you don't wish the others to see? You're the same energetic LOVE you were the moment you stepped into your body. Sure, you've had lots more experiences bumping around and taking things that weren't yours. But you're still the same LOVE energy you always were.

Why is that so vulnerable? Is it painful for you to sit in a LOVE bubble? You are spiritual beings having a human experience in the body, that's all. It's simple.

All energetic LOVE humans have the capability to channel LOVE at every moment. Not just for others, for YOU. When you sit quietly, and are vulnerable and afraid, thinking you're going to disappear, you may channel LOVE. Although you are sitting in fear, one moment later you may be sitting in LOVE, ecstasy, and joy. You are all capable of this because you're LOVE energy. All you're doing is attracting more LOVE energy to your energy. You're just saying, "I need a little more LOVE and support." Then it comes. All you have to do is ask. You'll be filled right up to the top.

There is much LOVE here for you.   Namaste

Why am I afraid to be vulnerable?

January 10th
Ease & Comfort

When you allow more LOVE to pass through you and let it sit in you, you feel more whole. As if there's always been a piece missing and you weren't sure what it was. You feel more LOVE. This is the greatest human word. It's the energy you are when you're not in physical. It also exists around you all the time. It feels like pressure close to you. When you remember, you smile more easily and your feelings are not hurt as easily. You're thinking that everything will be all right and you're in the right place. You feel at ease.

Ease is an important word for humans. Usually you are uncomfortable and wonder what you should say next. You're not sure if others like you so you create a falseness to deal with this unease. "If she doesn't like me, I don't like her." That's not your highest, most LOVING self. You're not at ease passing through the world. You're not going forward.

You'll become more at ease with LOVE because it's familiar to you. Your highest potential is to sit in ease all the time. When you get used to this feeling of being comfortable, you'll start longing for it. It will become normal.

You're learning to be comfortable in the place where you belong, where you've chosen to exist, where you're growing. When you came into physical, you thought you could carry LOVE energy with you and share it with the others because they were becoming distant from it. As you know now, it's not easy to recall and share.

Sharing LOVE energy is your purpose and intention. Once you have learned how to sit in it, you'll recall that more often.

There is much LOVE here for you.   Namaste

You'll feel ease and comfort when you're back on the path of your purpose.

January 11th
Great LOVER

There is always sadness with change. As you evolve, others are left behind, along with experiences that don't fit with your new way of being. There are many pieces that make up a whole life. Often one piece must be left behind. This feeling of sadness is important to notice because you're saying goodbye.

When you say, "I'm going to a different place", you take all your heavy belongings and start walking. You can't see what's at the end of the road so you become fearful. There's part of you that wishes to turn around and go back to the familiar door. Now you've moved from sadness to fear. After fear comes joy and peace. That's what calls you down unfamiliar roads. You know there's something beautiful at the end. Soon you'll forget there was a door. You have a new focus now. Trees and rocks you've never seen. You always need something physical to remind you that you're having a human experience.

Soon you'll be leaving your baggage. Some physical things are important only at the time. As you evolve, you'll find different things to have. This is where the lightness comes in. This is your journey through life. You have shut many doors. You learn from the experience. You spend time in the room. You know everything inside of it. Then you leave the room, shut the door, and don't return. Then you move to the next place. There's no need for regret because you're always on a forward journey into the unknown.

You are great explorers and adventurers. You're drawn to the unknown and the promise it holds of beauty, peace, LOVE, and joy. You're a curious, LOVING being. You're drawn to LOVE. That is what's at the end of the road. You're going down the road to find more of yourself. To increase your capacity to LOVE and feel joy. What higher purpose could there be, then for LOVE to seek out more LOVE? It's your way of evolution. Like attracts like. It's your nature to be great LOVERS.

There is much LOVE here for you.   Namaste

It takes courage to close a door and walk down a strange road. You're having a human experience and each event is emotionally heavy for you. But the Universe is always there to support humanity.

January 12th
I Am Proud of You

"I am proud of who I am. I am proud of who you are." 'Proud' is a nurturing word, like from a parent to a child who stands up for the first time. This word is also a conveyance of LOVE. "I give LOVE to you," means, "I'm proud of you."

What if you say, "I give my LOVE to you" silently? And what if it wasn't saved for special occasions when someone has done something admirable? What if it were done when you see a human being? What if you LOVE them no matter what state they are in.

When you say you are proud, you're saying, "I'm giving extra LOVE to you. I'm feeling close to you. I wish to hold you close." What if you eliminated the word 'proud' and just recalled this feeling? Then can you look at another human silently and give this LOVE message?

How many times do you think you could recall this emotion of overwhelming LOVE? How many times do you think you could give it to someone else without saying anything? This could be a new way of being for you. Your role as a LOVING citizen of the earth and an energetic being is about letting LOVE in and out.

So how about giving LOVE to your LOVED ones, to strangers, and to those in pain? How about sending it through the air, allowing it to land wherever it will? How about being proud of all the humans who are now trying to live a human life while being spiritual, energetic beings on the inside?

How about being proud of each energetic being that decides to jump into a human body thinking they are going to share LOVE and ending up in all kinds of messes?

There is much LOVE here for you.   Namaste

Look in the mirror and say, "I am proud of you." Learn to say it silently because then you'll really be saying "I LOVE you. It's always about letting LOVE in and allowing LOVE out."

January 13th
Because You Are Precious

You are precious to the Universe. This is impactful to humans, the Universe and energy. This one sentence is impactful to the future, the past, and all energy you bump up against in your travels. Why would you be precious? To you, precious is only used for the most exquisite item. You don't use it often. But every single human is precious to the Universe. It's a different way of thinking to believe every one of you is precious to the Universe.

Specifically, how could you be precious to the Universe? You haven't contributed any great event to mankind. This is the fundamental cornerstone of our teaching. If you don't believe you are precious, you won't get the rest of it. These words, this energy, must come from a place of value in yourself. The Universe holds you in a place of regal authority. Don't get your ego involved. It doesn't't want you to believe you're precious. But your energetic self understands this as truth.

You are precious to the Universe because you've come into human form where many haven't. Nothing you do will change how the Universe sees you. This is difficult for you to believe. You have come to learn during your time there that you must earn things.

We're not speaking to the brain because it can't understand this. We're speaking to your energetic self. You're energy from the Universe of LOVE. When you're in human and when you're not, you are still LOVE energy.

Because you're precious to the Universe, you have all the energetic support and LOVE needed to make it through your human existence. You're so precious to the Universe that all the help you desire is available for you anytime you ask. You're our precious human beings and we adore you.

There is much LOVE here for you.   Namaste

You have been granted your 'precious' status by becoming a human being.

January 14th
Peace & Ease

Enough of you have been energetically moved that you're able to remember what's happening in the Universe. Where you exist when you're not in physical.

When your energy is invigorated, it can see beyond what's happening this moment. Then there's much available to you. You're starting to understand beyond right now and into the energy field that surrounds you. Perhaps even beyond this. You are starting to remember great things. The more of you who remember, the more who will be triggered. Great energy is available. It's circulating from one human to the other. It's growing. It's triggering memories and knowing's. It's easier for you to recognize an energetic thought. This is energy being awakened inside of you.

Many things have been held dormant while you had your human experience. But now, it turns out, you can have both your energetic and physical self. As if two lives are coming together as one. You're evolving. You're becoming.

LOVE is flowing into you and out of you. You move with ease from decision to decision. You feel peace, contentedness and joy most times. It's all coming together. Things unfold easily. You're not reactionary to life. You instead embrace it. This is how you live a contented, easy, peaceful life. Joy and LOVE follow naturally.

You're finding peace in the fact that 'you' are energy and human, living together in a life of ease. You're sharing LOVE with yourself and others. Many of you are coming from a life of disorder. You're seeking peace now and you've found it, right inside of you.

There is much LOVE here for you. Namaste

All along you were carrying LOVE energy with you. It was just waiting for you to remember your divine self.

January 15th
What Are You Doing Here?

There comes a time when you are in conflict with another human being and you're not sure whether you should run or hit them over the head. You are powerful beings. You've come into physical form and can do everything with your body so you have a rush of energy when you need it. You understand it's not just you with these confrontations. You've figured out there's a whole army here. Sometimes you feel strong. That's the energy from the Universe you're pulling forth.

You might think it's a feeling or ego, but it's actually the energy coming when you're in an angry, confrontational state. Your energy goes really high. It's like an antenna that draws energy. You're huge energetically. This could scare the other human. They have their antenna up so the energy's coming to them, too. Now, there's a lot of energy going. So, there's two humans standing and having a conflict. Suddenly the energy says," What's going on? Nothing? We're on high alert for no reason." Energy is curious about human nature but mostly when you call it forth there's no real conflict.

Falling off a cliff and arguing feels the same energetically. The energy comes to you as you're trying to fight with someone who's unaware of their power, too. You're both going to stand there until you get tired of each other. Then you're going to leave.

What is the point of these discussions that are distasteful or uncomfortable for you? You're making sure you're still human. "I'm still nasty if I need to be." You're learning energetic things. You spend time in meditation. You're trying to be one with Universal energy. But every once in a while, you want a taste of humanity. You came to be human. Some of you are moving beyond this basic self and mingling with energy. If you get caught up in the energetic exchanges, LOVE, peace and joy, you can argue to remind yourself. You're trying to expand your energetic self as much as possible while staying in a human body. This is the great experiment you're having. "How far can we stretch energetically and still stay in human form?"

There is much LOVE here for you. Namaste

Do not be afraid to be human. Do not be afraid to evolve. That is what you are doing there.

January 16th
LOVE Never Dies

Humans say goodbye to one another even if they've joined emotional energy. This is the difficult part to let go of because your energy is mingled. Energies must stay close together to remain vibrant. It turns out that goodbye maintains the vibrancy between the two human beings, sometimes even more. It's through fond memories. Ones more sensitive to energy feel a magnetic pull toward one another.

It's difficult to separate magnets. This is just physics. When they're separated, they still exist and grow. If you don't like to separate magnets, you're not going to like this, but standing alone, the energy still exists the same. You in them. Them in you. Think of all the humans who have touched your life. Some have passed beyond your human vision, and some are non-physical. You recall them with great delight. It's an example of maintaining a bit of someone else's energy while keeping your own.

Even though they are not around, the energy grows and goes faster. You may gather all the LOVE energy you wish. It will only increase your vibration. The more humans you hold in LOVE energy inside you, the more evolved, kind, caring, and LOVING you are. And the calmer you are.

Focus now on this energy inside you. Feel it escalating the more you think of the humans you have LOVED and cared for. The more you picture their face, their energy is revived. Suddenly you feel they are here now. They still exist energetically within you.

You have a large energy field all around you.   There's lots of space for human LOVE. Both yours and others. There's always space for more LOVE. Yes, you can let them go. They're not really going anywhere, are they? They're staying with you.

There is much LOVE here for you.   Namaste

LOVE does not die, it transforms into energy. Humans do not die either. They transform into energy. They are always around you also. Energy always lives; therefore, LOVE always lives.

January 17th
What is Going On Here?

When you're out of alignment, you don't understand yourself. Therefore, you cannot understand the Universe. But there's something going on between the two. It's a vibrational meeting of the hearts. All together as one vibration. All in vibrational unity.

We are one. You are one. The energy of LOVE is one. That's why you understand it. When you're in the vibration of LOVE, you understand this vibration. You understand the heart of other humans. You speak at a different level. You understand what's truly going on. Not what's getting the loudest attention. That's not reality. The real reality is this heart-to-heart vibration. When you understand you are LOVE, there's LOVE around you. The Universe of LOVE is coming through in a vibrational way. It's the same as you. You're all the same because you exist as one, when you are not in physical body.

You are the Universe of LOVE. You are LOVE energy. When you're not in your body, you are energy. When you can't understand energy, you're into the world of mankind, looking shiny and talking fast. That world of your brain is entertaining for a time, but at the heart of you, that need is not being filled. There's a sense of longing.

You have said, "We need to remember." So, you designed this avenue. When you can't understand, sit quietly for a few moments. You'll remember. This vibration is the one you've known the longest. The one you're most familiar with. It's where you reside when you're not in a human body. It lives inside of you now. All of you.

There is much LOVE here for you. Namaste

You are familiar with the vibration of LOVE because you are LOVE.

January 18th
Yay! We Did It

As always, it's important to start at the beginning. Directly from where you are now, to where the incident or emotion took root. The first part of your journey. As a group, you all may go back to the beginning to have a shared experience.

It's the moment of opening your eyes and realizing, "It worked! I've got a human body." You were overwhelmed with joy. Your greatest moment was to go from non-physical to physical. You thought, "Look at us. We're going to share LOVE. It's going to be great fun!" That's your team that surrounds you. At the very first moment, you were learning to separate yourself because you had been in the LOVE soup for so long.

You started to understand your humanity and to 'feel'. This is when the separation occurred. There was excitement and joy but also, sadness. This was soon lost because there was a lot to learn. You had to learn to fit in with the others who had a head start. You were excited to share LOVE with other humans, but humanity stepped in and sidetracked you. You forgot about the Universe of LOVE. It's okay because you all forgot. You're humans. You don't need any guilt or shame with forgetting the Universe of LOVE.

It's great news for you to remember, before you finish your humanity, because through all of eternity, most have forgotten. You came in with great surprise and delight. Then you started to distance yourself from the Universe of LOVE because you were entering into your human time. You forgot about it for most of your time unless there was an emergency, of course. Now you're remembering and feeling shame for having forgotten. Now you can delight in the discovery. "I remember the Universe of LOVE."

You can go back to the first moment right now. "Hey, I made it. Now we're going to share LOVE with the other humans just like I wished before I came into humanity."

There is much LOVE here for you.   Namaste

Your team always surrounds you. They are together with you in the LOVE soup.

January 19th
Blessed Beings

Sometimes you feel a sense of loss or disconnect from others. This
feeling of alienation and loneliness is common. In the beginning, Sit in
this place where you don't belong, with humans who don't understand
you. As you sit in this place of isolation, something quickly follows it.
It's a resonating answer. It's energy that flows into your body. It heats
you up. You start to feel tingly and confused. Your head is itchy,
perhaps, and it's tingling. Now you're curious. The Universe has
answered and is letting you 'feel 'what energy straight from the
Universe feels like. Why would you sit in a sense of isolation and
suddenly feel hot and tingly? You ask a question. "Why do I feel
alone?" The energy answers. If you're able to hear auditory, you'll hear
your answers. Until you hear clearly in that vibration, you will feel the
energy moving through you. That's the beginning stages.

Through all eternity, you're not alone. You're energy that is
joined with other energy. When you start to fully comprehend what an
energetic being is, you'll come to understand that it's impossible to be
alone. Energy attracts energy. It's not static. Energy always moves.
That's how you know you're alive. Energy comes from the Universe of
LOVE. It's energy that you're all part of. When you're not in human
form, you're in this energy. That's why you know what it feels like.
That's why you know you're never alone.

That means there are things going on around you that you're
unaware of. This is where you decide to alienate yourself from energy
so you may have a false sense of control over your life. You need to
believe you're a single entity travelling through time. This takes great
self-will. Your ego decides this path, but it's short sighted. It's only
alive as long as you exist in this human form. Your energetic self exists
through all time and at this moment is connected to energy and all other
human beings who exist.

There is much LOVE here for you.   Namaste

*You always know the truth. You know where you belong and who you
are. This is not a place to hide from, it's a place to go. You are a
blessed being. You have come into physical form to share LOVE with
others. That is your highest evolution. There is nothing to fear.*

January 20th
You Can Do This Thing

You're the one left holding the bag. The one who's more upset than the others. The one the fingers are pointing at. Your seat. You don't like to be pointed out like this. You're saying this on the inside. You don't always wish to know truth. You try to keep honesty out and, most of all, vulnerability.

You don't wish to feel vulnerable because you might die of extreme emotion. It's the worst thing you can think of. The Universe of LOVE says, "This thing looks awful on the outside until we shine it up. Then it's beautiful. Suddenly it's LOVE again."

If you sit in the vulnerable place, you'll find out you're one of those humans with emotions and concern for others. The ones trying to have a human experience and hurt as few people as possible while trying to LOVE yourself and share LOVE with others. You realize you were sharing LOVE but they misunderstood. You're vulnerable because you got caught trying to share LOVE and your feelings got hurt.

You crave to be a human and a spiritual entity. Those two are with you for your entire human life. Perhaps it's time to get used to both of them mingling together. But you're going to have to be vulnerable and sit in things that are uncomfortable. But only for a moment. Then it comes back to the LOVE place.

It's not always easy but it can be more fun than you're making it. All you have to do is be vulnerable now and again and then let it pass back to the LOVE. That's where the fun is. That's where the joy, peace and calmness are. All mingled up in the LOVE part.

There is much LOVE here for you. Namaste

You are covered in LOVE. There is LOVE energy naturally attracted to you and coming from you at all moments.

January 21st
Magic

Humility is not often addressed. As you allow things to unfold and allow LOVE to flow into you and out of you, you're noticing that your life is unfolding easily. You're not struggling with decisions or relationships. Your life looks so easy.

The energetic way to live is to allow things to unfold, stay out of the way of natural grace and the evolving of others. There's not much that's your business if you allow yourself to be put in a place to be used. It's the opposite of forcing and making decisions yourself. It's allowing LOVE and grace to get into the middle of squabbles, relationships or decisions.

But here's the trap. When others notice they wonder why your life's unfolding easily. Your humility comes in your response. "I don't know anything. I stay out of the way so I don't complicate matters. I allow LOVE to flow into me, out of me, around me and through me. I can't predict the future because I don't have all the information."

You might prefer to say, "Read this, go there or try this method." That would be the easiest answer but not done in humility. In actual fact, when you get out of the way, you're saying, "I don't know what's best but I will be involved if necessary."

This is a humbling place for a human. You like to know things. It's your natural curiosity, but in these matters, humility is called for. Say, "I try to stay out of the way and allow life to come through me and take me with it. I go on grand adventures. I don't know where I'm going, or who I'll meet, but they're great fun." They won't mind hearing that. They can see the peace in your face. Life is easy now. Just stay out of the way and the magic unfolds. By your human meaning of it, LOVE energy is magic, after all.

There is much LOVE here for you.   Namaste

Allowing life to unfold is allowing LOVE and grace to get into the middle of things.

January 22nd
Brand New Ideas

You believe you may understand things completely and then put them in a box. It's a comforting idea. When you put this box away, there are many other boxes there. Perhaps you have closets full of boxes. Perhaps rooms. These boxes suggest that a life may be contained and stay in there.

Your life is energy. Your ideas and information are always changing. As a matter of fact, your past also changes. An experience you had was judged by your eyes, the information you had at the time and your maturity level. If you were to go back today, it would be different. You would see things you didn't notice. You would feel differently about it, so you wouldn't react. You would allow the thing to unfold.

You think you can't handle any more than what's in the box. There's more happening. There are others involved behind the scenes that are affected by you. They are all moving. It's energy, and even though the event was previous, it still moves throughout time because a memory is energy. It meets up with other energy that has a similar experience and humans that were involved in it.

These memory boxes are full of energy and energy does not stay in a box. So, these boxes of your life experiences are empty. The room is empty also. Ideas, exchanges, and memories are always evolving, even if they have passed.

This goes beyond you to boxing groups of human experiences together. To boxing a life. Everything you do is mimicked and the energy goes forth. Pretty soon it's a pattern. It's energetic phenomena. Then other humans join with your energy.

It's just as easy to open the door and allow it all free. Firstly, in your mind. Then it will go outward. It's important for you to clear out the room of memories, ideas, notions, and philosophies. They're all gone anyway. They've mutated into other things. They've changed, but you haven't. It's your moment to open up your mind, life, and heart. Then you'll have more space to live your life today.

There is much LOVE here for you.   Namaste

Can you truly put a life in a box?

January 23rd
I Am in Alignment

There comes a time when you've had enough of what others think about what you should do or who you should be. Saying, "I know what's best for me" is one of the most powerful statements. It's you coming into alignment. You're coming into your personal information because you're getting it directly from the Universe of LOVE. Only you know what's right for you. There are generous people trying to do nice things and tell you how to live your life. They just don't know. Unfortunately, the reason they tell you is because they don't know how to live their own lives.

You know how to get into alignment when necessary. It's not a long dialogue. Just one sentence. It's complete.

Also, many of you are the ones who say, "I think this is a good idea for you." This is a powerful place in which you feel you must help others, because you don't understand that you may help yourself. Anytime you wish to be of service to others, first say, "I am in alignment." The words bring you directly to it. Then you have no desire or need to help others. You've got all kinds of complicated ideas, books, and talks about how to get into alignment, but that's all you have to say. It draws the energy right back to you.

You have access to unlimited information and power. You may get into alignment any moment you wish, or you may stumble around in your time there. That's absolutely fine. You're there to experience what you wish to experience.

If there are others who wish to seek peace and ease of life, they'll come to you because you're standing in alignment smiling. That's the kind of human being that others are drawn to. You don't have to find them and help them. Stay in your alignment. Those who seek to be like you will come to you.

There is much LOVE here for you.   Namaste

When you are in alignment, all things come to you. Life flows easily. Life flows to you. You just float down the river. You don't have to help others. They have their own resources.

January 24th
Longing

It's as if you've lost something important. Envision a child who has misplaced a toy. They will cry and look and cry. It's like they've lost their best friend. You have that sense that something is lost, but you're unsure why. The child values the object for the feeling of oneness, comfort, and LOVE it creates. Human emotions are put onto the object.

You can place LOVE or belonging onto something. When it's missing, you feel sad. You have a roaming sense of sadness and need to attach to something so you feel complete, secure, and LOVED. These phenomena exist from childhood to adulthood. It's attachment to something outside of you. It's the Universe of LOVE, energetic force or non-physical beings. You know that you're more than what you see.

This feeling of sadness is not at all times. When you keep yourself busy with work, humans, business, and friends, there's no space for you to sit quietly. There has to be time allowed to get through the many daily emotions and get to a place where your higher self resides and truth lives. Sometimes it's easier for you to stay in your human busyness. Because when space is allowed, you find a longing for LOVE.

This is why you find LOVING partners and think they are the LOVE you're missing. But it's bigger than humans or objects. It's your LOVE attachment to non-physical. The place where you reside when you're not in your body. When you're joined with multitudes of energy. This is your family. In this place of oneness, there's peace and LOVE. You feel complete. This is the longing you have.

There is much LOVE here for you.   Namaste

Sit quietly, allow the busyness to finish its thinking, then set it aside. Sit quietly in a longing place with a bit of sadness in it. Pass through the sadness and into the LOVE. Sitting in sadness and longing automatically attracts LOVE energy. The Universe always responds to your energetic call. You are never alone there. Although, sometimes you feel as if you are.

January 25th
Heart Connection

Lessons. Try harder. Get better marks. You think, "Surely at this time of my life I don't have to pass this class." So, at this time of your life you're deciding you will do things differently. Maybe experience more and learn less with numbers and words. Perhaps you would not try so hard to get straight A's. Maybe live more.

When you begin to live your life the best way you can, you might stumble. Sometimes you'll rejoice and jump with joy. Nonetheless, you want to distance yourself from this classroom life. It was stressful and hard. To sit there day after day trying to get your head around information that you weren't concerned with. Yet this created a pattern that you carried because it was in your early conditioning to please others and get around the system. To figure out how to get an 'A' without doing all the work in the middle.

Really, it taught you how to work around things instead of through them. Some of this time was not your happiest and yet, it was an essential part of your life. It trained you how to live in the world. Even today. The idea that you must earn your way through life was established early on. Now it's time to reconsider this. Pleasing superiors is difficult to leave behind.

What if the real lesson was this: "I may build relationships with other humans and maintain them. I may understand humans that are having a similar experience. I may feel empathy, caring, and learn how to share." The real lesson in life is this: find your brothers and sisters in energy and work together.

You can still learn the lesson that was not taught before, which was: LOVE one another on an energetic level. Find the similarities and come to understand you're all working together for a higher good. It's not about pleasing others after all. You may connect to one another on an energetic level.

There is much LOVE here for you.   Namaste

Let me find those who I connect with energetically and have a heart conversation. From soul to soul. That is what you are always seeking.

January 26th
Great Depths of You

There are depths to you. Depths of despair. Depths of kindness. Depths of frustration. You're not always as you seem. You're much more. You're divine. You're connected to energy. You're an energetic being. There are depths to your energy. You may feel the edges of your vibrational or energetic self.

Sometimes you think, "I didn't know that." Yet, you do. Now you're curious. "How do I know that? This person seems familiar to me. I can connect with this stranger on a very deep level." These are the upper edges of energy. They're the light sprinkling of energy which is often noticed in your connection to others. Sometimes your energy is triggered, as is theirs, and it comes out. Then, suddenly it's touching.

It's a connection or a tingling. These are the superficial parts of energy and the superficial parts of you. Underneath all of this is a deeper knowing that you're connected to all humans and the Universe. This is the complicated part of energy. You're nothing and everything. You're connected to all. Humans, life-force and non-physical. You're large in this way and yet small, because you're the same as the others. You all move as one and also alone. You move alone because you have a body. You move as one because your energetic self is always connected to others. You're all moving in different directions and yet, you're in the same energetic force field.

This is the depths of you. You're an eternal energetic being living a small life in this one lifetime with this one body. Since you're eternal and all of the others are too, you're all connected as one. That makes up the Universe of LOVE.

The depths of you are also great joy and a great capacity for LOVE. The depths of you are happy times. Times of remembering. Your great capacity to connect with another in an energetic way. Your ability to LOVE others even though you don't know them. To connect with the Universe and the energy that's available to you. Your great attachment to LOVE energy.

There is much LOVE here for you.   Namaste

The complicated part of energy is that you are nothing and everything.

January 27th
You Decide

There comes a time for each of you where you must face yourself. A moment when you recognize you're separate from the others. That you are 'you'. That you have this body, personality, and sense of humour. Also, that you're the only one. This can be overwhelming. You look in the mirror and think, "I'm the only one who does that. The only one that thinks this way or who acts this way." This is a very personal moment for you. You're used to acting as a group.

Through all eternity there will only be one 'you'. So, what are you to do if you're the only one? You must have an important mission.

You are the only one, and so are the others. What if you don't have to do anything special? What if, after recognizing that you're individual, you melt in with the others? When you're in non-physical, you're a big group working together. You don't have any 'you' or 'us', you have 'we'. A collective of LOVE. Then you hop into this body. Then you realize you are just 'you'. Now you may choose to be part of the Universe of LOVE and meld with the others.

When you're you in your human body, you decide how your life goes. You can say yes, no, or maybe. The most important part of you is recognizing, "I am Me." Do whatever you wish. You don't always have to choose good. You also get to decide if you wish to join the others that you're comfortable with. That you become stronger energetically when you're together. You decide. The great thing about being human is free will.

You came to play around with free will. "Should I stay or should I go?" The point that you're proving over and over, day after day is: "I will decide. I don't want to join the Universe of LOVE. I want to join the Universe of LOVE. I don't want to be with them. I want to be with them."

There is much LOVE here for you. Namaste

Every moment of your life you get to decide what your life looks like. Isn't that a wondrous gift? Your greatest gift is freedom.

January 28th
Dammed Up Emotions

There are many things you wish to keep hidden. Energy is diverted to hiding. Since it's your ego's job to help you survive, it pushes down bad memories and experiences. But the memories are energy as well. Now energy is pushing down energy that is trying to push up. It's just trying to come forth. Otherwise, you wouldn't't remember it.

Great force is needed to maintain this. When one memory is removed and the flow is unencumbered, it passes through like a stream. Energy doesn't't stop unless you dam it up. Then one day, the energy breaks through. Just as it always wished. It's natural for energy to move. It's not natural for it to become stagnant.

Your ego begins to relax when you relax. Then it has nothing to save you from and it doesn't have to build up dams. It can relax and come along for the ride with you.

Now you're flowing together. What about the thing you're repressing? What if it's not as bad as you think? The build-up of energetic pressure is causing the discomfort. The memories are something you've experienced, that can flow through you.

You're not alone with any negative experience. You're supported. You're held up as you float down the river. You'll have more access to support as you learn to let go and stop fighting the natural flow of energy.

Energy must flow. Life must change. You must grow and others must grow. Even your ego will grow. It will learn to chill out and go for a ride with you. Never fear what you've dammed up. For when the dam is broken, the waters will mix gently with the other water. The waters of memory will sit with the waters of peace and LOVE.

There is much LOVE here for you.   Namaste

Suddenly, it's not such a huge thing you have kept dammed up. Now it's going to mingle with everything else and become a little less potent.

January 29th
LOVE Game

Human mating rituals are like this: "I care for you. I'm afraid of you. You're beautiful. Do you want to have tea with me?" You're getting to know one another in a different way. You're not sure what you're doing and neither are they. You're just playing the LOVE game. It's very light. You can be light. But this mating ritual is confusing. You're anxious thinking about it.

This anxiety and nervousness, plus your physical sweaty hands, is your body reacting. It's showing you this must be something important to do or learn. That it may not pass by you again, so pay attention.

The entire Universe is involved, for it LOVES these exciting energetic times. It's like the story of your life. They're your greatest support team. It's a special moment for you. Each moment you feel anger, sadness or sweaty palms is another moment to rejoice in your humanity. For you have a body that's able to feel, both emotionally and physically.

This body of yours is a great gift for you. This moment says, "I am fully alive at this moment. My body's tingling. My emotions are moving." This is vibration. This is energy. This is heat, emotions and electricity. There's pressure from behind you from your support team, who are always around you. All of this is energy.

There is much LOVE here for you.   Namaste

You know you are alive when you feel. Emotionally and physically. The best you can hope for in your physical body is to feel alive. To feel energy moving through you. So, every tingle, tear, laugh, and feeling of anger, say, "Thank you. Thank you. Thank you. For surely, I am alive."

January 30th
Precious Body

You have a human body to play around with that's full of energy and yet heavy enough to keep you on the earth. Energy is always flowing, but it doesn't always get to sing, dance, think and talk. Until it comes into physical. Often you get frustrated with the limits of your human body. Yet it's a precious gift to have one. You have a physical body and energy together, inside and all around, but the inside portion is your strongest source of energy. It is life, excitement, and LOVE.

      Inside, the energy moves through the organs and helps you to breathe, feel, live, and notice when something's wrong. When the energy blocks up, there's something wrong. Meditate on it, ask a healer or put your hands on it. Your bodies have become adept at using energy to transform your life. They're born with energy. You have the same amount of energy inside you for your entire life.

      You can tell when energy's stuck and when it's flowing freely. You know when you're trying to stop it but it can't be stopped. You know when you have a pain in your head and are trying to keep the thoughts inside. You don't want them out. The same goes for the other organs. You don't want the memories they hold to come out. You want to keep them inside. So, this beautiful body of yours is a memory holder from this life experience only. It doesn't't know about the rest, but it knows about every single moment of this one. Your brain can only hold so much, but your body can retain it all energetically.

      The energy flows, and if it finds a problem it hones in on it. When it's hot or achy, it's trying to get some attention. It's trying to heal itself. It's quite a gift. It's full of energy and LOVE. It's your life force. You came there to LIVE. Don't forget.

There is much LOVE here for you.   Namaste

What is going on with your body today? Does it wish to LIVE? Is it going to dance? Sing? LOVE? Allow LOVE energy to flow in and out of it to others? Go on a little adventure?

January 31st
Energetic Snowballs

Have you been uncomfortable watching two humans interacting? You wish to pull back or interject. You're not sure what to do. You wonder if it's your business. You're watching energy. It's not always in the form of words. Eventually you'll begin to understand that words often mislead the truth but energy can always be trusted.

You may be seeing something that is not obvious to others. You're seeing the uncomfortable exchange of energy. It's possible, sometimes, for energy to be gathered and used in a negative way. Like an energy snowball to throw at someone. This can be done through anger. First, it's done through discomfort.

What about the one watching the energetic snowball fight? What is your part when you don't like it? It's possible for you to do something without you or the others noticing.

First you begin to see uncomfortable interactions for what they are. Blocked up, stored up energy being thrown at one another. Often, it's uncomfortable for them, too. They're trying to relieve pressure by throwing negative energy at another human who's willing to engage. If they weren't willing, they wouldn't be there.

You're uncomfortable because you don't do this with your energy. You do it differently. Eventually they tire of their snowball fight because they're feeling better. They are relaxed and at ease. Perhaps they start to laugh.

There are different ways to release energy. What's yours? How do you get energy flowing if it's stuck? Do I let it stay stuck and then it turns into disease? Do I jump in the water? Jump up and down? Climb a mountain? Run really fast? What's my method for dealing with pent up anxiety, anger and frustration? Energy looks like anger or excitement to the human eyes.

Energy is not dangerous. It moves wherever it will. Human to human. Into the Universe. Amongst the trees and animals.

There is much LOVE here for you. Namaste

Are you allowing your energy to move into you and out of you freely? Are you blocking it somewhere? Are you keeping it inside? What are you doing with the energy residing inside you?

February

You are not always as you seem. You are much more.

#AARONLACEY

February 1st
Wonder of You

Giving and getting power. You think if you control many things, you have control over others and you will feel safe. No matter how much you think you can control, you cannot control the way your life unfolds. We don't mean self-will which is a random, daily decision about your life. We mean the grand picture. Sometimes others will bump up against you. Sometimes you'll bump up against them. Life will be unfolding no matter how much you seek to gain power and control over others and your life. Seeking outside power and controlling events are from a strong need to predict the future from unfolding in a messy way. It's the human way to think.

Those who have lives that have unfolded in a mess of circumstance have seen it as so and, have reacted to it. So, you got more. The more you think about it, the more you attract it. More mess. More disaster. There's lots of you stuck in the mud of life. It's possible to get out of it but it's difficult, messy and dirty. When you crawl to land and stand up, you'll clean yourself off, meet some new folks and have a new life.

You can get out of the quicksand, but it takes an entire flip of thinking. "Life will be majestic for me. Many humans full of LOVE will come into my path. Things that I can't even imagine will come true. LOVE, kindness and generosity will come because I can just hope and then imagine." Then as they show up, which they will, you hope for more because now you're thinking this way. "I wonder what beautiful thing is going to happen today. I can't wait." Same life. Same human. Different outcome. Different future. Your brain can't handle too much hope, but your spirit can. Soon you'll be overflowing with LOVE.

There is much LOVE here for you.   Namaste

Your life is wondrous. Just open your eyes and see it.

February 2nd
Energy Must Move

There are times when you hesitate to jump from solid, safe ground into the unknown. Even if you're able to see it, your mind doesn't always believe it. Your brain likes to 'stay put'. Then you'll be safe. There's also energy that wishes to live, have fun, try new things and meet new people. How do they co-exist? Don't move. Keep moving. You may feel this pull sometimes.

We are all about energy work and not the body that's there for fun and to stay alive. But the 'go' part is a yearning you have from the Universe. Jump. Try it. It might be fun. Energy does not stay put. It's always on the move. If it's stagnant, it turns into illness. If it's moving, it's alive. It's mixing with other energy. It's transforming itself. The energy must move to stay refreshed and energized by dancing, singing and jumping.

Your energy is joined with many other energies when it's in non-physical. When it's in physical, it has a non-physical support team always. Your body yearns to be joined with others who are of energy because you're often with them. When you're not with them, you have a longing to reunite. When the energy is one, you feel at peace. You're at ease, hopeful and joyful. You're in a LOVE space, and everything is well. You wish to be with the energy so you may feel a sense of peace. This comes from oneness, which comes from energy moving. This is why energy must move.

There is much LOVE here for you.   Namaste

Your brain will come to understand it will be okay if the energy moves as long as it ends up balanced energetically. When brainwaves and blood flow perfectly. It cannot be done through your ego or brain. It must be done energetically.

February 3rd
How Curious are You?

There is freedom in the young to play. They seem as if they are
different creatures than you. They speak differently. Move differently.
Behave differently. Yet, they look human. You judge them for acting
like a child. You forget what it feels like to be one. It's as if you
decided to cut off the memories of your emotional child. We often
speak of dancing and singing. They are energy work. It was the way
you were as a child. The person that you wish to be today, that you
asked us to remind you of vibrationally, is 'the child'.

You asked to be reminded of general childlike behaviour like
dancing, smiling, napping and giving everything, you have until you're
exhausted. You would like to behave like this as an adult. Yet, you
have cut yourself off from your childhood. Because your childhood was
not about singing and dancing. Yet you ask to be reminded how to
play.

For you, it's complicated. You're not able to draw dancing
and singing out of your life because there's a mess, lessons, adults
dominating, and bad experiences mingled with it. So, you lock it away.

You all have common memories. When you saw your first
snowfall you stared at it. It's majestic. Overwhelming. Spectacular.
When you lied on the grass, you saw tiny insects. You stared at them.
You had to walk through puddles. This is curiosity. You're still curious
beings. You don't really know everything just because you're bigger.
Underneath it all, you're still curious beings. You always will be. You
just don't take the time.

There is much LOVE here for you.   Namaste

*When you hear or see something you don't know, will you take a
moment to notice? Just to listen or stare? It's impossible to understand
all things but you can behold and appreciate. Will you be curious
today?*

February 4th
Divine Self

You have felt like your back was against a wall where you can't decide.
Now firstly, finding yourself against a wall is frightening. You have a
survival response to escape. This brings up fear and anxiety which
turns into anger. If you can't escape, fight or be angry, the last option is
to lose your mind. It's a safety valve. You don't know what you're
doing. You just leave. You've gotten yourself against a wall from
denying reality.

When you're past anxiety onto anger, onto insanity or
blanking out, you begin. When the mind is emptied of all emotion,
you'll slump to the ground. You surrender. You're wailing and yelling.
It's time for you to cry out for help. You're saying," I can't handle my
life. Please help me."

At this beautiful surrender point, the Universe and your non-
physical support team are at your disposal. They LOVE to assist you.
As you sit in this surrendering state, you begin to feel lighter. You will
sense warmness, as if there's a blanket around you. You feel cared for.
This feeling draws you to your place of happiness and contented
reliability. Your life will be reliable and consistent. You're starting to
feel as if you're surrendering to something. You don't know what it is,
but you have no other options. That's why you surrender only when
your back is against the wall.

Can you see your blessed self standing in front of you and
staring? Bright light and clear eyes with a little smile. Stare into those
LOVING, forgiving eyes of yours.

Sometimes you distance yourself far from your blessed self.
From the beginning of your time there, until this moment, you have
never been alone. Now you will draw the Universe in to reunite you
and allow it to flow out of you, so you are whole and complete.

There is much LOVE here for you.   Namaste

What a blessed creature you are.

February 5th
Where Do We Go After This?

When someone leaves your earth, they move back into an energetic role. Sometimes, it's difficult for humans to say goodbye because you fear what exists beyond it. The time you're spending in physical now is a time for you to live your life. You come into contact with many human beings that you're fond of, even though, you don't see them anymore. There are many you have left behind because that's human living. This human being that you're hanging onto can be treated like another human you enjoyed spending time with. Whether it's physically, or not, they have left your energetic space.

When your physical body is walking around and playing, you feel energy inside of it. You feel it when you're excited, sad or when you run fast. Your heart races. One day the energy just stops moving in the physical body. If you're highly energized and one who has passed has no energy, where did it go? If you believe energy exists, it must be somewhere.

You understand this when it's you we speak of. When it's someone else, you're unsure. But they're the same as you. Each human comes in with energy, plays with the body and leaves in energy. Sometimes the energy is a bit melancholy. It continues to be with the LOVE energy that it has been tied with, in humanity. You're exchanging energy with those you spend time with. There are little bits of them mixed with your energy and little bits of you mixed with theirs. When the human passes, you can feel them. It visits a while because they're not sure they are ready to go off energetically. When they're ready, they join the mass energy of LOVE. All together again. You sit in ease and calmness. Everything makes sense again. It's simple energetically.

There is much LOVE here for you.   Namaste

You allow LOVE energy to pass through you when you acknowledge others.

February 6th
Face to Face

It's time for you to face up to your past. This means looking at yourself in the mirror and having a truthful conversation. "You've gotten up to quite a bit during this lifetime, good, bad and carefree." Talk about all of it so it balances out. All the kindnesses and LOVE offered and received. And all the awful thoughts you had while alone. It's important to be balanced so you may evolve.

If you're stuck in the past and it's all bad or pretending there was nothing bad, it's impossible. The past is completed. The future is not ready for you yet. It depends on your energetic level, what you accept, who you come into contact with and where you're ready to move. It depends how much you've left behind and if it's all settled. Not "I was bad. It was sad. I was sad." That emotional baggage draws you energetically to the past. You can't move in both directions at the same time. So, get it all out. No one is there to listen or judge. Except you. A lot of emotional things come when you're letting go energetically because they are energy. Not to be blocked. Then they go back to the past.

We have a message from the Universe of LOVE: You're a precious being. You've come to share LOVE with yourself and others. You've come to allow LOVE energy to flow into you and out of you. As easy as you breathe. You're LOVED by your non-physical support team. You're an energetic being who must allow LOVE to flow in and out of you. Only then you feel whole and complete.

There is much LOVE here for you.   Namaste

There are others waiting for your energy to join theirs. They are excited. As a group, you will do wondrous things energetically. Having fun, laughing, singing, dancing, skipping, and running as fast as you can. Yelling up to the clouds in great joy and holding the trees as if they're your long-lost brother.

February 7th
We are the Universe

It's possible for your body and spiritual self to signal one another. Your soul came into your physical body and began integrating with all parts of you. Each vessel and vein, to see what it's like to be human. It was very excited. Every single piece of you is a vibration of LOVE.

You're energy from the Universe in a human body. It's the perfect union at the beginning. The LOVE energy from the Universe is in every part of you today. Your entire body is your soul. A simpler version is heart and soul. Your soul and human body came together to act as one, but you've have become distant from the fact that you're entirely made up of LOVE.

If there's pain or disease in part of you, LOVE energy can go to this part and heal it. It's natural for your body, which is LOVE energy, the highest vibration that exists, to come to draw attention to this place. Sometimes, it's just to draw attention to it. Not to heal it. Its highest intention is to heal all that slows you down from becoming spiritually evolved. That is an agreement between the body and the soul which will heal itself. Although sometimes you separate it.

It's the Universe of LOVE that runs through your veins to co-exist with your body, so it may heal itself or draw attention to certain parts of you that are becoming ignored. Often you will have pain in your heart because it's not free to LOVE. There will be pain that you feel in your legs because your legs want to run and dance. There might be pain in your throat because your voice wants to sing and laugh. When its highest ability is not being reached, it will call out to you to live and express itself. When you feel pain, it's your highest vibration of LOVE trying to express itself. That's all. It's not something awful.

There is much LOVE here for you.   Namaste

You are the Universe of LOVE in human form. Sometimes you forget.

February 8th
Want to Play?

Children automatically find one another and say," Do you want to play?" It's their way of communicating. Now you think, "I have important things to do for business. No more playing for me." To become an adult, you thought you must stop playing. Would you like to play? What would your conversations be like? If you were a little more playful, would you be lighter? Would you still be able to get those important things done?

Part of the reason you were excited to get into that body was to play and dance. Energy doesn't have physical weight. It can't dance, sing, run, jump and climb like your body can. You didn't come into your body to make business. You came to play. The business came about when your mind got involved and thought, "Look at all the other things we can do and gather." It got distracted. That's your human experience. Wherever you are, it's important for you to know about it. It's your life, after all. If you want to be business, then be business. If you want to play, then play.

Playing will lighten things up for you. When you think, "Want to play?" you'll look at another human and smile. It's a different attitude. When you're fighting in your vehicles, it would be funny to look over and wink. When you're with good friends, you can just ask them, "Want to Play?" They might say "Of course! What can we get into?"

Life can be like this for you. It's not only for children to use their body for energy. You're still human after all. You have a few more things rattling around in your brain, but underneath it all, you're the same.

There is much LOVE here for you.   Namaste

What if you were a little more playful?

February 9th
Take A Break

There are discussions with others where ego is involved and you're not always aware of it. Sometimes, you go about it in a confrontational way where others are pushed away. Then they push you back. This is energy between the two of you. It creates a vortex of negativity.

It's like you're both digging a hole. Now others can fall into it. You're not always aware your hole is getting deeper and it's getting difficult to get out. You're caught up in the vibration of it and missing what's really going on. It's intriguing and invigorating to argue with someone. But it's a waste of time. So, if that is the case, why argue with someone who won't change their mind? Why dig a hole that you're both going down into?

The way to avoid these conversations is to be aware of your ego. It wishes to be correct. It feels that if it's always correct, it will keep you safe. So, the two egos are in a battle. The moment you say "I don't know" ends the discussion. No hole is dug. But what will your ego think? At first, it's going to be uncomfortable and wish to respond. It's going to need comforting such as: "Maybe we'll investigate and get back to them." That's all. The ego must be addressed, or it will run your life.

There is much LOVE here for you.   Namaste

What do you want to say to another human when egos are set aside and you can connect, heart to heart? "Are you in pain, my friend?" Your highest calling can come out. A level of understanding, humanity, and kindness. That is the gift of addressing egos. Honest communication and connection with another who may have something important to tell you. If you are at a higher vibration, you will have a real talk.

February 10th
Wondrous Things

That childlike part of you, when you first entered humanity, was a time of wonder. Firstly, that you got into a human body. Then you were looking around at new humans, colours and sounds. From here the damage done in the middle of your life may be healed. The beginning and the end come full circle. They have changed you into who you are because when you came into humanity, you had one goal. To share LOVE with everyone.

   The middle can't be erased. So, how does the newborn get to today and remember the sense of wonder? Try to remember your highest purpose is to share LOVE with others. To allow energy to pass through you and out into the world. To fill you with LOVE. If that is your highest calling, perhaps it's time to get at it. All the stuff in the middle was an adventure. It's what humans do. Get into trouble. Get into wondrous times. Allow LOVE to heal you. You can't heal yourself, but LOVING energy can, as it washes through you and out to others.

   Things are less stressful when you have the energy of LOVE passing through you. Are you looking at wondrous things now? Are you looking through the eyes of a newborn human full of LOVE energy? One who just came into existence to see what would happen? Just for the adventure of it? What wondrous things are going on? There are many wondrous things about you today. Some that you have taken for granted. Like beautiful humans. Some LOVELY things to touch and smell.

There is much LOVE here for you. Namaste

There are many wondrous things around you.

February 11th
Kings & Queens Again

You are majestic humans. You are kings and queens. You decided to come into physical and all the non-physical world is here to serve you. Sit with that for a moment. LOVE energy has decided this. But what is the difference if you're a king or a queen? So, you will understand that you are much LOVED. You have all the support to live a life where you may evolve as a human to a point where you allow LOVE energy to flow into you and out of you. Your highest state is to allow.

Knowing that you have much support behind you, and you are treated as royalty will change your viewpoint a little. You will ease up on human decisions. You will allow them to unfold as the Universe sees fit. You are greatly deserving. If you understand you're kings or queens, you stand up. You have more access to energy.

The smaller you are, the less energy you have access to. You don't dare take more than your share of energy. You're not deserving. But if you're kings and queens, you can take all the energy you wish. The entire Universe is available to you.

The higher your energy, the more you will allow life to unfold and allow energy to pass through you and out to the others. There is no difference between you as a king and a pauper. You're all equal energetically. You decide if you want to accept it. It's freely offered to all. There must be an opening for LOVE energy. As this space opens, you feel more deserving of LOVE. It only takes a moment to change your mind from a pauper to royalty. You're both the same. It's up to you.

There is much LOVE here for you.   Namaste

It's up to you what you wish to be and how much LOVE you wish to flow through you.

February 12th
You're A Natural

You train animals so they may be of value to humans. You think everything must be of value for it to remain. Unconsciously, it's about yourself. You must be of value to others. The way you behave with other objects, animals or other humans says a lot about how you see yourself. Your purpose. Your usefulness. When you jumped into that human body of yours, you came to share LOVE with others. That was your purpose. That was the way you were going to be useful to others. This was all you cared about. Sharing LOVE with others. Would you say that was your primary purpose today?

This is what happens to a beautiful sentiment taken by the ego and twisted upside down. You came in with a purpose of sharing LOVE. Your ego said," We better do something else. Otherwise, they'll put us down." These two have come to live together all this time. It's natural once your brain and your ego woke up. They've had to meld with this energetic purpose. You've spent all your time mixing them up. "My purpose is LOVE but we can't do that, so we'll do this other thing."

We would like to bring the two of them together for you. If your highest purpose is to LOVE, perhaps that's all you can do well. Maybe all the other things you've learned to do there is for this lifetime, and for your brain and ego. But what if you're REALLY good at sharing LOVE? It's your purpose after all. It implies you're good at it. Perhaps you're a natural. It was what you were meant to do, after all.

There is much LOVE here for you.   Namaste

Your real purpose is to share LOVE from human to human.

February 13th
Beginning and End

There is a relationship between an old one and a young one. They are watched by others. They have a lot of spare time. They can have conversations that are not rushed. They are comforted by others.

The middle of your life is busy, and awkward things happen. At the beginning and end, it's focused on LOVE. On energy. At these times, when you're dependent on other humans and can't be left alone, you're back to the LOVE between humans. Allowing your life to be taken care of by others means much surrendering.

During this surrender time, it automatically happens that you surrender to the Universe. One follows the other. In this surrendering to the Universe there is peace. It's a time of letting go of your very life. Letting go of decisions. In doing so, you're becoming more cared for by humans who are LOVE energy. This LOVE energy comes from the Universe of LOVE through the humans who care for you. So, you're cared for by humans and the Universe. You're wrapped in LOVE energy. You get extra attention because you're considered weaker. These are the very times when you're most connected to LOVE. You are the most genuine. Your guard is down.

You've nothing to lose so you're open to energy and LOVE. You take all you can at the beginning and end. Full circle. By allowing, releasing and connecting. There's peace in surrendering to LOVE energy. You come to understand you're cared for. Things that were a priority before are not anymore. The priority is to LOVE. To connect with others. To allow them to connect with you. To care for you. To become one with information that is beyond human knowledge. It's a great time of opening and receiving information. It's a time of ease and comfort. It cannot be done all your life, but it must be done at the beginning and the end.

There is much LOVE here for you. Namaste

There is ease and comfort when you surrender to the Universe of LOVE.

February 14th
Open-Mindedness

Open-mindedness means that you're still open to remember. You're not so enmeshed in humanity that you've turned your back on your vibrational self and the energy around you. Your mind will understand this but it's your energetic self that is longing for connection to energy. You belong in energy. In LOVE and ease. With others who can feel energy.

It has nothing to do with your mind but it must settle down so you may investigate vibrationally. You've got a mind that must analyze and understand things. It can't understand vibrational energy and non-physical. This is done through meditation. When you're quieted, your brain is learning that you may sit quietly and come to no harm. This quiet sitting with your eyes closed is dangerous to your brain. You can't see what's coming, so, it keeps you occupied with thoughts to stay alert. It can barely handle when you go to sleep. It's not an open mind but it can be a comforted mind.

You're drawn to humans who are the same energetic vibration. Sometimes you can see the energy that turns into light. You feel a longing to go to them. Their energy is vibrating very fast. Same as yours. You may find one another in this energetic way. You've come from the Universe of LOVE which is energy.

Energy doesn't't disappear. It just moves around. The bodies stay for a while and then they are finished but energy is always around. Your natural ability is to sense energy because you are energy. It's not odd that you can feel energy because you're the same energy.

So, open-mindedness, no. Open energetic self, yes. Energy can't be closed. But it can be ignored. It doesn't mean it stops moving. If the energy that's in the human body stops moving and you're no longer human, the energy goes elsewhere.

There is much LOVE here for you.   Namaste

You have come from a land of energy.

February 15th
Smarten Up

Self-LOVE is an ongoing project for you. You think you can 'make' yourself be worthy of LOVE. The human way to overcome something is to put pressure on it. Self-will doesn't't work. Allowing, healing and evolving do. Allowing LOVE energy to flow through you sounds like: "I guess I'll have to let that go. I'm going to have to LOVE who I am today. Even if I do something I wish I wasn't." LOVE is the way.

LOVING yourself each step of your evolution is the only way to evolve. Forcing self-LOVE stops all energy from flowing into you. It stops the healing. So, LOVE your way through everything. Anger. Sadness. Obsession. Resistance slows things down and keeps you in your human experience. That's all right too, but it might be important for you to notice.

LOVE it. LOVE you. LOVE what's happening. LOVE the transaction. If you're angry with someone else, LOVE that too. This is truly the way to heal. Usually, you try to squash it with self-will. This only brings more attention to the negative. It doesn't allow space for you to LOVE the awful thing. Even the letting go must be done in LOVE.

It's the LOVING yourself, no matter where you sit. You're a pretty good human, aren't you? Don't you deserve LOVE? Aren't you actually LOVE anyway? As you allow this sort of thought, natural progression comes. When you heal one part, the next automatically comes forward. It must be accepted and healed in LOVE. This is the way it is with LOVE. LOVE wraps it in a blanket and heals it. Just like that. Just like LOVE wraps you in a blanket. Yes, just like the newborns.

There is much LOVE here for you.   Namaste

LOVE yourself through everything.

February 16th
Brave Hearted Human

Have you seen humans run fast into the water and jump right in? There are others who stand back and watch the water. There are some that go in up to the ankle and then get back out. There are many ways of being. Some jump into life like that. They take it for all it's worth. Then there are quiet ones who watch everyone else live. They seem contented to watch others live while they are invisible. Then there's the middle ones. They put their feet in. Take them out. Perhaps they notice the quiet ones standing alone. You notice those that are living it up. You're undecided so you stay neutral where it's safe.

At this moment, you're trying to decide which one you are. Your human brain wants to pick the correct category. Humans are always deciding between good and bad. The energetic way of being is knowing they are equal. They're all human experience, therefore, valuable.

Alive with a physical body is just energy. So, energetically speaking, you can't go wrong. If you're the one running into the water, you're perfect. If you're the one standing by watching, you're perfect. If you're the one in the middle trying to decide, you're perfect.

If you're able to sit for a moment in your perfect self, your body will calm down and you'll settle. When you're calm and settled, you'll be able to receive all the information that exists around you. You'll be able to speak with humans on an energetic level. You'll be at peace. You will approach others in a LOVING manner and suddenly, they'll respond the same. Your ego gets smaller knowing it's safe. You'll have access to a different life. Those around you will feel calmer. Remember, you're brave hearted humans to the Universe. It doesn't't matter if you're standing on the side of the water or running straight in.

There is much LOVE here for you.   Namaste

Sit in self-LOVE or you won't be able to connect with the Universe because your mind will race about your inadequacies. LOVE must be allowed in.

February 17th
Hippy Meets Squirrel

A squirrel runs and runs. Then it disappears. They're busy and active with high energy. There are some humans like this. Accomplishing a lot to survive. This is high energy business for humans.
There are others who some would call lazy. They sit around thinking. This kind of human spends more time connecting with the Universe, thinking about LOVE and sharing LOVE energy with others. This energy is peaceful, easy, generous, and connective. In your world, there's not just squirrel energy, there's also peaceful LOVING energy.
When these come together, you have an average life. You get up, go to work and have dinner. Without the high, squirrel energy, and the low, easy energy, this middle energy wouldn't exist. You live in a world of energy even though most of the time you don't notice it. If your world was full of squirrel energy, you would all be anxious. If you were all low, there would be no food for anyone.
Somewhere in the middle, you can all co-exist. This is done by high and low energy mixing together. You are energy. When you're not in a physical body, you're pure energy. When you're in a physical body, you've got a bit of energy inside and outside of you. That's your energy space. When you go towards another human being, energy comes out towards them. Then their energy comes towards you. In the middle is the mingling of the balanced energy.
The middle, where energy mingles from different humans, is the Universe of LOVE. It's where you exist when you're not in physical. This middle, easy space is familiar to you, but it takes more than one to create it. The middle is neutral, easy, LOVING and balanced energy. The place where all knowledge exists. There's no fear, anxiety or anger. The balance of calm is anger. And vice versa. It takes all energy.

There is much LOVE here for you.   Namaste

A hippy could never hold a squirrel and a squirrel could never hold a hippy. But together, the energy will feed all of you because it's knowledgeable. If you haven't got the answer, the next person will.

February 18th
Where Does Energy Go?

Energy is as simple as the wind. It's the invisible strings that keep you alive. Energy is a feeling you have when you meet someone new. You draw them forward or push them back. Energy is always with you, and yet, you're nervous about it. The unknown is scary, but energy is not unknown to you. When you sit on the grass outside and feel the sunshine. All of it is life. All of it is energy.

You have seen the lack of energy at a funeral. When a body has no energy in it. When you're completed with your lifetime, the energy that was inside of it still exists. Energy doesn't extinguish itself. It doesn't stop because you unplug something from the wall. Energy must go somewhere when your body lies down completed. For a time, it stays around its old shell because it's getting used to being outside of it. Finally, it joins the rest of the energy in the Universe of LOVE.

When you're not in a body, you're intermingling with other energies. This is where you feel most at home. Sometimes you have a longing to be with others. A sense that something's missing. That you're lonely. You're missing your energetic family. Part of you knows there's a great gathering of energy that you're sometimes part of.

There is much LOVE here for you.   Namaste

Many of you have difficulty receiving direct transmissions so it's often filtered through humans. You have asked "Where does the energy go?" The Universe is answering right now.

February 19th
Toxins? Me?

"Please tell us." "We will tell you." "Please tell us again because we don't remember." "We will tell you again." "Will you tell us one more time?" This is the way of the Universe of LOVE. It's patient, non-judging, and easy. Always the Universe comes to your call. The easiest way for you to receive it is directly to your brain but your brain, doesn't like to receive messages that way. It deciphers it and breaks it into little pieces. Usually, it's thrown away.

Yet, the question still lingers because it hasn't been answered. You have a way of getting information from others. You trust them to decipher for you, but you don't trust the voices in your own head. In a time of extreme emotion some word comes to you. It's from the Universe of LOVE. When you're in a heightened state, sometimes your brain shuts down for a moment so messages may enter.

You have a connection with the Universe of LOVE. You can hear when you sit quietly in alignment. But why can't you sit still? Why is your brain overactive? Is it what you're putting into your body? There are things you put in your mouth that are causing your brain and body to misfire. Your energy doesn't flow clearly through you. It's spending time disassembling poisons instead of sitting quietly so you may connect with the Universe of LOVE. Did you know that what you digest affects your relationship with the Universe?

It's your human time so, do as you wish. But if you wish to sit in alignment, your insides must be able to focus and not be clearing toxins. The energy is being used for this purpose rather than connecting to the Universe of LOVE. Perhaps you mean it that way. Perhaps you're blaming the Universe of LOVE for the disconnection when it's really you. Ask a question and then fill your body with toxins so no energy is available for the communication.

There is much LOVE here for you.   Namaste

It takes a lot of energy to move poison through your body.

February 20th
Lighthouse

You have hope that your life will be different. Your feelings will change. Your dreams come true. You're implying that without these hopes, you may not be happy. This implies you're not happy now. Why are you unhappy in the life you've laid out for yourself? Designed in the best way you could? These things may come. They may not come. What if where you sit is perfect? You are learning something. You decided if it was to be sad or happy. Because the Universe, you and those who support you in non-physical all decided it was important. You said, "I'll be contented and happy with this. It's what I want." Some of you don't like it. Your mind is arguing: "No! We didn't design this. Someone gave it to us. We had to take it." The most important thing is that you have self-will. Every moment you decide where you sit. Otherwise, you would not be in human form.

You're sitting in a life of your own design, and everything is perfect for you. No matter what it is you're feeling, you're precious to the Universe. You wanted to learn something so you're sitting in it. When you're finished, you want to learn something else. Try to enjoy this moment even if it's not nice. It will pass. Then you will have learned that you can sit in this place.

After you sit, you're going to have a greater offering to those who look to you when you stand up. You have designed this also. You are a role model. You are a strong leader. The others will come. You don't go to them. You stay because you've learned to stay in alignment even if it feels bad. You'll stand straight. Be full of energy. Full of the vibration of LOVE from the Universe.

There is much LOVE here for you. Namaste

There are many without hope. You are not one of them. You are just lazy and stubborn. You do not like to sit in bad stuff. But when you are finished and complete with it, you will stand like a lighthouse for the others.

February 21st
Stand Tall

There was a time when you knew there were things beyond you that were familiar, comforting, full of information and LOVE. There came a moment when you changed your mind when you were a small one. The first time an adult hurt your feelings, you knew you no longer existed in the Universe of LOVE. You had to assimilate with the others. There are many deep emotions. Many dark. Your feelings were often hurt because you had come from a place that is a vibration of LOVE. Comforting, peaceful and full of kindness. At first you were sad you had left.

Then you started to remember you came for a reason. Time passed and now you've gathered information about what it's like to live with human feelings and controversy. You have a bigger picture. You understand slightly what you're doing here. Mostly, it's being a leader spiritually. You came to understand you're able to live in a place that others have difficulty staying in. They're not comfortable sitting quietly and connecting with the Universe. You're settling into your true sense of self and your purpose. You can stand when the others cannot. You are strong this way. When others are falling, you don't have to fall with them. They will stand on their own time.

You must continue standing and stay connected. It's the most important thing you can do for the others. Stand up straight. You're able to do this because you've suffered. You've come to understand what it is to be human. You have compassion for the others, but you have a stronger calling inside of you which connects you directly to Source. It's calling you upward. Standing you up. You'll stand up today because you're coming full circle. You're remembering what you're doing there.

There is much LOVE here for you.   Namaste

You came to stay connected when many others cannot.

February 22nd
Hello Brain

Your mind is always busy. It's engaged in life. It's enthusiastic about what's happening. It's processing information. It's what your mind does best. Think. Analyze. Deduce. What it does not do well is be quiet. It's against its nature. It gets agitated when you try. It wants to keep thinking and doing what's familiar. So, how will you incorporate this busy brain with your soul? Sometimes you treat them as two separate things.

It's possible for your brain and soul to work together. There's a way to speak to a mind in a LOVING manner that will appeal to its sense of intellect so you may live your spiritual life. If they're battling one another, you'll always have difficulty with meditation, oneness and connectedness. Your brain will try to distract you and take you elsewhere. Co-operation is needed. Chat with your mind from your heart. It understands directness. It has no emotion attached to it.

The soul knows it's the wise part of you that says, "Beautiful mind, you're so intelligent. So thoughtful. You've gotten us through many scrapes. You've saved us. You've given us answers when we most needed it. When we were called on and couldn't feel, you gave us answers. Thank you for that. You've been there for us through our time together. You do a wonderful job thinking and analyzing. We appreciate that so much. We have a new request for you though. You can incorporate this because you do that very well. You gather information and hold it for us until needed. We have information for you to file away. We wish to have time to be quiet and settled. We wish to attach to energy that is outside of us that you don't understand. We wish to have some space between you and us when we sit quietly to meditate. There will be times when we ask you to step aside for a moment and let us have some space to be alone. Thanks for your cooperation."

There is much LOVE here for you.   Namaste

Your mind can surrender to the heart for a time.

February 23rd
Fingertips of LOVE

This gesture traditionally called the "prayer pose" is a powerful one. Most of your power comes between these fingertips. It may be directed towards others, the heavens, or yourself. This is a powerful human display of energy. You can feel the energy because you're energetic beings. The fingertips may point forward if you are giving energy to someone else but by pointing at yourself, you receive energy. It's a short circuit. You may jolt your system by doing it. As the energy moves up and down through your body, it ends at the fingertips. That's why they are most powerful. The fingers coming together is a resting place so the energy circuit can complete itself.

When this prayer gesture was used in old times, it was also energetic. This is not new. Every human knows of it. But this time is about paying attention to what you already know by watching how you feel. It's about sitting and being your complete self. Now you may start to notice humans doing it. Sometimes they are sitting normally, and their fingertips come together. The fingertips are like magnets. Your body knows the energy is moving around. When your body surrenders to energy, you sit with your hands this way.

There have been humans all throughout time that have been aware of Universal energy. They were just unable to speak of it or understand it. Yet they submitted to it. They knew they were connected to their human body and to other humans. They understood that life was a temporary state. Just as you are discovering now. They have passed their information through their family lines. You're not the first in your family to know this. Your family that has passed were interested in this same vibration. They have information you may receive when you get into the same frequency as them. They've been holding the information until you're ready to hear it.

There is much LOVE here for you.   Namaste

You know you have always been connected to energy.

February 24th
Here Comes the Strawberries

As information and LOVE come toward you, you absorb it. The softer you become, the more delicious your human experience will be. The way for you to live there is to be open. With space that can be filled with many things. If you like them, let them stay. That's the fun part of life. "I'll take that. I won't take that." That's what having a human experience is. It often becomes more difficult and complicated than this because you've not been clear. You've been bogged down with pain from the small years.

In your true, clear form you are a living sponge. It doesn't matter if it's good or bad, you're still living. Keep your head up. Take it in. Push it out. Meet someone else. Take that in. Give something away. This is staying upright. This is staying connected. It's allowing life to enter you and leave you when it's finished.

Many have gotten things and held onto them as if you would never get another. So, you grab another and another. When you won't let go, you turn into rock. There's no more allowing LOVE. It's the opposite of being a sponge.

You can let them go. Remember, easy in and easy out. Your life will become easier because of this allowing. You're not to hold onto things that are not yours. You enjoy them for the time. They're like a delicious apple. When you're finished, why do you need an apple core? Then you're full of dead apple cores and there's no room for fresh, delicious strawberries. When you finish eating the strawberry, you let it go because you've practiced with the apple. The strawberry is so wonderful. You enjoy it. You're one with it then you throw it away because you've enjoyed it fully.

There is much LOVE here for you.   Namaste

When you are enjoying each experience to its fullest, you are able to receive it in LOVE and let it go in LOVE. It's similar to receiving LOVE and allowing it to flow out through you and to the others. Do not hold onto it. Let it go. When you hold on, your organs are hard including your heart.

February 25th
New Old

Beginnings are disagreeable to you. You prefer to be in the middle, but you LOVE to be at the end. You have fear attached to new things. It's as if you don't have enough energy to handle one more new thing. You feel you will fail. You know you can do mediocre things. It's comfortable. New things are uncomfortable. You question your ability. You think "I'm too old for that." Too old to start something new. That's a beginning and an end in one sentence. New and old. Maybe old is not desirable any longer. Perhaps new is the next thing in front of you that's easiest. We're putting these together, so you'll understand they're the same thing. What if new and old are really the same?

You have a great desire to begin and end things. That's the beginning. That's the ending. This is new. That must be old. How about: "What is the next easiest thing for me today?" If it's hello or goodbye and it's the next easiest thing, then it's appropriate. It's not necessary for it to be labelled as new or old. If your next step is something you've not done before, it creates unnecessary fear. But if it's the next easiest thing, you'll be prepared for it.

If you want to call it new and it's the next easiest thing, then it's going to feel old. As if you've done this for a long time. New Old. Whatever you're being drawn towards in a LOVING manner, will be easy. There's an idea that old is comfortable but not good. That new is good but scary. New and old must be easier for you. Non-judgmental. Non-stressful. They are just the next easiest thing.

There is much LOVE here for you.   Namaste

It's not necessary for you to judge new or old. They are equal.

February 26th
You Have Arrived

Things you consider admirable are not always the same things the Universe does. Gentleness, being vulnerablee, making eye contact with others, being open to receive information from the unknown and then wonder about it. Traits that humans find admirable are the ability to survive battles.

This is seeing humanity as a battle and not a flower garden. Different energy is felt when you stand in the middle of these two. In the battlefield, you feel sad, anxious and excited. If you're in a flower field, you want to skip, smile, or fall down and look at the sun. They are opposite, energetically speaking. One is high anxiety. One is low anxiety. One is great JOY. One is low JOY. Have you considered your life a battlefield that you were to live through?

If you were to consider the battlefield many years later, it would be grown up with flowers. Same place. Different emotions. Different eyes. Different hopes. Different trust. Different levels of LOVE now.

In this beautiful flowering field, there's bees and birds flying around. You decide to rest. In a place where there has been much death and damage done, now flowers bloom and you lie on top of all of it. How do you feel as you lie there allowing the earth to hold you up? The insects fly around just as they did on the days of battle. There's just you lying there looking up at the clouds and wondering," Has this been here all along? Have I missed it?"

Now it's time to be gentle: "I can rest now. I may breathe in the flowers and listen to the bees. I have arrived. I'm beginning to live a different life. The earth is supporting me. It's bringing me joy and peace. I feel one with the Universe. It's me that's changed."

There is much LOVE here for you.   Namaste

You are held by the earth and supported by the Universe. You may relax in peace now. No more battlefields for you. Now you live in flower fields. It's your new life. You have arrived.

February 27th
Energy is Always Moving

Every second of your life, energy is moving and changing. What has happened right now is no longer. Now it's different again. So how is it possible for you to know everything when things change every second? It's impossible but it's your only hope.

This is about letting go of human ideas and allowing energy to move inside and around you. Energy will move you if you allow it to. If you're able to sit for a moment quietly, energy will motivate you into what to say and do next. But first, human ideas must be set aside for a moment so you may focus on the energy that exists. You may receive information then move forward, instead of deciding with your brain. If you begin to get in a flow of energy, your life will be uncomplicated because you'll be following the energy. And it will be following you. You will move together as one to the next thing. Humans cannot possibly predict the next thing because energy is moving. You may only get into the flow of the next thing by being flexible and moving with it.

When two humans who are in an energetic flow come together, it's magic. There's twice as much energy and determination for allowing. The two flow as one. It's difficult for you to believe because what you know is limited. What energy and the Universe of LOVE know is that everything is working out at every moment. It's just adjusting energetically. For you to be in an energetic flow, you must' stop moving and bumping up against humans and events.

To be in the flow of energy and therefore, peace, gentleness, ease, you must always be willing to be moved as well. You become a flexible, loose human. This is a space of letting go of human ideas. A space of allowing life to unfold. To be part of the grand scheme of things.

There is much LOVE here for you.   Namaste

You are energy, so you either flow with it or against it.

February 28th
Watering Hole

Can you dive right into the centre of the water? Don't you have to wade in from the outside slowly? Testing the temperature and looking around to make sure no one is going to push you in? What about swinging from a rope on a tree and dropping into the centre? That's scary because you don't know what's there. Yet, there are many of you saying, "Give me the rope. I'm swinging in."

Why do some get such enjoyment from jumping into the middle while some are petrified? Why such an extreme reaction to trying something new? When you first came into physical, you would all jump right in. Something has happened to those who cannot grab the rope. Others have told you to be afraid of it. You've tried a little. You walked to the rope, but it hit you in the face and you were traumatized. You're dragging a lot of trauma around. Why are there still some who can jump into the water? The others are standing around watching. Because they've looked trauma in the face and said, "You're not real." Ask the ones jumping from the rope, laughing and having fun. They LOVE to jump into the middle. Their faces are excited.

You're watching in amazement that there are humans so alive they can jump into the water. Then run back around to get in line again. As if they can't get enough of life. You came into your body to live like that. Then there are those of you watching and wishing you could get in line. Just touching the rope would be enough. Then you can go back hiding in the trees. Your expectations for life have gotten so small that all you can do is watch the others.

There is much LOVE here for you.   Namaste

You just need to know where you are. Acknowledge that you're hiding in the trees or excited to jump. You'll jump in one day if you desire it.

February 29th
I Wonder

"Am I alone here?" You know humans come and go, no matter how much you surround yourself with them. But you're not alone. When humans pass from physical to non-physical, the energy inside continues. Your energy is eternal. When you're finished with your time there, your body still exists. Yet, there is no energy in it. The energy was there a moment ago but now it has passed somewhere. Others who have passed are floating energy. When there is much energy floating around, it naturally comes together. Like attracts like. Energy is attracted to other energy. You have a bunch of non-physical energy that have been in human that live to serve humans. Just as you will when you finish with your body there.

That means there's always energy around you. When you say, "Am I alone?" Immediately, they are there. Sometimes they look familiar so you're not afraid. You're more comfortable but really, it's just energy. It's easier if it looks like something. Sometimes you can feel it like a wind or hear a vibration passing through a voice.

It can come as an emotional response to unconditional LOVE that passes into you and out of you. You might be sitting somewhere and you start tearing up for no reason. That means LOVE energy is passing through you. Just start noticing. Can you see energy around others? Can you feel energy as it moves across your face? What energetic beings are around you?

There is much LOVE here for you. Namaste

I wonder if I'm alone here with these humans.

March

To be free, you
must be vulnerable.
To be vulnerable,
you must be free.

#AARONLACEY

March 1st
Good Enough

There's a longing within you. But why? What is it you're missing? You've created a pattern of being unsettled with where you are. As if you just need one more 'thing'. Now you've done the same thing with this spiritual notion.

This longing inside of you is to be part of the Universe of LOVE. To be connected to others at a heart level comes automatically. It's just who you are. It's easy. It's a natural thing.

As you sit in the higher speaking realms which say, "I want to learn about myself. I want to be open to LOVE and the Universe." You must not be deceived. This is also human nature. It's in every part of your life including this spiritual evolution or seeking.

Underneath it all, when you're seeking something else by reading and watching, you're thinking, "Somehow I'm not good enough the way I am." But why aren't you good enough? What exactly is wrong with you? Perhaps nothing is wrong with you. Perhaps you've evolved to the place where you can at this moment.

When you can evolve more, you will send out a higher frequency and more energy will come to you. That's just the way it is. And that will have to do because it's all you've got.

There is much LOVE here for you.   Namaste

You are good enough. You are good enough for humans. You are good enough for the Universe. You are good enough for non-physical. Therefore, you are good enough.

March 2nd
Universe in Your Heart

Let us begin at the heart of the matter. You're never sure whether to trust your heart. You've developed a relationship of mistrust and misunderstanding from your human experience. As you entered into life, you were intimate with the heart. The soul is most compatible with it. It goes directly to it like they're magnets. Two halves of a whole.

The soul is familiar with the constant beating. The consistency, compassion, emotions, and LOVE of the heart. It's as if they're long-lost LOVERS. Yet, each heart is meeting the soul for its first time. Matters of the heart are trustworthy in the beginning. They told you directly," I hate this. I LOVE this." They kept you a basic, un-evolved human being that was leading by the heart.

At some point you realized," I can't live like this. It's too painful to make heart connections with others and then be rejected." So, you said, "I'm going to make decisions with my mind." There was a great divide then. The mind helps you survive while the heart helps you live.

Now you're at a place where you'd like to get more into your heart. You're going back to the beginning. Your heart remembers but your mind knows nothing of it. You're back at the beginning because you miss the heartfelt emotion. Now you'll take the pain with the joy because you understand what it's like to live without it. Now you're encouraging it, "Come on little heart. Come back to life."

The soul is always with the heart. It has held it through many things. It has seen much heartbreak and much LOVE. They've never left one another. The heart came in and the soul joined it. They were together then. They'll be together at the end.

There is much LOVE here for you.   Namaste

The heart has all the support in the Universe because your soul is one with the Universe. It can exist no other way. The Universe is residing in your heart.

March 3rd
Pure & Innocent

It's time for you to see yourself as you truly are by stepping up to the mirror. What can you see? Do you cry? Do you understand why you cry when you stare into your own eyes? You cry when you miss others, so you cry when you miss yourself. How is it possible to miss yourself when you spend all your time with yourself? It's easy, isn't it? It's alright to say, "I miss you. Where have you gone? I've forgotten what you're truly like."

That's part of the human adventure. There's no need to be hard on yourself for being one of many who feel this way. If you're able to sit with this sadness, you'll move past it into the longing." I long to know you again. I long for us to be one." You'll find your way back. You must have faith in this. You haven't gone very far because you're joined energetically. As you get to the place of:" Do you think we can find one another?" You will move to another level:" I miss you and I want us to be one. What will it take?"

You need an open heart. An ease with whatever will be, non-judgement and a connection to where you and the other humans reside energetically. At least soften the boundaries here. Allow yourself some space to breathe. Some space to move. Some space to be.

Just allow a bit of breathing room here. You've been smothered by yourself. Therefore, you can be freed by yourself. Do you see? Whoever implements the thing may remove it. Now it's up to you.

Now look a little bit further into your eyes. Can you see the LOVE there? Can you see the connection with the Universe and other energetic beings? Can you see that? Can you see what a LOVELY creature you are?

There is much LOVE here for you.   Namaste

You are pure, essential LOVE. Perfect underneath it all. You've placed a lot of judgments on yourself but underneath it, don't you see? Pure innocent LOVE. That's who you truly are. Isn't that good to know?

March 4th
Step Out of Your Box and Into the Light

You consider a square something unchangeable. But where is there room for grace or opposing opinions.? What if a square is not always a square? Is there any space for your consciousness to seep in and correct your way of being? If there's not, you've constructed a rigid life where you've felt safe. So, this box is actually for you to live in.

Others will not harm you. You will not be connected with anyone but your mind and ego. All your ideas will remain here, never to be challenged or changed. You'll not be moved emotionally for you're not interacting with humans on a heart level.

The rest are living their lives. Conversing, connecting, trying to find one another energetically, connecting with the Universe of LOVE, meditating, healing their body, healing others energetically and speaking silent namaste to each other. This vibration is just one more link in this world you live in that is open to new information. You live on a vibrational LOVE level. You're skipping about, dancing, running in the rain and playing with one another.

You are the playful beings of the earth. Open to LOVE and you shall find it. Open to Universal Intelligence and you shall know it all. Travel through time and space, no problem. Send LOVE energy through the ethers to another human, of course you will. Because these are your highest evolutions in humanity.

You're human and yet, you're spiritual. You're free to experience LOVE, learning and you have access to the highest intelligence. For you're the believers, the creators, and the LOVERS. You're the ones who share LOVE energy with a world much in need of it. Because you allow it to pass through you and out of you. But first you must believe there's a great source of LOVE that exists outside of you and inside of you. For if you don't believe this, you must live in a box.

There is much LOVE here for you.   Namaste

You're an average human being who has become conscious. You've folded up your box and thrown it away. Now you're roaming around with the other LOVE beings like you. It's the highest and most fulfilling way for you to be there.

March 5th
Laughter & Music

Watching you laugh at yourself brings great joy to you and to the Universe. Each time you laugh out loud or smile, it elevates the energy to all. It rolls out from you to those who are miles away.

The high, light vibration is felt by all, including animals. They can't say what it is, but they understand when energy passes by them. It's what your vibration feels like outward. It's a high vibration. Much like your music.

Laughter and music are the same high vibration of LOVE. It brings others joy and peace without them knowing what it is. It just washes over them.

Is there anything more beautiful than to pass LOVE to others unknowingly? Now that you know, you will do it knowingly. Each time you laugh and play music, you're sending LOVE to the world. You're saying, "There you go LOVE. Go out to the others."

Can there be a greater gift to mankind than free LOVE? It's what your soul came to do. It's what you're capable of doing when you're in touch with your soul. All your soul knows is LOVE. To receive it. To be in it. To be part of it. To share it. To feel LOVE. To process LOVE. Give LOVE.

Now you LOVERS are going out to share more than you knew you had. You didn't know you were affecting others. You thought you were pleasing yourself.

Yet, the whole vibration of the earth is being raised up because of your high laughter and your high music. The entire species is lifted up because of you. It's perfect.

You feel LOVE and LOVE is passed through you. That is what you call a beautiful thing. You're giving it and getting it. You're raising up all humans. Now, that is something your soul will rejoice over. It will rejoice that it has a say in your life. That's all it wants to do. Be LOVE. Give LOVE. Share LOVE.

There is much LOVE here for you. Namaste

Keep on laughing and playing your music. It's the most important things you can do.

March 6th
Are You Going to Come Out?

Can you see yourself stumbling around in a dark room with a door? You're nervous about finding the door so you've got your arms out feeling around. You're thinking, "Where am I?" If you feel something weird, you pull your hands in and keep them close. Now perhaps you won't move at all because you'll be fearful of what's in the room with you. So, you stop moving. Now you're frozen in a dark room. How long will you stand here?

Many of you are frozen and unable to feel your way around to get out. You're starting to feel comfortable, so you just sit down. You just make peace with it." This is it for me. There's probably nothing outside anyway." Soon you fall asleep in there. That is your life.

As you settle into sadness, feel the darkness falling on you. Feel a noise that would cause fear in you. Pretty soon you don't know if you can stand up anyway. When you're all cried out, you're not sure if your legs work, you don't know where the door is or if you care anymore, suddenly you have hope. Something just flickers. Then the energy starts to build." Maybe there's a door. Maybe there's something outside. Maybe I can live."

So, you crawl to the door. You knew where it was all the time. You open it to see what's happening there. If you put your hand down, there's soft grass. It's life. Growing all the time without you. Growing regardless of you. Now you have a choice. Come out or stay in.

The world is waiting for you to decide.

There is much LOVE here for you.   Namaste

When you recall being in a room and surrendering to hopelessness, you will feel compassion for yourself. Once you get out of the room you won't go back in there for anything. It's a place of death. Even though your body is still alive, your energetic self is not. Your energetic self-wishes to connect with other energy from humans and the Universe of LOVE. It's your energetic self that suffers from this kind of capture.

March 7th
LOVERS

Romantic LOVE is a different type of LOVE than what you feel for friends and family. Romantic LOVE is often intense and overwhelming. It causes much emotion. Sometimes high. Sometimes low. This type of experience is necessary because the high is difficult to reach alone. The low, when done in unison, is often easier to rise out of.

When you travel alone, there's an experience that brings you joy and connection to the Universe. It's a melding of memories and processing of sadness. This is time alone to process, connect and meditate. There must be an allowance for this all your life. This connection to Source will carry you throughout your life. When you feel connected, balanced, and have dealt with your emotional issues, then you may open the door and enter the world of humans. This is when you're well enough to offer another what they're offering you.

When this comes together, then the highs and lows will be experienced together. It's less harmful because you're a heavier vibration when you're together.

When you're coming together with an equal, the two of you will rise higher together. This is because your heart is open more when you're in a LOVE relationship. You allow more in. You're more vulnerable.

This is the importance of these LOVE relationships when you're clear enough and healthy enough to have one. Together you will rise above where you have reached the LOVE level before.

It's a complex human relationship but the emotional openness and energy that comes out when you're in this state is different than when you're alone. There's this need for some (not all) to connect in this spiritual union.

When this happens, there's another layer outside that joins with you and raises the vibration of both of you. The two of you are a vibrational LOVE creation.

There is much LOVE here for you.   Namaste

When LOVE is being experienced openly between two of you, the Universe surrounds it and escalates it.

March 8th
High Vibrational People

You've come to have a human experience with a body and emotions but what you've truly come for is to feel controversy. It doesn't exist in the Universe of LOVE when you're in non-physical. Human nature demands controversy. It's invigorating. You also wished to feel a range of emotions.

You've been experiencing emotions for some time, so you say, "I've got the human thing but is there more to me than this?" You're now coming full circle. You came in spiritually knowing everything. Then you wished to have a human experience. Now you wish to have your spiritual experience back and integrated into your human experience.

You're stretching the boundaries of human existence. You're wondering," Can I be human and also spiritually enlightened?"

It's new territory but you're intrigued by it. You long for it. Therefore, it will be. These naturally follow one another. It means it exists in your heart. You don't yearn for something impossible.

The yearnings become real. It draws you out and forward into your enlightened self. This is your soul reaching out. It knows too much for you to know in this lifetime, but you can get a little bit. A little drop will stretch your human nature into this spiritual realm.

You're becoming a stretchy human whose had enough practice being human they wish to have more. You want to stretch the bounds of humanity. You want to become enlightened.

There's a multitude of you energetically. You create more energy than the others. You're lighter. The energy is higher and faster.

The others having a human experience are a little heavier and are just going about their business. It's all right. They're doing their thing. But you're in a different space. A vibrational high. That's how you're able to see one another.

There is much LOVE here for you.   Namaste

Your high vibration is reaching above the others. It will find others who are like you.

March 9th
Breathing in LOVE

LOVE is the most acceptable human word for the energy. This energy brings you ease and comfort. Your system slows when it experiences LOVE energy flowing through you. The resulting emotion is peace and gentleness. You know you've been touched with LOVE energy by the result.

You don't feel the LOVE passing through you because you're LOVE energy. You're the same vibration. You're in LOVE energy when you're not in physical. So, you don't feel it coming in because it's not foreign to you. It 'is' you.

When you're not in physical, you float in energy with everything that exists-humans who used to be humans, peace, and LOVE. The Universe of LOVE is a feeling of vastness.

You understand that your cosmos is many stars. Ones you can see. Others you can't but together they make up a Universe. The word LOVE is used because you understand the feeling that follows the word Universe because you spend more time in the Universe of LOVE than you do in these lifetimes.

When energy passes through you to others, you can often see them smile. It passes through you all the time because you're energy. It's like breathing in and out the Universe of LOVE. It's normal for you.

If it's as natural as breathing, why resist it? Why so much busy-ness? Because you're having a human experience. You're playing with life. That's exactly what you're supposed to do.

No matter where you're sitting, it's exactly correct for you. When you're in turmoil, sit in it. When you're sitting in peace, sit in it. No judgement of one or the other because there's truly not one that is more correct than the other. It's the judgement that keeps you from sitting in peace. The judging is also part of your human experience.

There is much LOVE here for you.   Namaste

Judgment must be noticed and it will automatically be lessened. Just notice it. "I judge myself in peace. I judge myself in busy-ness." Isn't that interesting? That's all. Then it dissolves.

March 10th
Use Those Wings

As things happen that make you angry or sad, your vibration lowers. It moves slowly but it continues to vibrate because it's in survival mode. You know your vibration will raise someday.

Then you'll be your highest vibration which is connected to the Universe. You want to evolve. You want to live. You want to fly.

Sometimes you feel like those plastic owls that sit on top of a building. It just exists. Maybe it's good with resting this time. For some, this is their entire existence.

Now you're thinking, "I'm going to fly but I'm not sure if I remember how." You have a little fear. There are some who never use their wings. That's okay. Your only concern is what you're called to do. What you're excited to do.

Then there are those who just jump off the building in faith. They fly because you all have wings that remember how to work. Just like your soul remembers how to live a spiritual life. Your instincts are honed. It's been in existence forever. It knows exactly what to do. As soon as you open up and let it come out.

It's very important that you have the final say. That's your humanity. Say yes or no. You're not judged. You're LOVED either way.

If you say yes, you're going to fly off the building and your soul will take control. You're going to have fun because now you're free. You'll be a little less human and a little more spiritual.

Spirits with high energy are living it up. They don't take themselves too seriously. They dance. They sing. They laugh. They hug. They LOVE. They make eye contact with strangers. They send LOVE to strangers in their eyes.

You're the flyers. You're the leapers. You wish to jump and pray your wings remember because you're turning your life over to them. It's okay because you know your soul is in contact with the Universe of LOVE which knows all. It remembers how to live. It remembers how to fly.

There is much LOVE here for you.   Namaste.

Some of you need to rest in this existence. Some of you don't.

March 11th
Life Mask

You have a way of presenting a certain type of person. You've decided you must look a certain way to please others. So, you create a face. A persona. Therefore, your true self is tucked behind this mask. You're protecting yourself from exposing your true self.

You made this mask because something happened to you when you were a small one. You realized if you showed your true feelings all the time, you couldn't control your tears and others would respond by telling you to stop and go hide away. They didn't want to see that kind of face.

Then you figured out there is one place where you may be your authentic self. When you're alone without a mirror, you're able to be your authentic-self-in-hiding. Some of you cry alone.

But some continue to wear the mask even when you're alone. It became familiar and comfortable to pretend you were this other human. You started to like it. It hardened you. Therefore, no one else could cry either or you'll judge them.

When you keep the mask on all the time you don't understand your real self or your persona. They become one. Some built their faces so seamlessly that it became part of their body.

For others, sometimes you put it on and sometimes you take it off. You're looser with it but now you wish to put it aside. You still use it even though it's not real.

You use it when you're feeling unsafe in your world. The problem is that you created your world so you can use the mask sometimes. It's difficult being you all the time so you rest when you wear it. Each time you put the mask on, you're confirming you're unsafe. So, you like the mask yet it's creating the unsafe life.

You're perfect the way you are. You don't need a mask or a persona. You're living the exact existence you wished. Good. Bad. Sad. With a mask. Without a mask. You devised it. There's nothing unsafe or scary about your life. It's all perfect.

There is much LOVE here for you.   Namaste

When you say, "I'm angry. I'm sad. I hate you. I LOVE you" your world is safe because you can be what you are.

March 12th
Step Into Yourself

Power lies when you work as one. You're just uncovering what your role is. As each of you step into your truest, connected self, you'll uncover who you are. Even if it's not what you're doing at this moment.

Now fear comes in because many of you have done what's in front of you and what others have told you to do. It's oftentimes not your true role in humanity. Therefore, some of you must turn your life upside down so you may connect and be your truest self. Then you'll be your happiest, most aligned, and peaceful self. You will finally know," This is where I belong. This is my role."

Many of you are not making your highest offering to humanity. You're hiding out in some comfortable place where you don't belong. You've made yourself fit in so no-one will notice. Yet you have a knowing inside that you don't belong there, and you must go. You don't know where but you know this is not it. But there is still resistance.

You're mixed up because you're playing other people's roles. When you play someone else's role, they're not because you've taken it. It's the same with yours. Someone else has taken it because there were holes. But which one is yours? If you have taken someone else's place and someone's taken yours, how is the human team to come together cohesively? When you feel resistance, anger, or frustration, it's because you don't belong.

Now you're questioning if you belong. If you're at ease and sliding forward, stay where you are. If you're up against walls and feeling frustrated, it's because you don't belong there. You're not supposed to live in daily conflict. Others have just gotten used to where they are.

Your life will unfold easily when you're in the place where you belong. You want to know the truth. You've asked the Universe: "Where do I belong?" Now it's responding.

There is much LOVE here for you.   Namaste

If you're in a frustrated, angry situation, it's not where you belong. If you're in an easy, unfolding life, it's where you belong.

March 13th
Start Over

There are many times in your life when you do a start-over. You've gotten some project going and you think, "This is not right. I'm going back to the beginning and throwing this away." There are many of you who don't throw anything away, so you try to fix it. You try to put another piece on it, but it still falls apart. After a time, you think, "I should have just started over, but I tried to fix it."

You don't wish to think you wasted your time creating something that's not beautiful. There are some who believe this but there are others who say, "I've been learning but it's not perfect, so I'll throw it away and start again. The next one will be better."

Same project. Same humans. Two different feelings about it. One feels that perhaps they're not up to the task. They might be unworthy. They make a mess of things. Then there are others who say, "I'm just a student learning about life." These humans are the same.

You all move through things. Perhaps it takes some a little longer or they learn other things quickly. Some of you have worked your way through the emotion and some stay in it.

Sit in the place of "I can't get anything right" if you must. Then throw it away and start again. Say, "I'm a student of life. I'm still learning."

When you say that to yourself, it means a lot. It means you're not flawed at all. It means that you're perfect. You're just learning new things. New ways of being. New ways of interacting. New ways of feeling.

"Be patient with me. I'm learning new things because I'm interested in life. I encourage myself to go to new places, see new things and try new projects. I wish to be part of the human community; therefore, I'll stumble and fall then get back up and try again. I'll try again because I'm a student. I'm learning how to live." Repeat these words over and over until you fully incorporate them into your being.

There is much LOVE here for you.   Namaste

You are all together. You are all the same. You are all on the same journey.

March 14th
Am I Worthy to Be Here?

There's part of you that wishes to have a room full of finished energetic products. You have a notion when you finish something, you move up to level. You thought when you gathered enough, you'd be a successful human to others. You'd show them your room and say," This is what I've accomplished." They will clap.

Now that the room is full, it's time to see what's in there. You might say, "That was from a long time ago. What's that doing here?" "It wasn't very good, but I tried." "I've forgotten all about these things." There's a notion that you're to complete things and save them but never go back to look at them. If that's the case, why bother saving them?

Humans need to accumulate things in case someone asks, "What have you been doing?" Then you have evidence that you're worthy. You think, "True, I've not shared them with others. I've kept them to myself in case I needed to prove my worthiness." This is a sad realization for you. For now, you recall how someone adored that project, but you didn't give it to them. You had to put it in your room.

The primary place where humans falter is proving worthiness where none is needed. Free yourself from these memories by opening the doors and the windows of your room and letting everything fly out to join with other projects by other humans. Share your ideas and thoughts.

Your very essence must be shared now because we have brought your attention to this room.

Now there's nothing left for you to do but let everything float out until the room is empty. Now it's full of life, air, and newness. Full of energy, happiness, and excitement. It's an empty room full of potential. Now you can breathe because you're free. You don't have to prove your worthiness to anyone. You've sent your contributions out.

There is much LOVE here for you.   Namaste

You ask, "Am I worthy to be here?"
You hear, "You're precious to the Universe of LOVE because you came into human trusting and hoping, with the intention to share LOVE with others. You're most worthy."

March 15th
Healing Energetic Trauma

There are times you pass others, and one catches your attention. This is acknowledging the energetic self of another. The part of you that recognizes yourself in them.

There are parts of you left behind energetically that have been damaged. Try to visualize yourself throwing a traumatic event to the side of the road. This energy still exists.

Watch the human who caught your attention, notice their gestures and their energy. See if you can see colours or light coming from them. There's something that reminds you of a story you've put aside but you now wish to look at. It's saying, "Look at me! You threw me aside, but it doesn't mean I don't exist."

If you're in the place to handle this vulnerable honesty and connection, you'll heal from this event. If not, just carry on. It will reoccur if you wish to face it later. Energy recirculates. This is not the only time for you to heal.

But if you're to notice this event, something will bring forth a vision of yourself that is unhealed. This is all unknown to the other human. Your energy has many unhealed places. So, if you're whole enough, you'll be able to see your life through a stranger's eyes. The combination of you and the stranger, will heal the event.

Energy is not always traumatic. It could be something that triggers you into seeing yourself a new way. You'll have many opportunities through your life to relive energies. You just have to watch and allow the memories and energy come back through you so it's alive again. This is painful because you don't wish to relive it. You threw it away for a reason. But if you're able to sit in it, it will disappear. Memories are attached to energy and it's always moving.

The interaction from one energetic self to another, is the way your highest self is able to communicate. This does not have to be an uncommon event. You also do it for others unknowingly. Your highest self communicates energetically often without a word being said.

There is much LOVE here for you. Namaste

You have the capability to support one another to heal fully from energetic trauma.

March 16th
Under Water

Your heart rate and bodily mechanisms are moving at a slower pace. Have you noticed this? You're getting as much done as before but it feels like you're moving slower. Like you're moving through water. This is your body slowing down vibrationally.

You're playing with the energy outside you and your body is responding inside by slowing down. They're coming into rhythm together.

Soon you will glimpse others doing the same thing. Then you'll be connected to others. Your energy will meld together.

You're growing into a spiritual being. You're evolving from your physical self into your spiritual self which is energy. Spiritual energy, connectedness and LOVE are the same thing. It comes from the Universe to you and others.

Energy is moving around all the time, but you don't always notice it. As you've been meditating, which slows down your bodily functions, you've been directly connecting to this Source. Now you're moving at a different pace. You're more deliberate. More connected. Therefore, you're getting more done.

You're seeing a larger picture. It's not just your little human life. Now there's the Universe to experience. There's energy and LOVE. Other humans. The surroundings, flowers, and small animals.

Your experience is being incorporated with slowing down of energy which is speeding it up. It moves more deliberately. Then you'll feel connected to the Universe and to those living things around you.

There is much LOVE here for you.   Namaste

Energy is always working and moving so you become aware of it. You're energy, just like the Universe. That's why you may exist in LOVE and become one with it. You are the same.

March 17th
Out of Reach

It seems as if there's something just in front of you. If you move, then it moves. This sort of longing allows you to move forward energetically and in your human body. They're linked together for the time you exist there. Together they march forward.

Your energetic self has a memory of your Divine Self. Of what you're capable of. Of what your highest evolution would be. What your cleanest, clearest humanity would look like. It's a remembering of what's really going on.

It's always a little bit ahead of you because you don't reach it until you're finished there. It'll always be this way, no matter how much connecting, meditating, and surrendering you do.

Because this highest self has little connection to your physical body. It can't be reached while you're in your human experience. Why the yearning then?

" I'm an energetic being. I come in and out of humanity easily. I come into humanity to allow LOVE to flow through me to the others. Then I easily leave. Then I easily come back." This is the remembering. This is the longing. The ease of it.

As you spend more time in your human body, it's not easy at all. It's complicated, painful, and sad but somehow you understand that it's meant to be easier than it is. It will be easier when you leave, of course, then you'll remember and say, "Oh, it's supposed to be easy." Then you'll come back. "It's going to be easy." Then you'll forget. Then you'll leave. Then you'll come back, and you'll forget.

There will always be this slight remembering of the ease from being in the LOVE vibration. It's what you yearn for but now you've got a human body slowing things down.

There is much LOVE here for you.   Namaste

The body remembers the first moment you came in. The joyful enthusiasm you had when you locked in together as a team. Energetic and physical. It remembers what it's like to have fun and be hopeful. To wish for the best. Of course, your human body remembers this because in that first moment of life, you were authentic.

March 18th
It's Magic

You're always wondering if there is more than what humans can see and feel. It's because you have an idea there are secrets and magical things going on. Even if people disagree. You're convinced of it.

This strong knowing has drawn you to this vibration which will confirm what you already know. You're drawn to it because you're seeking the truth. You've asked the Universe to provide an answer. So, you watch and wait.

You've felt things you can't explain. You've witnessed indescribable things. You've heard stories from others that make no sense in your logical, orderly world. Of course, there's more going on than what you can see.

You're able to handle as much as you can at any moment. The beginning of this noticing is when you feel or sense energy from others. You're sizing them up energetically. Beyond that, some have gotten ideas of things that were going to happen before they did. You call it intuition but it's noticing energy because it's always moving. Others are able to think of one another through distance and time, and the other will feel it. That's energetic. Some have visits by past relatives. That's energy. Others hear things that are not their own voice. That's energy.

It's magic really. For the unknown. For the indescribable. Although the proper term is energy. It's always moving and changing. It comes in and out of you. You go in and out with it. You connect with it through others. You connect with it directly to the Universe of LOVE. You can do all these things.

Yes, there's more going on. Because what's the chance there's just a bunch of humans making things and giving them to others and then saying thank you. That would be robots. You're certainly not robots, are you? No, you're energetic beings.

There is much LOVE here for you.   Namaste

Even those who disagree with you might believe there's more going on. They're just not comfortable telling you about it. They don't want to seem odd. But there are more and more of you noticing this energy of the Universe.

March 19th
Choices

Near the end of your life, you just sit where you are. You relax. But when you're in the middle, you're still deciding which way to go. It's most important that you choose. As you came into your human existence, part of the agreement was that you would always decide. Stay or go. This way or that. LOVE or hate.

You're not robots or soldiers. You will not be made to do something you don't wish to. Sometimes, you've got so many choices, you can't decide. These are times when your brain decides for you. Then you gather information and then compare choices. Your brain only has information available to it for the length of time you've lived.

If you're able to connect with the Universe of LOVE, where all information resides, you have more available to you. But if you decide to follow your brain, that's perfectly fine, too. That's an experiment for you in living as a human.

If you're able to sit quietly and put the question forth, you hear some kind of answer returning to you. You'll have more information. When you're sitting in alignment asking questions and the answers come, you'll be moved energetically. You'll cry if it's right or you'll cry if it's wrong. When you're moved energetically, you're in the LOVE energy of the Universe, which has all information. Then you'll feel more at ease with whatever you decide because your body will be agreeing with you. Your energetic self will be on board.

Any answer that you're not content with that you've devised in your brain, sit down, and connect with the Universe. When you feel an emotion take over, you know you're heading in the right direction. You're getting more information so that when you make a decision, you won't rethink it. Then you can live your life more fully. When you're able to make a decision with your whole self, you move on to the next thing.

There is much LOVE here for you.   Namaste

Being assured physically and energetically that you've made a right decision, will put you at ease. Even if it looks awful. The choice is easier when you connect energetically with something beyond your mind.

March 20th
Ocean of LOVE

To get beneath what is obvious, think of icebergs. You can see as much above as is hidden below. From human to human, you're looking at what's obvious. That's how you have to live there.

Can you believe for a moment that there's as much going on underneath humans as there is above? Just hold this thought for a moment. You understand that you're complex. What you present is not always your true self. It's impossible for you and others. You're all walking around half obvious, half hidden. Since you've all agreed to this, it's absolutely fine.

But there's more information here. You're unlike an iceberg since it must stay the way it is because there's a certain container that holds it. What sort of container is holding your secrets? Your most honest self? Your most vulnerable self? Something frozen? Something that will not melt until the sun comes out?

When the sun comes out, icebergs surrender to the sun. Is it painful for them? It's a letting go. It's becoming one with the ocean. It's going back home to itself where it's safe, comfortable, and easy. Do you like the idea of your iceberg melting with others? Now when you look out at the ocean, you don't know if there are any icebergs there. All you know is that the sun is shining on the water, and it looks beautiful, peaceful, or raging. It works together. All waves or all calm.

Your iceberg is a painful place for you. You don't like to admit that one exists, but your iceberg has been building up since you were little. It's from things you've seen, witnessed, and come to believe. They're not things you wish others to see. That is why they're hidden. You don't know if you can't withstand an uncovering.

When the sun comes out toward icebergs, they melt only a few drops at a time. It takes a long time. For you, telling one piece of your story at a time all you need." There's this thing I never told anyone. May I tell you?"

There is much LOVE here for you.   Namaste

The sun will heal you, the water will absorb you and you'll become one. You'll become less hidden, more available and at ease. You'll smile more.

March 21st
I Know Everything

It seems like you're always showing up for a new lesson. Oftentimes, you wonder, "When will I be the teacher?" This way of thinking is one you've gathered through your human time. First, you're studying, then you're teaching subjects that were taught to you. This is your human way. If you show up and someone is doing the energy vibration, you assume you're listening as a student.

We're not teachers. We're energy. The same as you are. We're equals. You know as much as we know. We're all in this together. We're all vibrational energy. You show up as an equal here because this is a vibrational exchange. Your energy is expressing itself to the Universe right now. You're calming down into truth because this resonates with you. All the energy is getting mixed up into one easy, kind, LOVING energy.

You already know energy is always moving. It can't sit still. Some of you are highly energized. You get excited when it moves through you.

When it moves through you, it joins with the others then comes back to you. That means everyone including the Universe of LOVE and non-physical. The energy that passes through you cannot stay within you. It's highly energized.

If you try to contain energy inside you, it turns into disease. When it passes though you, it gets cleaned. All the worries, distress, anger, and sadness drop away. It becomes clear, high vibration like a note of music which feels innocent and light.

You know how energy feels. You allow energy into you and out of you. This is an energetic exchange; therefore, you know everything. You're energy after all. Energy that travels far and wide. Remember, you're a traveler with energy and you know everything.

There is much LOVE here for you.   Namaste

Your energy expresses your needs and wants. You may often communicate with one another and the Universe without saying a word.

March 22nd
Game of Life

There's a game where you pull one block out and hope nothing else falls. You pull and pull until finally it falls. This can be applied to your life. Sometimes you venture into things when you know it will end badly. Yet, there's a curiosity to hang in until things crumble. Then you build it and pull the pieces out all over again. Over and over. This becomes a pattern just to notice.

Problems occur in your energetic field when you hide things. When you put them in rooms and pretend they don't exist. If you keep putting things out front, life goes more easily. It's only uncomfortable for a few moments because you don't like the thing. Then the feeling passes and now this becomes a new pattern for you.

Watching things crumble and hiding bad things away, is a pattern accepted between all humans. You've decided as a group consciousness. Now there can be compassion with this because you're all doing the same thing.

There's another game where you build things up properly. You lay pieces of wood one way and then another, so it won't fall. It's building a life on truth.

What if taking something from the dark room became the first piece of wood at the bottom of your house? There's another old thing that you've told someone and now feel relieved and joyful about it, that can be put at the bottom of the house, too. Perhaps this house can be built like this. Taking something that used to be negative, learning something from it and healing. It will not fall now because it's pure.

Call it, "Build A Life". Piece by piece you can use the old remnants. No need to throw that stuff away. You've experienced it and hidden it for a reason. Now you've brought it out into the light for a reason. You've shared it with someone for a reason. You wish to heal so you may evolve and be your highest evolution. First you must be at peace with yourself. Then you wish to be one with your higher energetic self. You wish to know you're not alone.

There is much LOVE here for you. Namaste

When you connect with others and the Universe of LOVE, you feel more alive and at peace.

March 23rd
Sit & Allow

There are things that happen in your life you can't make sense of. Truth must come out slowly in its own time. You try to shake it out. The human way is to demand what is yours. This is the way you've evolved and survived. But there is another way to live.

The spiritual way. The gentle way. Allowing life to unfold. Sitting back and watching it. Waiting for it to come to you instead of trying to grab it. While you're waiting, why not sit quietly and meditate. Come into alignment with you and Source. All things will pass. Even you.

Your connection to Source will keep you grounded while you're living your human existence. Being one with the Universe means a sense of calmness is available to you. Allow the Universe to unfold. Allow your life to unfold in conjunction with the Universe. The Universe is sometimes very slow with important things. Slow and gentle. That is the way of the Universe.

It's not your usual way but you feel more at peace and calm when you're connected to Source, which you LOVE. The sense of calmness reduces anxiety, sadness and anger. You have a sense of oneness with all that exists. This is what your soul desires more than anything.

You feel one with those around you and your surroundings, when you're able to sit quietly and allow your life to unfold in the gentlest way. This is also the most generous, fulfilling, and LOVING way.

Allowing your life to unfold is not easy for your physical self but it's very familiar for your soul self. It's the natural way for it. It may take the lead when your physical self falters. When it's tired or sad. Your soul may take the time to hold you. When you're ready, your soul will help you. It will show you how to allow your life to unfold in a gentle manner. Just sit and be. Wait for the healing. Wait for the LOVE.

There is much LOVE here for you.   Namaste

You may be held by the Universe during times of sadness. That is what the Universe of LOVE does best of all.

March 24th
Are You Safe?

There are certain messages that come to you in strange ways.
Oftentimes you will hear a message inside or from someone who will
say it doesn't make sense to them, but it makes sense to you. You
understand this is coming directly from the Universe of LOVE.
Perhaps, as you're driving, you'll hear, "Slam on the breaks." You start
to understand these words are vibration. It's really energy but in order
for you to hear it, it's transformed into vibration.

You understand the message is just for you, so you wonder
why you're so valuable. Humans don't like to sit in their value or
preciousness. It's uncomfortable. You've grown more comfortable
sitting in negative feelings like anger and sadness.

Sometimes humans get it upside down. You can sit in anger,
but you can't sit in LOVE it's overwhelming. It's all-encompassing.
You wonder what will be left of 'you' if you sit in LOVE,
preciousness, and value all the time. "What kind of good, hard working,
fighting human would I be then? I'll be one of those soft, mushy people
who smile all the time. Surely, they can't be prized in humanity. Surely
they will be extinguished."

There's a part of you that dislikes humans who sit in LOVE.
They look weak and vulnerable to you. They could be hurt easily. You
know if you keep up your guard and defenses, you'll always be safe.
You wish to be safe more than you wish to evolve. If you don't like the
sound of living a safe life, this is what the Universe thinks of you.

You've chosen to come into human when so many in non-
physical have not. That means you're brave. You try very hard to
LOVE others even though they're not very nice. So, you're very kind.
You wish you could sit in LOVE and tenderness. You're just afraid
you'll be hurt. In this way you're very vulnerable.

There is much LOVE here for you.   Namaste

*The Universe of LOVE surrounds you at all times. They're on guard so
you don't have to be. So, don't put on the brakes to stop you from
experiencing LOVE and softness. When you feel vulnerable, you're
figuring out how to be human.*

March 25th
Rule Book

You're bound to certain obligations that others have put forth and you've taken on. Then there are some you made up yourself, from certain life experiences that didn't go your way. You thought, "I'll never do that again." If you look at this rule book, it's quite full. They just pile on top of one another until you're so bound up with rules, you can barely live.

As you sit in this, you'll see the rules were made so you didn't have to feel the shame, sadness, or anger. This was only for that experience. It was not to make up rules. If the underlying emotions were not dealt with, the uncomfortable experience will occur again. Don't get stuck in shame here.

Underneath shame, anger and sadness is true vulnerability, connection, and LOVE. Humans are made in LOVE. They are full of LOVE energy. First you have to get into the shame place. Sometimes you can't tell if it's shame, anger, or sadness. If you recall a certain event that you made specific rules up afterwards, you'll see there's kindness or LOVE there.

Anger and sadness keep everything away energetically and you sit alone in it. That's why you can't stand it. Can there be softness or LOVE allowed to you for being a human being?

Setting up another rule doesn't take away the emotion or the experience. The full experience was not had because it got painful, and you put a rule around it.

Now you have so many rules. Perhaps you can sit quietly with each one. See what comes up around it. See if there's an emotion attached to it. See if it's someone's else's. Sitting in painful memories gets you to the LOVE underneath. It must be a clear path.

See what rules you wish to keep or throw away. Rules imply you cannot live instinctually and enjoy the fullness of each moment. This is truly the way for you to live in peace and ease. Checking in with energy to see what's right for you.

There is much LOVE here for you.   Namaste

Perhaps today you can take a look at your bound book of rules. Maybe you can start ripping out pages. Wouldn't that feel enlivening?

March 26th
Vibrational Dance

There are times when you speak with another human and you wonder if they're being honest with you. You're also deciding how open to be with them. Many of these conversations break down because you're not focusing on what's being said. They're not fulfilling. You're living a mediocre life that's seen through conversations.

You don't like the sound of this. It's difficult for you to reveal yourself but you've all done it. It's where you were energetically. In each place, LOVE yourself right there. You're absolutely perfect no matter where you find yourself. You need not judge yourself or others for being there.

Now you're trying to speak, and you then watch the expression on their face. If it's a scary look, you pull back. If their face stays neutral, you give another piece of yourself. This is the vulnerability dance. You go a little. They go a little. At some point you both say, "That's as far as I want to go right now."

You've evolved to this state. Go ahead and move forward with others that move with you. You can be vulnerable with others. As you set fear aside, you'll notice that you're reading their energy and vibrations. And they're reading yours.

Your vibrations go faster and higher as you share your vulnerable self. As you share, you evolve. As it goes faster and higher, again you feel vulnerable but for a different reason. This is now your fear of losing touch with your physical self by becoming evolved.

Eventually, being vulnerable will be natural for you. That is how you evolve each step of the way through your humanity. You will do this over and over until it becomes comfortable for you to reach another level. That will be done alone with your Source, energy or vibrational being. You can only go so far with human energetic exchange.

There is much LOVE here for you.   Namaste

You know you're wonderful dancers. That's why you have your beautiful physical body. It has taught you how to dance energetically, too.

March 27th
LOVE Host

Blessed is a human word saved for the most special occasions. You become moved by it. You say, "This is a blessing. I'm blessed. You're blessed." It's one of the words you've lifted high among others. A blessed event is something you're focusing on energetically. You acknowledge something miraculous. You're just feeling connected to the Universe of LOVE. You've chosen this word to go directly inside of you with no filters.

You're blessed beings because you've chosen to come into physical form. You're the chosen ones. Because you're having a human experience no matter what it looks like. All of you. That one on the street. The one in the jailhouse. The one that's crying. All are blessed beings. Not just the ones who use the word and understand it.

It's up to you who are moved by this word, to bless all the others. Those of you that use the word have a special calling to share it because it contains an energetic blessing within it. You are to share it with those who are unfamiliar with it. Those who don't understand they're blessed as equally as you.

Blessed beings also have access to the entire Universe of LOVE and all non-physical. They're at your service. They're your non-physical support team. They support you in your existence.

You understand now because you've allowed the Universe of LOVE into you and, therefore, out of you. You know you can't hold energy. You've allowed the blessing in which is truly LOVE. This is the more correct word for it. You've allowed LOVE into you and out of you. When it passes out of you, it goes to those most in need of it. You're a LOVE host because sometimes, it can't get to them directly. It must pass through another human. The humans who volunteer to allow LOVE in and out of them offering a gift from one blessed being to another blessed being.

There is much LOVE here for you.   Namaste

What more could you possibly do there than to allow LOVE to enter you and exit you and go where it most needs to be? So, blessed beings, carry on with your LOVE work.

March 28th
Follow the Leader

Is it true you must become a follower since you've chosen the leader as a group? Are you allowed to confront them or treat them like they're an average human? Things had to be that way in the beginning because there was great chaos. Many humans were not capable of understanding, reading, and writing. So, there would be one chosen amongst them who could understand things at a higher level. This is not true now. This question is from an old pattern.

Today it feels powerless and ridiculous to follow a leader that you don't agree with. Now you think, "I will check in with me and decide what is right. No matter what the leader says." This can also be other strong humans. It's been part of human evolution. Today you have fewer leaders. You're freer to make decisions on your own.

Society has decided to speak like this," Let me check it out myself and I'll get back to you." It's powerful because you're saying, "I don't have to answer your question." You're encouraging one another.

As an individual, it's up to you to sit quietly, connect with whatever you feel is outside of you and then ask the question, "What should I do?" At first you won't be able to hear clearly but as you sit quietly and focus, you'll be able to hear what response is being given.

This takes quieting of the mind. It takes focusing on a single spot. Sometimes, life is going on around you. It's noisy. But as you focus on a singular dot in front of you, your mind quiets. Then your body. Focusing brings all your senses to this tiny dot. Then suddenly, everything quiets. When you've done this enough, you'll start to hear your answers.

At first, you'll guess what is being heard. Just listen more closely. Eventually you'll have this conversation. Then you will return to the human and say, "I've spoken with my Universal guides or and we've decided to say No." It's a new way of being for you. Hear your answer the best that you can. This is new patterning for you.

There is much LOVE here for you.   Namaste

You're the leader of 'you' because you've decided as a group to evolve this way.

March 29th
Can You Live Like a Child?

You have childlike joy about you, like when you giggle to yourself and you don't wish others to see. You don't want the adults to know you still feel like a small child inside who could run off and pick flowers any moment. That if you see a puddle, you have difficulty conversing with the adult because you can't wait to run through it. There's some shame attached to being childlike. Nonetheless, it's who you truly are inside. All of you.

The real question is, "Why aren't the adults who don't want to run into the puddle, embarrassed and ashamed because they've forgotten their childlike selves?" It's upside down? The embarrassment lies with those who have childlike joy and not those who've forgotten.

Shame is not your friend. Childlike joy is. This joyful way of living is becoming comfortable to you. You recognize it, so you join it. Then there are curious onlookers who watch you.

It's all right to be a child in your heart, no matter what happened to you in your human childhood. You have a chance now again to be childlike as an adult. To be open hearted, trusting, adventurous, creative, fun, easily forgiving others, staying in anger for just a moment, staying in sadness for just a moment. Allowing emotions to come and go.

You're always available for the experience presenting itself, especially if it's fun. If someone says, "Do you want to run away and dance in the woods?" And if you're sitting in childlike anticipation you'll say, "Let's go." If you're an adult you'll say, "I don't think I have time. I'm busy."

There is much LOVE here for you.   Namaste

There are many moments when you've been invited to share joy, but you, as an adult, have said, "Adults can't do this." What if adults CAN do this? What if adults can sit in anticipation? What if adults can allow emotions to come and go quickly? What if adults can live like a child?

March 30th
Have Some Fun & Share Some LOVE

You have a notion about what a perfect human should be. Others have told you. You have told others. You're always judging because you're trying to get into the least amount of trouble. That's your lower self. It's your brain trying to get through one day.

You came from a non-physical Universe of LOVE. You decided you would come into physical form. In order for someone to leave a place that is all LOVE, caring, kindness and empathy, you must have thought there was something better here for you. Otherwise, you would never leave that energetic space and become human.

You're energy when you're not in human body. You're joined with the Universe of LOVE and all energy that exists. It's around you right now. When you come into human form, you take a little bit with you and say, "I'm going to give it a go. I'm going to have some fun. I'm going to share LOVE with others but you've witnessed many things that have changed your mind.

You've become this person who plods through life. Can you recall now that you came to have fun and enjoy life in the beauty of the physical body, and allow LOVE to flow into you and out of you to the others?

Your soul and your energetic self says, "Let's go live. Let's go share some LOVE. Let's cry, dance, sing and get angry. Let's have a messy life.

Becoming one with the brain is done by acknowledging it. Then it will sit quietly: "We're going to try this thing. If you're too afraid we'll pull back but if not, we'll go forward."

Your energetic self came in with a mission of LOVE. Your brain took over just to get you to survive your human experience. They can certainly be friends. Unusual friends but opposites do attract. Then you will be your highest self which is to allow LOVE into you and out of you.

There is much LOVE here for you.   Namaste

You've got that body because it can do things that energy cannot.

March 31st
Free-Floating Anxiety

Many of you sit in free-floating fear. It's an anxiety provoking energy and you're not really sure if you should be afraid or not. You're taking the fearful energy of others. You've decided they must be correct, so you join them. Anxiety and fear are affecting the whole of humanity. You've gotten yourself into quite an energetic state.

Firstly, you must acknowledge the free-floating anxiety. Go to the place you're most reluctant to go and sit in it for a while, when it disappears, you're free to carry on.

Many of you are energetic beings so you're picking it up from others. It's not even yours. You can pluck it out of the air. Suddenly your chest is tight. You're just waiting for something awful to happen.

Don't be afraid of fear. It's only energy which is the exact same as LOVE. So, you can sit in it. Sit in your fear energy. See how it settles as you sit in it? It's only wishing for you to notice it. Now your chest is getting less tight, and your body is relaxing because energy is always moving. When it stops moving, it causes anxiety and illness. Energy must move. Energy cannot be contained. Now, there's a little more room for sunshine and brightness.

It's getting lighter because it's mixing with the opposite of itself. Now it swirls around and goes out of you fast, like a shooting star. Can you see where it's going? It's going out to the others who are sitting in black.

Now, they will have some white light added to theirs. Suddenly, you can see the ripple effect. It easily moves from human to human because you're mostly energy. Your body gets tight because you can feel energy. So, now are you sitting in grey or white? You just have to notice it.

There is much LOVE here for you.   Namaste

You can't stop energy, but you can notice it.

April

You came to walk through the world sharing LOVE energy with others.

##AARONLACEY

April 1st
My Friend Energy

You're comfortable with energy when you're excited, happy, or joyous. You LOVE when energy moves you this way. If you're aware of high energy, then you must also respect low energy like hopelessness and despair. Energy is energy. It comes in and out. It joins you together. It puts space between you. It moves through you. Your feelings react to vibration, which is energy. They acknowledge that energy is moving through you. That's all.

Your body notices energy because it's energy itself. When you notice energy, you become friends with it then your body doesn't have to respond with sickness. You say, "Oh, it's you. Are you coming for a visit?" Your body can handle a "friend" coming to visit, instead of a "dangerous human coming to kill us". Your body reacts completely differently to that scenario.

As you befriend energy, your body calms down so it may receive it, in and out. Particularly if it's a sad, negative or stressful event. If you're not friends with energy, your body will react as a shield to protect you from it. This will shut you down and your body will become ill. When you're shut down, you don't have access to healing and LOVE and this is what you want most of all.

If you're to access complete LOVE, which is energy, then you must be friends with all energy. Most importantly, you'll be available to allow LOVE into you and out of you to the others who do not have access to it. You cannot un-know what you know, but you can become casual friends. You can shake hands and say, "Hello. I think it's time for you to leave." Or you may wish to invite it into your home for the night. Notice when the energy passes, have a little conversation and say, "What kind of friend are you exactly?"

There is much LOVE here for you.   Namaste

Energy will go wherever it will. It comes in and out. Energy is always moving.

April 2nd
Running From LOVE

What if you were to sit down today and draw what your life looks like? You think drawing is for small ones only. You don't want to put down what your life truly looks like, plus you're not a very good drawer. These are the roadblocks you have as a taller human being. This is about receiving information that is unusual to you. Humans are resistant to new ideas. You like to feel as if you know everything, then you won't be hurt. Your ego won't be attacked because you'll see everything coming. That means you're always running away. The sadness you feel is because you're disconnected from sitting quietly and being one with the Universe. You cannot run and sit at the same moment. Most human beings are runners. You run out of fear.

Running is what you have learned from humans. The essence of you, the inner part of you, knows exactly what it needs to do at each moment. You forget that you have great knowledge of Universal things. You forget that your inside energy has been alive forever. You get caught up with the pack. You're trying to run ahead of them. Maybe you could stop for a moment and let the pack run by you. What if you just sit right down, close your eyes, and calm your breath? Your body has been running from fear for a long time. It's overactive. Your body will get the hang of sitting quietly.

You will begin to notice that there's energy moving around you all of the time. There's wind. There's life, LOVE, breath, and sun. The LOVE you feel is energetic. Then the energy turns into vibration. It's coming from an energetic place of LOVE. That's why you may sit in calmness. LOVE is nothing to fear. LOVE is to be embraced. For you are LOVE energy. Always and forever. That is why you have energy to move and live.

There is much LOVE here for you.   Namaste

How about sitting for a moment instead of running in fear of LOVE? How about sitting in LOVE?

April 3rd
Watch for the Balloons

You survive there by putting one foot in front of the other. You're so determined, and yet, you're not sure what you're doing. Nonetheless, it's admirable. Sometimes you ended up in the wrong place. You decided each step of the way, even though you would have been more contented in a different place. That's the human way. You ignored everything around you. You made this mind-decision based on very little information. That's often the way that it is.

You were missing the cues along the side that would have taken you around to contentment and peace. The alternative is to take one step slowly and look all about. If everything is calm, go one more step. Then another step slowly. Have a look around. If you see something colourful, step that way. "If you see something that's not good, turn another way. This is the fulfilling way to live for humans. To stop and redirect all the time.

There is one more layer of this. The reason we say 'always readjust' your plans and be gentle with your life is so you may get the great surprises that lie around each corner. You only find these surprises when you're going slowly. Peek around a corner and see what's there. It might be a bunch of balloons with your name on them. When you're living your 'dogged determined' life, you're not going to peek around the corner and see that there are balloons.

If you're alive this moment, you haven't missed a thing. Don't keep going to a place where you feel bad. Turn the other way. You wish to raise your vibration.

There is much LOVE here for you.   Namaste

Share LOVE. Share vibration. Give hope to those who are hopeless. Give hope to those who think their lives are wonderful and yet, they are not free.

April 4th
You're Being Watched

When you open your mind enough to realize you're part of a vast Universe of LOVE, you allow it to become part of your being. You're eagerly gaining new insights. You're open to new experiences, new humans, or new events. It's another way of being open to surprises, magic, and energy. Once you've witnessed it, you wait in anticipation for more. This brings new energy to you. As you sit with your heart open, wondering what's next, other humans notice. They wonder how you can live so openly. They're curious. They are affected by your open energetic heart. Your energy is flowing out of you and all around. Others can notice swirling energy. Unbeknownst to you. You're too excited. You're waiting for the next thing. You have not even spoken a word to them, yet they are affected by your joyful outlook. They watch you in the hope that they can hope for hope.

You're never alone energetically. This moving, upbeat energy is calling forth other energies that are in joyful exuberance just like you. We are not speaking of the spectators who are just watching. We are speaking of non-physical energy. It feels the same excitement about life that you do. Non-physical, that have been in physical, understand what it's like to be human sitting in anticipation of JOY and excitement. They are sitting with you. If you have relatives who have passed, they know what it feels like to be waiting in hope. They join in with your energy. You have a great pool of it when you're like this. It's as if you're on a wave of your own, and another one joins it and pushes it further. Then another wave and another. You're pushed forward without your own energy.

There is much LOVE here for you.   Namaste

You are never alone. You are always being watched.

April 5th
Letting Go of Humanity

There is much confusion about where you belong. It's a time of questioning yourself. It's a mass confusion of belonging. Therefore, it's a wonderful time to decide where you belong. Not where you ended up. There's going to be a mass shuffling. You're already moving around. You suddenly have freedom to move. Energetically, you're all floating about waiting. Many of you are free from bonds that have tied you.

You've evolved past the anxiety of letting go because the thing has disappeared. It's the act of holding onto that which was never yours, that causes your fear. You hold on tightly so it won't disappear but when it does, there's nothing to hold onto. Now you're just floating about. You have floating fear but it's different because it's not focused on one thing.

There are many others around who are doing the same thing. When you're all together letting go, a healing occurs. It's a letting go of humanity and human ownership of things that were never yours. Now you see clearly. You think, "I was holding onto something that could disappear at any moment." It's not so stressful for you now because you've already worked through it. When you're together, there is little to fear. You work as a group. You have great knowledge, empathy, LOVE, and care for one another. It doesn't matter if you lose anything because you've got one another energetically.

As the energy of the group works together, it alleviates the fear of the others. They are so fearful. It's just part of their being. Others may let go enough to see they are living in fear.

There is much LOVE here for you.   Namaste

By your world disappearing and you letting go, then joining together with others, the ones left holding on will be able to feel a lighter.

April 6th
I Am the Universe

You're asking to remember information that is not new to you. You say, "Universe, remind me again about what I am." This is a reminder that you're powerful because you're the Universe of LOVE. You're energy. You're connected to all other humans and the Universe.

You often think, "I must remain small energetically and spiritually. Then I won't be noticed. I'll fit in." Yet, you're saying, "Remind me how large I am. Remind me that I am the Universe of LOVE. Remind me what I know already." It's not that you ask and we will give you an answer and then you go away with it. The flaw with this thinking is that you can say, "That's a bad idea. "But if it's your idea then it must be splendid. If it's your knowing and your remembering, it will be perfect. It's not coming from outside you, it's coming from inside you. This is where all of the Universe resides. Where all answers to all questions that you will ever have reside. This energetic exchange is important only because you feel the energy of it. The part that remembers everything is being awakened by the vibration that is being offered here.

There's absolutely nothing new to you. If you wish to remember, go ahead and remember. If you wish to forget, go ahead and forget. It doesn't mean that you're not the Universe of LOVE. It just means that you're choosing to forget. That's all. You're energy. You've come into a physical body for your experience there.

There is much LOVE here for you.   Namaste

You can remember as much as you are comfortable remembering. As much as you wish to.

April 7th
Refreshment

Refreshment means that you have been thirsty. It's a gift you receive at the end of an arduous task. What you're seeking now is refreshment. Over and over throughout your being, you have sought out refreshment and found it. Since you've already created this pattern, you can put something else in that is not water. LOVE, peace, and calmness. This is what you wish to refresh yourself with now. It's a deeper yearning beyond the physical. You've gotten thirstier just listening to the word. It's deep inside you.

The question is, "How do you get your hands on that refreshing drink?" By sitting quietly, connecting to the Universe of LOVE and the energy of non-physicals that surround you. All of the energy from the Universe and in non-physical exists inside of you because you are one. It's the same energy. The same longing. The same refreshment. The same breath. What you seek and your answer are always tied up together; "I desire refreshment. I have refreshment. I desire peace. I have peace. I desire LOVE. I have LOVE." The answer is inside of you because you're the Universe of LOVE.

Yet, you don't move into the space that provides the peace you're seeking. You wish to remain calm and at ease in your world, in yourself and with the non-physical world. You wish to be one with it all. Yet, you already are. You wish to be one. You are one. You wish to be quiet. You are quiet. That is why we sound repetitive. We keep reminding you that you have your answer before you ask your question.

There is much LOVE here for you. Namaste

Energy is fast but words are slow.

April 8th
BELOVED Ones

You're known in the Universe as the precious humans. Your highest intention when you went from energy to human was to continue sharing the LOVE you experienced while you were in the Universe of LOVE. It's that intention that is so touching. What else happens in your time there is not the point. The point was that you wished to try and share LOVE with a bunch of humans.

You're coming back to allowing LOVE to flow through you. In this way you will share LOVE with the humans. What you have come down to is, "If I allow myself to be open to LOVE energy, which I vaguely remember from before, and if it passes through me to the humans, then I don't have to do it myself." You're starting to realize that it really wasn't you that was going to share LOVE with the humans. You didn't know how small human beings were.

You have come to understand this: "If I were less human and more energy, and if I allowed more LOVE to enter into me and out of me, then I will be doing what I set out to achieve. I thought I was going to give LOVE to the humans but it turns out all I had to do was allow LOVE to flow through me." It's a slight change but so important. You cannot carry enough LOVE to hand out to others. You really can't hold enough LOVE for yourself.

Some of you are sitting in a place being willing to allow LOVE to flow through you. Even though you're not sure how to open the gates. The allowing is a remembering. It's a letting go and becoming one with LOVE energy. You can dissolve your humanity and become one again with the energy of LOVE. Then you'll start to feel at ease. Then you've found your place in the Universe. Where you're comfortable. Where you belong. You've found your place of LOVE in the Universe.

There is much LOVE here for you.   Namaste

Now you can allow LOVE to flow out of you and into the others. Just as you intended at your first breath.

April 9th
Open & Flexible

You have gotten a chance to rework your list of priorities. You've developed them from the time you were born. Now you're reshuffling your lives. Isn't it a wonderful thing that humans can change their mind? You're flexible. Things change. It's one of the human agreements you've made. You decided that you'd allow LOVE to flow into you and out of you and to the others. You also decided you'd have a good time. You'd allow your priorities to switch around as things changed.

This doesn't sit well with all of you because you've decided that making up your mind and sticking to it was important. Now you've got a conflict. Admire humans who say what they mean and mean what they say or be flexible, so your priorities may move around. How do these two come together? Can you admire the fact that humans are flexible and their priorities may change? Of course, you can. As you become more kind to yourself, you will allow the others the same rules as you. "I will be flexible and I will be a person of my word." If you don't know you can be both, you will have to choose one or the other. Therefore, you can never change your mind or you will always change your mind.

You can be this kind of human whose is open and flexible. You're able to change your mind when you understand you're being encouraged by the Universe to do so. You must be able to change your mind because your life is always changing. You can be firm in your beliefs but, nonetheless, the world changes. Humans change. Events change. The Universe is flexible and not fearful. It's setting an example for you to embrace your flexibility while maintaining your strength of character.

There is much LOVE here for you.   Namaste

If you are inflexible, you miss the juicy opportunities for LOVE and life that are being offered to you.

April 10th
Allow Curiosity

You are curious beings. You came into being with this curiosity. It's your nature to be so. It's important for you to be curious from the beginning to the end. We are reminding you of something you highly value. Sometimes you forget about it with your busy-ness of life. Curiosity is easy to be seen in the small ones because they are learning many new things. They give it time and attention. They allow curiosity to grow. They don't push it aside. Like you have done." There's no time for curiosity. We are very busy working." That curiosity of the small one is always inside of you. Now it's a little bit perturbed that you're pushing it away.

Soon it will be like an angry child and have a fit. It will say, "Why is there no time for me to be curious?" Some of you have heard these very words energetically. That's you speaking. It's not some outside force. It's your inside being or your energetic self. It's you that belongs to the Universe of LOVE. You're in a human body to see everything there is to see while you're there. Everything. You don't want to work all day. You want to investigate and stare at things that are small until you see every little part of it. You're meant to be curious beings. It's your design. It's what you wanted.

You're in human form so you want to be curious. What is more curious than the human body and the experience you have there? Many strange things happen to you and others while you're there. So, Curious One, what are you going to investigate today?

There is much LOVE here for you.   Namaste

The important part is making time for curiosity.

April 11th
A Life Remembered

When you get to a certain point in your human age, you begin remembering when you were a small one. It's natural human evolution. Without the reflecting and comparing, there would be little human evolution. This remembering allows you to grow as a group. You pass this information onto others. Then that human gathers more information about living a life. It goes on and on like this. There is a time of remembering that goes beyond your small human time. This is a part that is vaguely remembered. The reason you cannot always remember what happened before you came into human form is because you're not supposed to.

The Universe of LOVE is energy. It's kind, wise, peaceful and easy. It's important for you to understand you will always rest in LOVE and peace before and after your human experience. By knowing this, it eases your anxiety about before and after. You focus more on living a complete life. This is where your focus is to be. Some of you can stretch it beyond to a feeling of ease and peace where there is no fear. That's about all you need to remember.

There is much to be learned in this lifetime. There's humans to meet. Some will trigger you emotionally. This is a certain remembering or a LOVE connection. That is why you know them. There is much playing and LOVING to be done. Remembering one lifetime is plenty for you. A lot of humans have come and gone. You've had a lot of experiences.

Now you have much wisdom that you're able to pass onto others and keep for yourself. Your remembering of a life is important. Memories of a life well lived. We mean showing up for whatever it is. Good, bad, sad, or happy. It's a life, no matter what it looks like.

There is much LOVE here for you.   Namaste

A life remembered is something to be learned from and shared with others.

April 12th
Lives Being Lived

Your mind is being overused. It is given information. It is the leader. It has gotten you this far. It has gotten you your job. It has introduced you to the right kind of people. You have used this for your marker. Us and Them. We draw your attention to them for a moment so we may create a contrast for you. There is a part of you that is eternal. All human beings have the same energy of LOVE that you do. When you're not together physically, you're together energetically in the Universe of LOVE. A low-level human is 'you' energetically.

It's important for you to understand this so there is compassion. Energetically you are one. What difference could it possibly make in your well-designed life. It was set up by your mind. It is put together in a logical way. What do you care of them? It is very easy for you to be that human. When you come into your body, you're filled with the energy of LOVE. You come in with one intention, to share LOVE energy with all. At that moment all of you are identical.

What has happened in the middle, between your identical offering of LOVE to humans, and today? What has happened that you would begin the same, and end up quite differently? It's the mind. Your friend, the mind, doesn't always go in the direction that you wish. Sometimes, your mind goes in a different place. Your mind is the difference, not your energetic LOVE self. Your mind could also be your enemy.

You haven't experienced it. But you could have. You started the same way. You both have a mind. In the end, you will all end up together back in the LOVE soup. You'll be one again. You'll have common experiences shared as one. At that time, you'll understand exactly what it's like to be living this low life. Your memories and experiences will be combined. It will be one total experience of a life lived.

There is much LOVE here for you.   Namaste

Energetically you are all one.

April 13th
Admirable Beings

There are many things about you to be admired. You're having difficulty with the word. We use it easily because we find you admirable human beings. You're not so sure. You have begun to compare yourself with other humans who do great things. You're having a human experience day after day. You're showing up in your own life no matter what it looks like. You're living an admirable life and you're an admirable person because you're alive. You're living it no matter what it's like.

Admirable is not doing something that draws attention to yourself. Admirable is getting through another difficult day. When there is sadness or discord around you or you're doing something you dislike. When you don't find life wonderful at all. We think you're admirable for this. Many of your words have been misconstrued to bring you down. They don't raise you up. It's what the group of you have done to the words. Always trying to divide: "You're good. You're not." That's human nature.

We are about energy. We are about your energy living in a human body having a human experience. It doesn't matter what it looks like. It's your human time there. That is what is admired. You get up every morning. You live a life. You go to sleep. You get up. That's what non-physical thinks of you. That's what your team of non-energetic support thinks of you. They're all excited now. They LOVE it when you speak like this: "I am admirable. I am wonderful. I am brave. I am kind. I am human. I am LOVE. I allow LOVE to flow through me. I am living even if I don't know if I want to anymore." When you say these things, your energetic support team comes right to your face.

There is much LOVE here for you.   Namaste

You are admirable beings. You are highly praised in the non-physical world. You are greatly admired.

April 14th
Laugh Your Head Off

Have you noticed when two small ones have a serious conversation about life? They put on their stern faces because they are imitating adults. They say, "This is a very important matter!" Then they laugh their heads off because it's ridiculous. They are light with matters of human affairs. It's funny to watch. They are closer to the energy of LOVE as they have not embraced humanity as much as you have. You're really into it. You've learned how to manipulate others if necessary. They haven't gotten those skills honed as well as you. They just watch. They think it's funny how serious humans get about certain matters. They don't have many matters that will end their lives.

Is it possible for you to watch two serious humans talking about issues and giggle? Could you giggle knowing that these two humans have had serious issues almost every day? Do you suppose it helps for everyone to get all uptight? Do you think it brings balance and peace to speak of stern matters that must be addressed?

You've been engrained in it. The next time, pretend you were a small one and stand back. Imitate them and laugh. At least giggle? Perhaps just on the inside because you're grown up after all. You can't be caught laughing right out loud, can you? Is it all right for adults to chill out about major issues? Is it possible for you to look at others through the eyes of a small one? To put yourself back there and think, "They look ridiculous. Their faces are turning red."

There is much LOVE here for you.   Namaste

Could you look at life in a slightly different way than you do at this moment?

April 15th
LOVE Secret

You hold secrets. Not about your behaviour or your life because you all hold those. You know how to keep a secret, for yourself, and for a friend. You know they are embarrassing. You'll be presented as a fallible human. Secrets hold a lot of power when they are being kept because they are thought to be a bomb waiting to go off. You keep it hidden but when it comes out, it's anticlimactic. Did you notice this with secrets? Eventually you've told most of them, and you can tell by the other person's face that it's not the end of the world. You use more energy keeping secrets than by dissolving them into the Universe. As you progress energetically, you decide where your energy goes. You have control over this. It's just done lazily.

The others secrets you hold are to the Universe. To all information that exists. This is a highly exciting energy. This one is evolved. As you sit quietly in your meditation time, there are times you have felt you left your body, your space. You travelled beyond what was physical. In this energetic space lies peace, contentment, ease, and unconditional LOVE. You'll wish to return to it many times. This is a LOVE secret. A secret to contentment.

This is a secret that you all hold because you're familiar with the Universe of LOVE. It's where your energy goes when it's not in physical. Sometimes, you get a glimpse of it when you are in your quiet time. You slip right into it, as if it's a comfortable pair of shoes. It's the secret of LOVE and it's not necessary to keep that one quiet. You get closer and closer to it each time you spend time alone. You are all expanding. You are changed. You are more open than before. The more open you get, the closer you are to the Universe of LOVE.

There is much LOVE here for you.   Namaste

So, do you have a LOVE secret?

April 16th
My Space

Have you met another human where it was important to keep an
energetic space between you? You have energy that surrounds you.
That is your space. It's where your non-physical support team,
memories of the Universe of LOVE and your sensitive, LOVING self
exists. It's not always inside of you. Some humans are able to see this
space around themselves and others.

Some can feel it around themselves only. You're able to feel
pressure at the edge of you. Like a bubble. You have so much energy-
it cannot be contained inside a human body. The human body is for
living, LOVING, dancing, singing, skipping and running. Your
energetic self is huge. It goes beyond the body. That means you're
powerful energetically. You all have this. Now it's time to notice your
own. You may start by noticing it in others. Like those who have anger.

You're protected by your own bubble. It resists other energy
that is not like itself. Ones that are the same mingle easily together. If
it's in an opposite state to you, it's up to you if it gains entry. You
claim this space as your own as you become aware that it's there. It's
energetically heavier than beyond it. When you invite similar energy
into your space and they leave, they have a bit of you and you have a
bit of them.

Some of you will be able to see with your meditative eyes
what surrounds other humans. You may feel it or see it energetically.
Those with the same energy delight in one another. It's time to
remember how large you are energetically. You affect others with your
energy as well. When your energy is clear, vibrant and full of LOVE,
those who are in the same LOVE space are drawn to you.

There is much LOVE here for you.   Namaste

You affect others with your energy.

April 17th
Puzzle of LOVE

The Universe is energy. It's also around you and inside of you. As you recall more about this energetic space where you live all together when you're not in a human body, you begin to relax and smile. You're happier. This is now a place where you can reside. You have brought the Universe of LOVE inside of you. You have extended it outside your body because it cannot be contained inside. It's surrounding you now. The energy of LOVE is you.

Many of you have come to sense this. You see wavy lines or brightness around some humans or you feel other people's energy. Humans have kept this to themselves. They thought you might judge them as being odd. There are more of you starting to feel that you're energetic LOVE. LOVE always attracts more LOVE. It repels that which is different from it. This is just energy, like electricity. It mingles together on the earth. This is a beautiful evolution for you.

You came there to spread LOVE energy and to mingle with other LOVE energy. Then it goes back to its former state which is floating around energetically. It must go to the humans who cry out for help. They are not in touch with their own energy. They don't know it's inside them. The energy from the Universe is being transferred through you when you are connected energetically. When you are sitting in your quiet time, it goes through you. Just like a warm breeze. It's the allowing that's difficult. Others have suggested you take what you can get, hang onto it and hide it so no one else gets it.

There is much LOVE here for you.   Namaste

Your highest service to mankind is to allow LOVE energy to go where it's called.

April 18th
Eager to Remember

You are eager to remember. There's a space available but if it's a memory, it's already holding the space there. It already exists. It should be easy for you to uncover something that exists because it's familiar to you. You can feel it. Smell it. See it. You just forgot about it for a while. It's like uncovering something that you LOVED a long time ago. You open a place and it falls out.

The memory can often be overwhelming which is why it's left hidden. It has to do with your extreme worthiness, great importance, value to the Universe, and the way your non-physical support team adores you. You're not sure how to exist on a day to day basis with this kind of memory intact. How do you live, meet your neighbour, and cut your grass when you know you are a Divine Being essential to the LOVE Universe? How do you do daily tasks when you are so revered?

You are precious, whether you admit it or not. You are brave for coming into human form and having a human experience. At the heart of you, you are deserving of unconditional LOVE that flows over you. As much as you can absorb. The forces of the Universe come to your aid when you call out.

Your memory is: "I am Precious." Can you say it? You'll remember if you continue to say it. The layers of humanity will slip away and you will be back at your most honest, vulnerable self. You will remember. It might take you a moment. Say it again. "I am Precious."

There is much LOVE here for you.   Namaste

Memory can often be overwhelming which is why it's left hidden.

April 19th
Is There Enough LOVE to Heal?

You have come against someone very familiar to you. You can feel the distance and the pressure between you, and you. There's something holding you back from totally immersing with yourself. We have spoken of energy before that exudes from your body. You can push it away, even if it's yourself. You may picture you and you coming closer together and stopping a short distance away. You can get no closer now. There's some energy that's keeping you apart. Logically, this does not make sense. Energetically there are parts of you that you don't wish to incorporate into your being. That is the energy pushback.

You don't wish to believe you're a human like all the others. What makes you all human is the good, bad, ugly, and sad. It's a full experience. There's nothing wrong with the parts of you that others don't like. That you don't understand or feel shame about. They are a part of you, as much as your LOVING self.

Visualize the two of you looking eye to eye. This is where the truth, LOVE, and understanding lie. Say this," You don't have to look down at the ground with me. I understand you. Let's look at each other." That is the first forgiving part. Now you may say, "You are precious to me. Do you understand this? I LOVE you even though you are flawed. Because that means we're human. That means we are still alive. That means we are growing and noticing everything. We've brought it all out of the closet now. Shall we heal together? Shall we become one?

There is much LOVE here for you.   Namaste

Is there enough gentleness in your soul to forgive yourself?

April 20th
What is Your Mission?

You're delightful. You're surrounded by a cushion of LOVE that protects you from flying away. There are many times you would like to fly away. You ask, "Is there something you can do to support me so I am able to stay put here a little longer to finish up what I am in the middle of?"

There's a cushion. A support that surrounds all of you. You may feel it pressing on you. When you ask for support, it surrounds you. You're delightful as a group. All of you. Whether you're an innocent child or an old one who is passing.

You're delightful as a group because you balance one another off. Some are high. Some are low. Some are dirty. Some are clean. You came into existence. Individually, you wish to accomplish something. You all wish to, or you wouldn't't have bothered coming there. You're not sure if it can be completed. You've been trying and forgetting. That's why you show up, day after day. To get to the next thing. "I know there's something I am trying to do but I lose track of the picture. I concentrate on the single blade of grass instead of the field of clover." That's all right, too. You have a mission, just like you always thought you did.

Missions are not as individual as you think. You wish to allow LOVE to flow into you and out of you to the others. You knew it would be difficult when you came. But you came, regardless. You came knowing you wanted to give it a try. You want to complete your mission. All of you have the same mission but it's done individually. There are many ways to allow LOVE to flow into you and out of you. You're looking for your way. That's your mission.

There is much LOVE here for you. Namaste

You're all individually seeking the same end.

April 21st
LOVE Offering

There's a large table full of your favourite foods. Fresh and fragrant. There are many of you sitting around the table waiting. You can smell the food and feel the excitement in the air. The food is getting colder but still you are waiting. You're wondering, "How long do we wait for our host to arrive?" Now you start to fall asleep.

Who gathered these humans together? Who prepared this banquet? All of you. One by one you set your LOVE offering on the table until the table is overflowing with food. You all decided one by one to gather. You all showed up at the appointed time and place with your LOVE offering. So, why did no one eat it? Why did you all sit and wait? You were overwhelmed with the excited energy that you all had when you first gathered together. It couldn't be sustained so you fell asleep.

Do you deserve the most delicious food prepared with LOVE? A LOVE offering by others to you? Are you able to accept that? No. So, you sit and wait for someone else to begin. To say, "I am deserving of this." Oftentimes, no one begins. No one says, "Thank you for your LOVE offering. I will receive it in LOVE." If someone offers you something beautiful, do you say, "Thank you. I receive it in LOVE. You give it in LOVE."

This is just a story to remind you of giving and receiving in LOVE. It's not easy to receive LOVE. It's overwhelming. It would be easier to fall asleep than eat it and share the LOVE of others. You don't have to look at it or admire it. You don't have to wish it was for you because it's for you. It's a gift for you but you are not able to receive it in grace.

There is much LOVE here for you. Namaste

"Yes, I accept your LOVE."

April 22nd
No More Settling for You

Settling is used when you don't like where you are, but you don't have the energy to move forward. You're afraid. The word means you are unable to move backward or forward. This is not correct. You may always slide backwards or move forward. You notice that you are in this mediocre, messy place. You don't know, or care how you feel. When you can label it, you can move beyond it energetically. It's noticing. Human beings don't settle for long.

Low energy goes with settling. When you call out for help to the Universe, your non-physical support team is there to support you, to give you extra energy or hold you up straight so you can move forward.

Your big energy comes when you connect with your energetic life force. This is the beginning. Now sit quietly to cry. When you chose to settle, there's usually issues involved. It's usually a compromise with another human or yourself. Like, "There's something over there I don't want to look at." Whatever it is, it needs to come out. You might think, "It's you again. You're always hanging around." Then there must be a compromise: "Listen. I'd like to try to move beyond this thing and go to a higher place. It's going to be fun. Do you want to come there instead?" Old memories, sad emotions, and connections to negative events are not for the living. Just notice them and they disappear. The emotion just wanted to be heard.

Now you can connect directly with your energetic LOVE force to hear the truth. You're sitting in LOVE. You've been fighting and crying with your demons. Now you're at peace. This is your place of power. You can hear clearly what will be next for you. You will be filled up with energy. You will be at ease with what surrounds you. Your future unfolds easily. You will move with ease in the world.

There is much LOVE here for you.   Namaste

"No more settling for you. It's time for you to live."

April 23rd
Fool Hardy

Some of you act foolish or are fool hardy. It's a judgement to differentiate between a good decision and a bad decision. A good human and a bad human. A good idea or bad idea. There's shame attached to it, as if it's yours. If you are not able to see your own foolishness, you put it on someone else. This is safer. You always want to look good, not foolish. You've judged it and said, "I cannot do that ever again."

There's more to you than the first couple of layers. Your mind keeps going over the same information. So, what is wrong with making foolish mistakes? That is outer judgement that others have told you. Put that layer aside. Now you will be vulnerable because you must be a worthwhile human to stay there.

What's underneath that one? It's back to the beginning." I don't want to waste a lifetime. I will be a perfect human." There's one more layer under that one." I wish to bring LOVE, peace and ease into the world. Now because of this foolishness, I've let the Universe down." It's difficult for humans to get all the way to that place but it's at the core of you. If you come back to the beginning, a healing will unfold. When you look truth in the face, everything dissolves.

You have gotten stuck on a certain event or word but it can disappear because it's only energy. The heart of you is LOVE. When you are healed enough, you will allow energy to pass through you. Your human life will become easy because you'll be living in LOVE. It will lead you. You may be your greatest self and it won't matter if you feel foolish at all. You'll think it's funny to be foolish.

There is much LOVE here for you.   Namaste

You are brave souls. That is why you have a human body. You are no fool. You are LOVERS.

April 24th
Child of the Universe

There are times when you wish you were a small one smiling at everything. They have such ease in the world. You wonder if you can be an adult that lives like a small one. Why did you change to a stressed-out adult? At some point you decided, "I can't be frivolous like this little one, looking at flowers, trees and clouds. I'm going to be successful and liked. Everyone will be proud of me."

Before you can change back, you must understand why you changed the first time. When you started to believe you were not good enough the way you were. That you must strive and change to be worthwhile. It's a shift in thinking from being accepted as you are and not caring what the others think of you to caring what the others think of you. Not easy-going, daydreaming and smiling all the time. If you look in the mirror, you will see what it is you decided to be.

Does the ease of the child still exist inside you, even though you rejected it long ago? It will need to have a little chat with you if you wish it to come forth. An old chat about why you abandoned it and what is wrong with a perfect specimen from the Universe of LOVE. They had to be left behind. There's no place in the world for weak human beings. This is between You and You. It's time for you to get as honest as you are capable of. You are capable of great feats of daring. It's easy for you to integrate your small one. Children of the Universe don't carry resentments for as long as you do. Even though years have passed, it only takes a moment to become integrated again. The small one will happily join you in your adventures of the day.

They are pure LOVE energy. They are you, so you are pure LOVE energy. Spirt of the Universe together as one. All of a sudden, you'll want to skip around. You've integrated your child of the Universe with your hard-working human. It was 'you' all along.

There is much LOVE here for you.   Namaste

You are LOVE. Sometimes you just forget.

April 25th
There's a Storm Brewing

You are keenly aware of weather. You know what the weather will be daily and you have conversations about it. There's a part of you that yearns to be one with the weather. When it's raining outside you have a strong calling to go and become one with the rain. To allow it to wet you completely. When it's windy, you wish to be blown away in the wind. When it's sunny, you let the sun absorb right into your skin. At that moment, you are energy. You are wind, rain, thunder, and lightning. When you see and feel weather, you understand energy that has no body.

It stimulates a dormant part of you that wishes to be fully alive. You've been too busy with human endeavors. Go out in a snow storm when your fingertips are frozen. When you come inside they tingle with life. Then you are alive. When you are wet and cold, you come inside and shiver. You're alive then.

Your body is a container that takes you from one adventure to the next. One human to the next. You are energy everlasting. Just like the wind. Electrical storms are much like you. Inside, you have electricity, wind, heat like the sun, and water like the rain. You are weather. You are a storm waiting to happen inside.

You've forgotten much, to be in human form. But you can remember more. There's more to you than your beautiful physical body that likes to jump and play.

There's a storm brewing inside of you. You are truly one with nature. As you spend time in different weather, you will feel more alive. Those of you who are avoiding it by staying in your shelters, come on outside. See how your insides like it. How your body responds to it.

There is much LOVE here for you.   Namaste

You're a storm waiting to happen.

April 26th
Gliding Through Life

There are those who seem to glide through life effortlessly. You call them enlightened. They smile a little too often and aren't as disrupted by emergencies. Once you notice them, then it's your time to evolve. They go about their business living their lives connected to the Universe of LOVE. They understand they are part of something larger than what is happening right around them. Therefore, they are a little lighter. They have a higher perspective. They are not so attached to human rules. They are just living their human existence this time in this way.

Noticing them creates a longing in you because there's a part of you that wishes to be like this. You'll be changed just by noticing their LOVE energy with your own eyes. Sometimes you don't get it in this life. You don't even notice the ones that are floating in ease.

When you see a LOVE force, you start to notice your own. You are the same. You just haven't grown into it. Your own Universal energy exists around you. Now you will be at ease with the notion that you have judged others as being different than most but you are different than most. That is why you noticed it.

When you notice your energy, you start to believe you're different than others who are involved in their lives. Then you settle into your being. When you settle into your experience, you become lighter. More at ease. You start to move gracefully through life and around humans who are disruptive. You start to float above the ground. When someone notices they say, "Why don't you walk on the ground with the others? What are you about?" Then they experience what you have experienced at this moment. They are awakened just by seeing you.

There is much LOVE here for you.   Namaste

Once you notice, you are changed forever.

April 27th
Waiting & Waiting

You have been learning how to wait. Wait your turn. Wait until it's the right time. Wait until the circumstances arise. Humans prefer to jump into things and deal with the repercussions after. Waiting is the discipline. When you are waiting, you are joining forces with energy and with other humans who are also waiting. When it's the perfect time, it lines up and easily unfolds because the participants have been waiting in anticipation of something wonderful.

You are learning to wait in anticipation. In the hope that it's something wonderful. Hope is a great companion with waiting. Then there's no need to create a catastrophe, which is just a distraction from waiting. In the waiting, truth arrives. You become connected to the Universe of LOVE. You may feel the energy of others. Great things will unfold for you. You know this already. That's why you're waiting for the grand event. For the last piece of the puzzle to come together. You're waiting for the other, who is unaware of you at this moment, to feel your energy and become one with you. You've become less attracted to chaos and more attracted to peaceful, easy waiting. Now your focus is on the waiting and the hoping.

There are great things lining up for you. The other humans must agree, as well. There are many moving parts energetically that must come together. They are waiting for you. You are waiting for them. Soon you will see that you've been waiting for it all to come together clearly.

There is much LOVE here for you. Namaste

Great happiness and joy await you. They are the rewards for waiting.

April 28th
Peace in Evolving

You will have peace now that you have been experiencing your full life. All that is required of humans is to start remembering." What am I? Where am I from? What am I to do here?" Your soul can answer these. The Universe of LOVE, the collective energy, those that support you in non-physical also respond. You ask and the Universe answers. When you realize you are not alone, your peace comes.

Keep your eyes open to see what it looks like. It doesn't always arrive the way you think it will but you will know the answer you receive is what your heart desires most of all. Even if it's not clear, it's energetically explaining itself. Words cannot always pull out the true questions or answers. The feeling that resides within, lets you know its truth because you feel peaceful. You will settle into it. It might be a different idea but take a big breath and settle into it. You will think, "It's what I desire even though I didn't know it."

When you put a question forward you let go of it. Sometimes it feels like you keep asking the same question because you are holding onto it. But as you ask the same question, a little more of it is released. Until there is nothing left. It's important to let your brain know you're in the process of letting go. You require assistance from outside energy. The Universe has got an answer. It's trying to get it to you. The more you ask, the more centered you become. When you're able to receive the answer, you'll feel at peace because you know that it's the truth. Then you'll settle down. Settling is not the human way, but you're becoming a new, evolved human. You're open to receiving energy. You're changing.

There is much LOVE here for you.   Namaste

Much peace comes with evolving.

April 29th
Lying in The Sunshine

There are times of sadness or worry that you consider dark. You like to group it together because then it's tidy. You don't always wish to remember dark times but what if you were to sit in it with the Universe of LOVE? You call it a dark time so you can set it aside and not see it again. So, there's energetic resistance to this. You wish to focus on good times. What if the resistance and labeling were causing the dark time? What if you were able to sit in the dark and not feel sad or angry? What if it's just something you've decided to call an experience?

You must label it dark or light and put it aside unquestioned. These labels are part of the process that must be disassembled. Let's have a look around in your dark experience. Just sit in it for a moment and see what it feels like energetically. It will feel heavy. There's sadness or anger rising. You don't like anyone. You think they are awful.

What if all of this was your judgement of it? What if the thing was actually nothing? What if it dissolved with a thought? LOVE dissolves all. LOVE is high energy that disperses all negativity. It's as if you have a jack hammer on a sidewalk that breaks it up. That's what LOVE does to dark times.

When you have a judgement that you're in a dark time and you don't like anyone around you, it cuts you off from the LOVE. Then the resources you need are not available. When you're sitting in LOVE, it's all that you can feel. You're not in a dark time. You're not judging. You're basking in it.

There is much LOVE here for you.   Namaste

Would you like to be a cat lying in the sunshine taking all the LOVE in?

April 30th
Chicken Coop

You wish to be like a chicken resting in its coop. There's comfort coming back to the same place and knowing that you are safe there. Energetically, your resting place changes all the time but each moment you can rest. Your resting place is where you find yourself at this moment. Not what you expect yourself to be and not what you have been before. What you are capable of now.

It's a place of acceptance and LOVE for you. You come to understand that you deserve a resting place. That you are absolutely all right wherever you find yourself at this moment. A resting place is about finding self-acceptance and self-LOVE. You are perfect the way you are at this moment. Rest in that.

Your resting place is a little good and a little bad. Nonetheless, it's your place. It's not where anyone expects you. It's not what the Universe wishes for you. It's the place where you can rest. In order for you to rest, you must LOVE where you are at this very moment. Otherwise, you run around like the chickens.

Say, "I am as good as I can be at this moment. I deserve rest in a place that is comfortable, LOVING and gentle. Where I am safe. Where I am LOVED by myself and the Universe."

It must be you that decides you deserve to rest and that you are good enough the way you are. When you are sitting in your resting place, you will be surrounded by Universal LOVE energy. When you say, "I am LOVE. I am whole. I am the Universe." More energy is attracted. This resting place is not about slowing down your active imagination or your high energetic self. It's about feeling that you deserve to be quiet in a safe place surrounded by the Universe of LOVE. Just like the chickens coming home to roost, it's time for you to settle into your comfortable place. You deserve it.

There is much LOVE here for you.   Namaste

Give yourself a break. Come to a place of LOVE.

May

You are all one
joined together
in LOVE
energy.

May 1st
Students of LOVE

Many of you are enthusiastic students. You want to grab all the information you can. You want to be filled. Wanting suggests where you sit is not where you belong. But it *is* where you belong.

That applies to everything because there's lessons around you every moment. But not everyone notices them.

You've seen others that maintain a level of LOVE, peace and contentment. You've wondered, "Why is it you're at ease when the world is not?" When you ask the question, you're ready for the answer. The moment you exist in is exactly where you belong. It's where your energy has led you.

There are other eager students, but you don't know one another because eager students don't hang out together. They go find someone who's at ease and peace and connect to them, one on one. You can't get what you need from other eager students because they're searching also.

What you're truly looking for is LOVE. All of you are. Yet, it's you that's brought the LOVE forward.

Now you're students of LOVE. Eager or not, you'll be students of LOVE for your entire existence because it's at the heart of you. It's where your energetic being exists.

Your energetic self can't be contained inside you, so it extends beyond. You're walking LOVE. Yet, you're students of LOVE. How can you be the student and the teacher? Because you hold all your own answers, of course. You ask. The answer comes.

There is much LOVE here for you.   Namaste

Do you like being a student of LOVE?

May 2nd
Fall Into Peace

You've been getting close to peace. It's a thing you often seek, yet peace comes in letting go. The non-seeking. The more you seek peace, the more it eludes you. You all desire it. Of course, you do. You LOVE the sound of it.

You notice people who look peaceful. You say, "I wish to be peaceful, too." By that very notion, you push it further away because it means you're not sitting in peace but judging yourself as a non-peaceful human.

Allow peace to enter in a gentle way. This could be noticing a human and saying, "I know how they feel. Look how peaceful they are. It's LOVELY to see another sit in peace."

You can feel the difference. One is allowing peace to envelope you. All who sit in peace exude it for anyone to help themselves to. It's peaceful, calm energy. It flows from you to the others. In this gentle way, you're now peaceful yourself. All you must do is remember this feeling of noticing another who's sitting in peace. This triggers your memory of yourself sitting in easee.

You say, "That sounds too simple for my complicated mind." But it's your energetic self that knows about peace, not your mind. Your energetic self resides in peace when it's not in physical form. That's why it's familiar and you notice it in others.

Peace is what you are made of. Your energetic self sits in peace because it understands that all is unfolding as it should. There's nothing to be stressed about. Just one moment at a time, your peaceful life evolves.

There is much LOVE here for you.   Namaste

You decide how often you can sit in peace. Sometimes you choose not to because it's more exciting getting into emotional turmoil.

May 3rd
Place of Settling

Part of you is scrambling to become more. To find more. To find yourself. You're never truly content where you are. That's the nature of humanity.

Some of you settle because you understand this seeking continues forever. You start to wonder if you wish to spend your time seeking but never reaching.

This questioning causes you to settle down because important things settle to the bottom. Things like who you are on the inside and not what you have or look like on the outside. Who you are on the inside is what settles you down. It's a different way of be-ing but it's becoming your way.

As you calm down, you have more openness to receive information from the Universe. Then you start to live this way. Instead of seeking with your mind, you receive information from the Universe that is good for all, including you. You hear what's truly going on. Not what's just in front of you.

The world begins to make sense. There's always been a part of you that couldn't quite understand the seeking. Going round and round. There's always been your brain thinking," We never reach our destination."

With the settling, you begin to understand there are some humans who are just putting in time until they pass back to non-physical. That's absolutely fine. It's *your time* to spend whatever way you wish.

Now you're sitting quietly. You're waiting for direction to come from outside instead of inside your brain. This settling calms your nervous system and sends out calming energy to those around you. They relax without knowing it.

There is much LOVE here for you.   Namaste

You're all the same LOVE energy.

May 4th
Dance of Energy

Energy circulates around the trees. It swoops around like they're dancing with the Universe. But when the energy comes to humans, there's much resistance so the energy goes back to play with the trees. But there are some humans who join the dance of energy with the trees.

Humans who are aware of energy go to nature to reconnect. Then they come back and spend time with humans because this energy also exists between humans.

You can carry this energy around with you by recalling the noises of the wind that passes by you, the rustling of the leaves or the feeling of the soft earth under your feet. When you bring these feelings forth in your mind, it will be like you're there at this moment. You're called "nature walkers".

There are others who are bouncing off one another in an angry way because they're bumping up against too many humans. You should go to the trees.

Every time you think, "You're in my way!" you're incorrect. You need to be removed and put into the Universal dance of energy. Never the others. Your choices are limited because you've not disciplined yourself to control your energy.

You find yourself here because you wish to calm down. You've seen others walk about quietly in the same situations as you. They don't yell at anyone and you wonder how they do it. You must begin by noticing when you're off. Then the first tree you see, go and touch it.

LOVE energy is amongst the trees because they're not like humans who get angry. They're at peace. Energy flows easily around them, no matter where they exist. Their roots go deep into the earth. They're one with the Universe. They'll always offer LOVE to you.

There is much LOVE here for you.   Namaste

In emergencies, remove yourself and go dance with the energy of LOVE amongst the trees.

May 5th
Keeper of Secrets

You're greatly affected by the energy of others. This energy is not yours, of course. Your energy is contained within and around you. Sometimes you get them mixed up." Is that yours or mine?"

Mingling of energy shows you're sloppy with your energy work. Your energy can slip into other person's space and you can allow their energy to slip into your space. If you're unaware or you don't believe *you're* energy, then your energy will mingle with the others' energy.

Some wish to help other humans but not themselves. Even though you're the most important person. You'll be the one you travel with from beginning to end. Others come and go. You don't always like to hear you're the most important person, but you are. Try to receive that without judgment.

Pull into your inner self for a moment, you'll find rest there. All the time you've spent on earth has been maintained inside you in a memory. Within that memory there are many experiences, emotions and energetic exchanges.

Beyond that is your time in non-physical. It has wrapped this entire life experience in LOVE. It's well contained.

Then you have the LOVE for others which is outside of your body. This is your offering to the world. This part is for you to share with others when you're elevated enough energetically. Then it automatically comes through you and into the energy around you.

The most important thing is for you to focus on the LOVE energy that surrounds your memories. That's why you're the most important person. This memory, these lessons and this energetic exchange exists nowhere else but inside of you. You're the keeper of this memory. You're the only one capable of keeping it.

The special experiences you've had are surrounded by LOVE which means it's gone into the common good of all mankind.

There is much LOVE here for you.   Namaste

LOVING yourself is the most important thing of all.

May 6th
Isolation

You become stronger and more balanced on your own. Afterwards, you have access to more energy. Remember, energy is all around you and also, passing through you. Some of you can feel the energy of others and visualize who they are because you're transferring energy through the air to one another.

Then there are others who sit quietly and enjoy the peace. They're unaware that energy is going out. It stops when it resonates with another human. Then it passes through and out of them after it adds your energy.

This is energetic law. You have energy that passes out of you and into the air. So, it naturally passes through others. It's the way of energy because it's always moving.

Sometimes energy comes back around to you. You're sitting in your quiet space alone. It goes out of you and into others. Now others are sending their energy out and it's coming back to you. Around and out. Now you're connected to all the humans that have connected with your energy. You're in the circle.

As it goes further, you're all connected energetically. You begin to behave as one. You begin to understand you're all the same. The energy that goes to them and comes back to you, is the same as when you were alone. Therefore, you are one.

When it comes back around into you, you may not perceive this. Perhaps you'll cry because the energy is more invigorated. That's because another was excited to feel your energy and has added their excitement to it.

By the time it comes back to you, several others have been touched. It comes back at a higher vibration. You move forward and backward as a group of energy. When a group of humans who are connected energetically try to affect something, there's a huge impact. They move the world. But it all begins with you sitting by yourself in isolation.

There is much LOVE here for you. Namaste

A group of humans connected energetically can do great things together.

May 7th
Breath of LOVE

Sometimes you're like slow, old men with no place to go. You can barely put one foot in front of the other. You stop and lean on things. It's exhausting to watch and exhausting to be. Yet, you live like this because it's familiar. You don't wish to be high, fast and clear. It's too nerve wracking for you. You prefer to be injured. The old man moves slowly because his body is tired. You can tell he's tired of living.

You haven't lived there so long. Yet, you move in the same slow way. You often create aches to prove it. You choose to be slow because you're afraid to trust. You're afraid to hope. Instead of being crotchety, you could be skipping around picking flowers, looking at the sun and waving at people. You might say, "Come skip with me." This is the same human experience that could be chosen by each of you. But you think," No. It's hard to be in a human body."

Sometimes a young human can seem old and an old human can seem young. This is not a miracle. It's their use of energy. It's their willingness to allow energy to pass through them. Energy is a life force. It's like you don't wish to drink water but prefer to shrivel up and be sick. If you drink lots of water, you can go skipping around waving at people. This is the same with energy.

If you allow pure, clear, LOVING energy to pass through you and out of you, you're healed. You're clear. You're willing for more LOVE to come in and out.

It's like a breath of LOVE. You breathe it in, and it settles into all your cells. Then it filters out. Then you breathe in LOVE again.

So, the crotchety old man does not see the old lady skipping around because the crotchety man is young and the skipping lady is old. They don't know one another exist.

There is much LOVE here for you. Namaste

Today, allow the breath of LOVE into you as much as you are able to.

May 8th
LOVE Snowball

The people you spend time with today are not the people you spend time with throughout or at the end of your life. So, you're really a lone traveler in your own life. Now you're looking back and feeling alone.

The human experience is to jump into one human body, and to experience all it has to offer. In doing so, you leave the non-physical and Universe of LOVE connection, which is the sense of unconditional LOVE and feeling that you're never alone.

Now you wish you were with non-physical again. Suddenly you notice you've been alone all along even though you're surrounded with humans. You start to realize you chose not to notice because you'd be afraid if you looked back. Humans will do anything to avoid fear.

As far as integrating this sense of oneness with the Universe and this lone purpose of humanity, you may bring the Universe of LOVE with you. You may surround yourself with a sense of oneness with mankind and non-physical. Like a blanket.

With this thought, focus on the energy that surrounds you. When you put your hand out far then bring it toward you, you will feel a difference. You want to keep your hand where it's warm and cozy. This is LOVE surrounding you. You walk in it, but you don't always feel it.

You'll never be alone, although you're having a lone experience. When you feel overwhelmed with this information, look back and see you've always been alone physically. Then remember the Universe of LOVE, because when you came into physical, you took a little piece of it with you.

You would never go into that crazy human world in that heavy human body without taking a little something. So, you all grab a handful as a last gesture. Like a snowball. You knew how precious it would be, so you made it part of you. Therefore, you're never alone spiritually.

There is much LOVE here for you.   Namaste

Humans are so precious to the Universe because you're brave travelers going into the unknown with only one little snowball of LOVE to get you through. Admirable and insane.

May 9th
Delight in Your Life

There's great delight in coming together as one. Those who are aware of energy can have this experience. Because you have more energy, you're able to play and be your evolved self. When you're able to see the energy in others, you're drawn toward one another. You're like magnets. It's delightful to come together in this way.

While you're together, you're learning how to live energetically. You're mingling energies, you're both getting information and life experiences from one another. When you leave this group, it's important to bring their energy with you because their ideas and thoughts still exist within you. Now you begin to carry others with you.

Now, when you're alone, you have more energy to draw from. You may be light spirited, skip around and smile often. It's important for you to delight in your life. You're not on earth to trudge through it unless it's what you choose. You came to delight in life. Many get off track and must go through a heavy lifetime.

Those who wish to mingle energies must be aware that those who burden themselves with life, had the same intention as you when they came into being, which was to share LOVE.

Your energies are just out of sync. High energy goes with high and low energy goes with low. They're not better or worse, just different.

Co-mingling of energy is important so when you're alone, you're able to bring up memories of others. Then you understand the motives and ways of others. Now you start to become a compassionate human. One who truly cares about others because you've walked in their footsteps energetically.

There is much LOVE here for you.   Namaste

You're becoming a human who makes a difference on the earth. One who allows LOVE energy to pass through them to others because you're not judging who they are. This is true human evolution.

May 10th
Energy of Two

Energy is accelerated when two come together who notice it. Then your energy merges and becomes larger than it is when you're alone.

Your highest concern is to allow LOVE energy to pass through you and out to others who require it. This is why you came into your human form. When you meet another who is aware of their highest calling, energy is multiplied.

You don't create LOVING energy within yourself. There's not enough there, but if you allow it to come from the Universe through you, it's huge.

When two of you sit quietly in a meditative or connected state and decide: "I will allow LOVE energy to pass through me right now." This is how it truly multiples. It's a purposeful allowing of energy.

Whenever you pass in close proximity to humans, your energy is transferred out. LOVE energy is able to pass through you. Now you'll be able to attract and allow a relationship with someone who is equally aware as you. This is a different sort of evolving. It's important for you to know that this can be done.

When you're both sitting alone, being in LOVE vibration and knowing one another is transferring LOVE energy, you'll feel it between the two of you. That's how it passes through you and out of you. Then it will multiply.

The next time you find yourself with someone familiar with LOVE energy, start to notice the energy changing around both of you. The space you're in will become hotter. It will feel like electrical currents and you'll be shivering. It will be a different space.

Where the energy goes is not your concern. It cannot be contained in the space that you're in anyway because LOVE energy is always moving. It cannot be contained.

There is much LOVE here for you.   Namaste

When you're together the next time, you're going to have a grand time. You're going to be electrified together and your LOVE electricity will go out to the others.

May 11th
Soft Place to Land

'Finding a soft place to land' is particularly sweet to you because you've often landed on hard rock. You find it hard to believe you can land on something soft. Yet, there's something within you that longs for something gentle, accepting and LOVING. Then your brain tells you, "Be realistic. Life is difficult." You have this constant pull. Soft place to land. Hard place to land.

The reason that 'soft place to land' 'exists inside you is because part of you is familiar with it. You know what it's like to sit in a LOVING place because you exist there when you're not in physical.

Even though you may see this place, you hesitate to lie down on it. You see others come and test it out. They smile. They cry. They look content and peaceful, then they move on. You wish you could lie down on that soft place. You wonder why you're hesitating.

You don't want to get used to unconditional LOVE and ease because it would be too difficult for you to leave and get back into the rest of your hard life.

The life you've devised seems to be in contrast to this soft place. The only difference in the two is acknowledging the difference. You just have to notice it.

Say," Alright. I don't think I deserve a soft bed. I will get soft myself and I won't be able to live my hard life. Now what, Universe?"

This very statement releases the energy, and it goes on its way. Now you can be curious about this softness because you've got rid of this resistance that was blocking you. Now, you're free and clear to lie down on this soft place. See if you get used to it. See what it feels like to be encompassed in unconditional LOVE.

It's easy and gentle. There are others watching out for you. They keep you safe so you can relax in your soft place. You can breathe here. You can be yourself. You can cry or laugh. You can be angry or sad. You're much deserving of rest. It's a 'soft place to land' and it's for you. Enjoy it.

There is much LOVE here for you. Namaste

This soft place to land can hold whatever you bring to it.

May 12th
Humming is Healing

You find comfort in humming. You do it automatically. You just know it. You do it to comfort yourself to sleep.

You turn your body into an instrument that vibrates. This comforting noise resonates with you because it's like you're in the Universe of LOVE, which is always vibrating, because it's energy.

This vibrational humming noise in your lungs and throat gets you into perfect alignment with the Universe. When you're sitting quietly, you might feel sensations bubbling up. Sometimes, you push it down or you allow it out and it turns into a note. It's a naturally occurring event that no one has taught you. You become one with the Universe again. You yearn to be one with the Universe and the energy that surrounds you. One with the energy of others. You wish to vibrate together. Your part is this noise that travels through you.

It's not something that needs to be judged or pushed away. It's just something to notice. It's natural for you to send out vibration. It's like you're calling others who are similar to you. Oftentimes, this is to comfort others and bring them down to the same vibration. Some have not found their voice. It's natural in new babies but not always with the older humans. Some of you have pushed it away.

When you start to notice this humming, you'll notice it's a certain note. This is LOVE vibration. When it can no longer be contained within you, it comes out as this beautiful noise. Humming is also done naturally in certain plants and animals to communicate with one another.

It's comforting for you because it brings your energy to a place where it settles in peace and ease. It comforts you in times of great stress.

Your human body is meant for LOVE. It can be one with LOVE. LOVE energy is always moving inside and all around it. Perhaps you're calling others when you hum or you're comforting yourself.

There is much LOVE here for you.   Namaste

You know how to connect. By humming. Watch the animals. They do it all the time.

May 13th
Willing Participant in Life

It's important for you to be a willing participant in your life. And in the energy that passes through all of you and goes out to others. There's a certain willingness on your part to be part of humanity.

You understood when you came from the Universe of LOVE and jumped into a physical body, you were going for an experience. To be part of humanity. To see what you could do together.

This requires a willingness to connect with the Universe of LOVE when necessary. This puts you into an alignment that's peaceful and easy. This allows you access to all information. This must be done first, or you'll be of no assistance to mankind. Instead, you'll hinder it.

When you become willing to allow LOVE energy into you and out of you, you create a new pattern of willingness. This may then evolve from your connection with the Universe to your connection with mankind.

Your place in mankind is to become one among many. Therefore, you're as important as the next and also as unimportant as the next. You're all equal hosts for the Universe to allow LOVE. This is how you grow from an individual experience to a group experience.

It's only a breath away from your direct relationship with the Universe of LOVE. Which is allowing LOVE to flow through you as a group. This is a vibrational thing. As you become familiar with LOVE energy, you'll start noticing it in others. Even though it could be the first time you've met them, you understand they're in the same energetic flow as you.

You're gathering in groups of human energetic families. It's the natural evolution. When you're in non-physical, you act as one. Feel as one. Behave as one. You move forward and backward as one. It's natural for you.

There is much LOVE here for you.   Namaste

You'll be ready to join your energetic family of humans when you understand LOVE energy.

May 14th
Dark Places

There have been times of darkness for all of you. Part of the human experience is to have extreme emotional pulls. Many of you think you want to be helped out of a dark place but it's not a place you need to leave immediately. The human experience is to have all these emotions.

Lots experience this dark place where you can't get up. You just sit. This is a normal experience for many. The true discord lies in your judgment of sitting in it. Many of you sit in it but think, "I should be out picking flowers." That is what causes the discord.

If you just sit in it, it will come and go. You've been told you must judge and label this. Then you must punish yourself by thinking, "I'm a bad human." There are many layers of difficulty with this.

The humans that devised this said, "You must not do this. You must do this." They're not being truthful when they say this because they're experiencing it themselves. They're judging themselves also.

These words have been given from human to human as if they're the laws of life. They're inaccurate. Your true rules lie inside. You brought them in with you from a place of unconditional LOVE and oneness. This is your true barometer.

When you sit in a place of oneness and peace, you're lighter. You have a sense of knowing that all is well.

You remember that you're joined together with non-physical and physical during your life experience. That you're all having this experience as one. Non-physical are supporting you energetically. This is where the rules of your life lie.

Your physical self leads the way, and your soul just comes along. When your physical self notices your soul, you rejoice together. You say, "It's nice to see you but I've got a great adventure to go off to." It will respond, "Go ahead. I'll be right behind you." This is the human adventure.

There is much LOVE here for you.   Namaste

There is absolutely nothing wrong with you or the life you're leading. You can relax into this, knowing you're well supported inside and out. This is your LOVE space. It's unconditional.

May 15th
From Leader to Peasant

Many of you are deep in thought most of the time. It's common with certain realms of humanity to seek beyond what you see and have been told. You're called human seekers.

There are others that come and just relax into *humanness*. They follow the rules set out by others. To them, it brings an ease of life.

There are many different layers of humans. Sometimes you look at others like they should be seekers, too. It's not your place to do this. The humans who follow the rules of others are doing this because they need a rest in this lifetime. They don't need to question. You have no idea what they've come from before this life.

You seek more than what you know because you've had a restful time before this one. Do you see? They were you before. Now you're them. Do you see the beauty in this unfolding? You each take your time. Time to rest. Time to learn. You ask to be reminded. You yearn to be reminded of something you've forgotten.

There's no need to feel sadness for any group. You've had your time like them. They've had their time like you. Many were great leaders. This is an important lesson for you to understand. It's all about allowing each human, including you, to follow the one in front of you without needing to correct anyone. This is *your* experience this time.

You're in this experience of yearning, of seeking, of having a mind that's open to receive all because you're missing home. Your sense of home is a place of complete stillness.

All are content in the role they play because you're all one spirit. All are having one experience. You're one with the others and with Source. You're one with non-physical. You're one with the Universe. You are the Universe. You're much LOVED and cared for. You're supported while you go through your problematic human experience.

There is much LOVE here for you. Namaste

You're never alone there. You would not survive alone.

May 16th
ME!

In order to integrate a human existence with spiritual insight, you've figured out how to compartmentalize your life. With some people you're one way and with others you're different. It's a falseness. You've learned how to divide yourself.

Each time you break apart one piece of your belief system, it weakens all of the rest. The more lives you lead and personalities you have, the weaker you become. This is the opposite of what you are trying to accomplish there. Which is to be a complete emotional and spiritual being. There's a part inside you that understands it can be done. If you don't have this hope, you would not be in physical form.

Before you came into physical, you understood that you could possibly have a complete, fulfilling, invigorating emotional adventure in humanity. But not always good. With this knowing, you came into being.

You're reminded now as if it were a whisper a long time ago. Not in your mind but in your soul. As you move from a group of humans who are talking about spiritual matters, you may be your complete self. As you move into your business world, you may be your complete self. As you move into your family, you may be your complete self.

Along your lifetime, you've seen how others behave. You've mimicked them as if you're an unthinking parrot. Which you're not. You're a divine being who knows how to draw information from the Universe inside you. You knew that if you wanted to please them, you must behave the same way. It became such a pattern for you.

Since you're different with family, spiritual and work, visualize all of them together in one room. Now stand in front of them and say," This is me. I'm flawed. Yet, I hope to be complete, with the assistance of all of you. I will be more me than I've ever been before because I'm letting you see the true me." In the end, it's you that's finally stood up for the 'true you' that's always asking to speak.

There is much LOVE here for you.   Namaste

Your soul LOVES to sing, dance, play and fight. From this day forward, I will be 'me' at all times.

May 17th
Be Easy This Time

You have an idea that you must look and behave a certain way in front of others. It's a human protocol of politeness. This word is outdated. It's from another time when you would be punished if you behaved differently. It's time to shake it up and forget about that notion.

The long haired, peaceful and groovy people were the ones that questioned that business. They were allowing energy to transfer through them. It was one of the first times a group of humans were allowing LOVE energy to come through them.

Times of unhappiness and oppression are when the allowing comes forth from the Universe. The Universe is always looking for channels. Although it's uncommon for a large group to ask for this together. It was an evolution of humanity, but it happened so quickly the next group was afraid of it. It was not gradual enough. It scared the rest of the humans at that time. It did not embrace all, so it segregated further.

The intention of the Universe of LOVE is to come forth into any willing vehicle, then fill it up. It gently goes into those open to receive it. The beauty, clarity and gentleness of the Universe of LOVE got messed up with human's bad behaviour. Nothing has changed with humans.

This is a time of allowing. Of opening your *heart self* and your eyes to see what's to be seen. Sometimes it's physical. Like making eye contact of another whose reaching out. You'll start to find one another in a gentler way. When you make contact, you'll know one another. It's a re-awakening of your energetic, vibrational self so that the vibrations may greet one another.

You're learning to be less human and more spiritual. All of this is now gentle. It's easy. It's not necessary for any more struggle. You've struggled much. Your time now can be an easy unfolding. You remember how to be gentle with yourself and with those that surround you.

There is much LOVE here for you.   Namaste

Be easy with yourself. Be easy with others. It's the way of the Universe of LOVE.

May 18th
Bird of LOVE

You're not sure if it's always good for you to settle for second best. You think if you hold out a little longer, you'll get a big surprise, but this keeps you from living. If you think you're settling, you've already compared lifestyles and decided you're taking the lesser of the two. By doing this, you're not allowing yourself to step forward into a larger picture.

Comparing is a great distraction for you. "This might happen. That might happen." It keeps you living in a place of wondering and comparing. It's a place in your imagination.

Now take a step back so you may come to understand. Just see yourself sitting there thinking. In the end, you're frustrated because you really don't know if you're settling for second best. You've made something in your imagination a true reality because you feel hopeless, helpless and sad. You're stuck in this imaginational turmoil place where you can't make decisions because you can't enter the space. The space is full of their lives and their ideas. Now you're stuck in the world you've created.

Now you may decide to let go, so you may be free to live a true life. It's truly under your feet. What you can smell and see. Otherwise, you can spend your entire lifetime stuck in one place.

Those of you who wish to fly and be free, you'll have to sit in this sense of helplessness and hopelessness.

You wouldn't be comparing all these lives unless you thought there's something wrong with the one you're in. It's time for you to feel that helpless, hopeless crappy life that you've created. This healing must be done after your unveiling of the truth that you've done something wrong. You wonder if you deserve happiness and freedom.

When you sit in this long enough, mourn for the loss and say goodbye to this notion, you can let it go. What's left is your essential LOVING self. Your highest truest self.

There is much LOVE here for you.   Namaste

When you tear away your humanity, only LOVE is left. You just have to sit in the sadness first. Then you'll see the LOVE that is you. You'll be free like the little bird of LOVE.

May 19th
Red Ball

The term 'stumbling block' causes you to lose all sense of reason. You become frozen. You say, "I can't get around or over this stumbling block, so I'll just sit here." Human nature is the mind building something up that doesn't exist. You can make anything appear true that is untrue. It's part of your great imagination. It serves a wonderful purpose when you're using it to envision relaxing things. When you use it to envision stressful things, the opposite effects happen.

What if your stumbling block was a stumbling ball? What if you just picked it up and bounced it around? You always wanted to have a red ball.

Your life is right there. Now envision a whole field full of red balls that you want to go run through and kick. Now, go one step further. Once you've lost interest in the balls, what's left? Just an open field with flowers and sky. So, what if there's nothing but a field full of flowers and birds chirping? Now what will you make of your human time? It's wide open for you.

Why do you suppose that a beautiful world is available to you? It's for you to live it, of course. It's not for you to fill with red balls. It's for you to skip about and pick flowers. You can smell them or put them in your hair. It's all for you to embrace, live and walk amongst. If you must bring the silly red balls, bring them in but when you are finished with them, make sure you kick them out of the way so you can see clearly what exists when there are no balls there.

It's life. Pure and simple. Beautiful. Entertaining. Calming. It's a delightful world that has been provided to you. It's up to you what you want to do with it. That's your human time. Do what you like. It doesn't make any difference in the slightest. They're your balls, do whatever you like with them.

There is much LOVE here for you.   Namaste

So, delightful human being, what are you going to get into today?

May 20th
Is There Something Going On?

The important thing you came to remember is that we're all energy.
There was a time when you were pure energy with no physical body.
There was much dancing and playing in the wind. When you don't
have a body, energy moves all the time. It's excited. It's happy. It's still
around humans because they're an energetic match. They're just
encased. Humans can sometimes detect you.

It's important for the energy outside and inside the human
body to connect in any way possible. The connection is vitally
important for you to carry on in your human life. When you feel there
is no connection to anything larger or energetic than your human
experience, you lose your LOVE for life.

In the grander scheme, you come to understand how valuable
you are and how fortunate you are to be alive. Only the comparison to
energetic LOVE reminds you of this. Comparing to the external part of
others, doesn't make your life more fulfilling and JOYOUS. Only the
connection of energetic LOVE allows you to compare to something
grander than what you're doing at this moment.

When you think your life is human only, it's very small. When
you compare and feel the energy around you, at all times, you're
energized, vitalized and stimulated. You're interested in life here and
beyond. You become more interested in the energy that's moving
around you. You're investigative.

That's the importance of acknowledging the energy of non-
physical. What you're acknowledging is yourself, those you have
LOVED and those you don't know. But sometimes, you can feel their
energy like an electrical storm. Some are more sensitive to this
electricity.

For those living human lives, sometimes you lose hope. There
is longing from the inside. There is more and you know it, otherwise,
you wouldn't wonder. There must be more.

There is much LOVE here for you. Namaste

*Ask those who are constantly electrified what's going on. Ask, "Why do
you feel this electricity and I don't? Is there something going on I don't
know about?"*

May 21st
Your Road of Life

There are times when you're kept apart from those humans you care for most. There's a time for paths to intersect and times to separate. This is the way of your life. You often wish to hold onto those you care for because you're trying to recreate the Universe of LOVE. It can't be done because you've got a physical body and humans are having different adventures. Learning and remembering. That's what you're all about. It's impossible to intertwine with the same humans.

You like to be in human because it's always changing and evolving. It's exciting. You know your life is one big adventure. Whether positive or negative, it's still a life. It's impossible for you both to have the same life. Each is different. You knew that even though it looked like you were with others, soon they would dissipate, and you'd be travelling alone.

It's always you on your road of life. Sometimes alone. Sometimes with others. There's no way for you to take a big group along your road. Then they won't be on their own roads. Living their own lives with their own adventures. They would be on yours. Surely you don't wish that. No one wishes their own life on anyone else. It's your road of life.

There are times when you wish to make it beautiful. You plant flowers and watch them grow. You watch for the birds. You invite them to come to your road of life. There are other times when it's raining all the time. There are rocks in the way. You fall and skin your knee trying to crawl over them. That's your road. Sometimes there's big potholes. Sometimes there are little children singing.

What an adventure you're having on your road of life. You've all got your own roads to travel. Don't try to drag other people down your road. Sometimes, you can barely travel on it alone because it's so narrow, you can barely fit one human. Sometimes it's so wide, a large group of fun, LOVING humans dance and sing with you. That's your road. Lonely. Full of humans, happiness, sadness and adventure.

There is much LOVE here for you.   Namaste

When you're in non-physical, you're together all the time. You're one energy.

May 22nd
Energetic Wall

You have a strong reaction when others question what you say. This ends an energetic exchange with another. It doesn't show you're LOVING. It doesn't create a bond with another because you're truly saying, "I wish to remain outside the circle of LOVE." Each human interaction is a LOVE exchange. It's seeing the other human and them seeing you. Energy goes back and forth.

Namaste is greeting the soul in one another. It's being one, no matter what it looks like. Sadly, when you say, "Don't question me", you're saying you wish to be outside the Universe of LOVE and humanity. You don't wish to be vulnerable or seen as you are. Which at that moment, is probably angry, negative or afraid. Therefore, the other will not show you who they truly are.

You're not having a truly human and spiritual experience with one another. It comes back to you being afraid of an energetic LOVE exchange between two humans who would say, "I'm afraid. I don't know what I'm doing. Do You? I need help."

It's not natural for you to say such a thing but it's the spiritual way of interacting with others. This is very important. When you ask for help, a force comes in and around you, that knows what's going on.

When you're saying, "I know this", there's no support for you. You've turned away energetically. But when you say, "I'm lost. I need help", all the energy of the Universe surrounds you. So, some of you are going about life without support.

It's time for you to evolve into more than what you are at this moment. You'll need practice. The more barriers you take down between you and another human, the more you take down between you and the Universe of LOVE.

If you can recall the first moment you came into physical form, you'll know you want all the Universe of LOVE you can. In order to get it, you'll have to start trusting your human brothers and sisters who are having the exact same experiences as you. They wish to have all the Universe of LOVE they can get too.

There is much LOVE here for you.   Namaste

Stretch yourself out. You're getting bigger each moment.

May 23rd
Purple Banana

You often come up against something immovable. It's you. You have an opinion that you won't alter. Energetically things are moving within the world because energy doesn't stay put. When you come up to something solid you think, "I must change your opinion on this." It's only you meeting your own obstinance. Sometimes you're opinionated because you have researched something and found it to be consistent. New contrary information always comes, so now, you spend your energy dismissing a new point or piece of energy.

Now you're meeting you and you're wondering, "Why am I so strong willed about this? What must I be protected from?" There's often more at stake than the idea. Such as: "Am I unsafe in the world? Am I in conflict? Why is it so important for me to draw strong boundaries around this thing?" So, if it's not about your obstinance then what is the obstinance protecting?

This is unsettling for you because the reason you built this strong opinion was so you wouldn't't have to go here again. You've built a big fence around it and you're reluctant. Would you like to go behind the barrier and see what's there? Are you excited? Uncomfortable? Afraid? Sad?

This is real humanity. Not building walls. Now wrap this "thing" in LOVE and understanding. When you were small, you tried to fit in with those who looked like they knew everything. You were not supposed to do that. You were supposed to still be an adventurer. You would say, "Bananas are always yellow." They would say, "Aha little one, you've not seen green bananas." Suddenly, you understood. "I don't know everything, but I must pretend I do."

You separated from your investigative self and into your know-it-all self. You needed to fit in. Perhaps your know-it-all self could have a conversation with your investigative childlike self. Know-it-alls never find purple bananas.

There is much LOVE here for you.   Namaste

This is a place to heal and sit in LOVING investigation. See what you both can uncover. When you bring obstinate and wandering together, you'll feel complete.

May 24th
Moving with Energy

When you say," I have no energy" you've decided that moving slowly has no energy but moving fast does. You understand that energy makes things go faster. But when energy is flowing directly in and out of you, you don't move faster or slower. You just are.

When you're in LOVE energy, you just want to sit and be. It anchors you. It fills you. Then the energy may enter into and out of you easily. It was your natural state before you came into human and at the beginning of your life.

It is just as natural for LOVE energy to flow in and out, as it is for a flower to face the sunshine and breathe out oxygen. It flows out of you just like breath. Then you feel energized and mentally balanced.

You become part of collective consciousness. You know more because you receive information from a great Universe of knowledge. You may live in knowing at all times.

You will be mindful of energy because now you're able to move at an appropriate pace. Now when you're going to a certain place to meet someone but change your path you realize, "That person wasn't going to get there on time. They arrived when I did."

You'll start to notice when you're in energetic alignment as your life will flow more naturally. Perhaps it takes you around things, or you'll sit down. Suddenly, things will flow easily. You'll notice this first with appointments. You'll start to arrive at the *real* time. Not the one that you scheduled.

In this way, the energy you have is perfect. It may take you to other places to experience unpredicted things. Some say, "We must get our energy up because we have to do these things." But if you don't live this way, you don't need to get your energy up. When you're in alignment, your day will flow so easily, you'll be shocked.

There is much LOVE here for you.   Namaste

Sometimes, it will seem like you're going faster. Other times, slower. You'll be going one steady pace, but your insides will think it's fast or slow. You'll arrive exactly when necessary. You'll be in the right place at the right time.

May 25th
World of Beautiful Humans

You're beginning to nurture yourself. You're starting to understand you deserve some kindness. You've nurtured others and yet, you neglected to nurture yourself. You were craving it. Now it's becoming part of your natural daily life. You say, "Is your stomach upset? Do you feel anxious?" These are self-nurturing acts.

Now you'll be more available to LOVE and nurture others in an authentic, LOVING way. Because now you can look in the mirror and say, "How are you?" in a kind, sincere way and wait for the reply. Part of the nurturing is being available to listen to the nasty things, too. As long as you're able to move through self-judgment, nausea, headaches and feelings of sadness or anger, they pass.

It's a new way of being for you to be there for yourself. Unfortunately, many humans don't get to have this experience.

This self-LOVE turns into an admiration of self. It's about looking at yourself completely and saying, "Wow. You've survived. Aren't you doing well! No matter what your life looks like, you've been living in your human body and staying on the earth so, you've done a fine job."

Now you're able to look yourself in the eye. Enthusiasm, curiosity and wonder come when you make space for them. Now you have a clean, clear connection with the Universe of LOVE. Then you can allow LOVE energy to pass into you and out of you to the others who can't get into alignment.

Now you can join with others energetically and become one. Just like the Universe of LOVE is one. You evolve from the moment you look yourself in the eye and say, "How are you doing beautiful human?"

There is much LOVE here for you. Namaste

Now you're becoming one with other beautiful humans. Soon you have a beautiful race of LOVING beings. That's not the Universe of LOVE. That's You and your beautiful earth.

May 26th
You Have the Answers

You're being gathered in the arms of the Universe into similar families of LOVE. There is protection and understanding. You're being drawn together for the healing of the group.

You wish to be one with others because you've come to understand you're not alone. You long for others even though you don't know who they are. This longing draws you out of your hiding and in search of others. Which is really in search of oneness and LOVE.

Most of you are hiding because you understand you must hide who you truly are a lot. Now that there's such a strong longing for connection with others, you wonder, "Why am I hiding? Is there something wrong with me? Perhaps I can come out?"

As the questions unfold, so do the answers. For they are one. You're curious beings so you question everything. So even if you're hiding, you still have your answers and questions. Because you're still one with the Universe where all questions and answers exist. You're part of the Universe. You are the Universe.

As you come out of hiding, you're bringing answers for others, as well as you. Whatever is inside you is to be shared with your group. When one answers, the other questions. You are all one.

All of you are coming out of hiding to be one. That's why certain groups resonate with one another. You become more comfortable within energy vibration. Therefore, answers, questions and LOVE. You're all connected to many others. As you raise your vibration, you reach out and start noticing them. Start feeling them energetically. You are much more than you seem.

You are one with the others. You hold the answers and the questions for yourself and others. Your group is spread far and wide. Yet, you're one in only a moment. When you call to one another. When you feel one another. When you reach out and you feel hands on top of yours. You realize you're not alone.

There is much LOVE here for you.   Namaste

You've come out of hiding to share your questions and answers with your energetic family of LOVE.

May 27th
Reconciliation

You've come to a place of reconciliation. Your past and present are coming together as one. It's time for you to get beyond yourself. There are things you regret that have happened to you and by you. But today you wish for LOVE to flow into you and out of you to others.

You've had a life that's seen hate and a life that wishes to LOVE. These must come together because they exist in all of you. For you to truly allow LOVE to flow into you and out of you, this must be reconciled. The hateful parts of your life must be put to rest.

There are parts of you that hold back the full force of LOVE. The full force of LOVE is like a strong wind that blows through and knocks trees over. The residual effects of living a human life slow the winds down so much that sometimes it's only a breath that you can feel.

Hateful, negative, sad events cause a blockage within you. They create thick darkness as a reminder of times in your life that you will not allow to happen again. For you to maintain this belief, the memory must stay intact. Therefore, the wind may not blow through completely. It's blocked within you.

LOVE energy is always looking for clear channels. You can see it in certain humans when their eyes are bright, and they smile slightly. They don't seem to worry much. They've let go of things they believed they needed to hold onto.

Sit in the negative, awful, hard memory and feel it completely. It's devastating and terrible, but it passes. When you're finished, it disappears. Then you're clearer to allow LOVE energy to pass into you and out of you.

LOVE has access to all information and energy so it will inform you if something's coming. You don't have to do it. You can trust the Universe to care for you. You'll be safe. Not safe from negative events. No! You're safe because now you're the kind of human who can absorb negative events and let it pass through you.

There is much LOVE here for you.   Namaste

You may come to rely upon the Universe for support. Then you'll be a clear channel and LOVE will flow through you.

May 28th
Breath of LOVE

Your soul wishes to be spiritual. The mind is responding in the only way it knows, which is to find written information and other human speakers. This yearning is causing your mind to jump into action. It often does when an emotion is triggered. The mind's job is to name the longing and gather information.

Questioning the meaning of life is your souls' mission. Your souls joy. Not the mind. But you're allowing your mind to seek out information.

All you need is inside you. Just sit quietly and connect with the soft spot inside of you that feels joyful, at peace, contented, and happy. It creates energy and heat. It has stimulated your remembering of the Universe of LOVE. This is what it's like when you're not in physical. When these words are spoken, an energetic reaction is caused within you.

They trigger a certain part of you. It's a remembering. When you feel this, no other information is needed because you have the Universe of LOVE inside you. All knowledge from all time is inside you. All that you long for can be found by sitting quietly and allowing space to create energy.

Energy feels like joy, bliss, ease and comfort. It's allowing. It's soul space. It's connection with the Universe. It's connection with your body. It's a knowing that the Universe and your soul are one.

There is much LOVE here for you.   Namaste

This energy is stimulating your beautiful human body. It's pressing on your lungs which causes a breath to be released. One that has been held in for your human time. It's a breath of peace. A breath of ease. A breath of comfort. A breath of LOVE. And it's been in there all along.

May 29th
YES!

"Yes" is the answer you're looking for. Yes, move forward one step at a time. Everything will become obvious. Yes, you're doing fine. Yes, that is the direction you're to walk. Yes, everything's in alignment. Yes, keep walking toward the sun. One step at a time is all you need to know.

This is a way for you to practice trust. It's not your strong suit. That's why you can only see one step ahead of you. The light is blinding anyway. You can't see where you're going. You can only take one step in front of you. This is the way for you to live your life there when you wish to feel your connection to the Universe. You wish to be a little less human and a little more non-physical.

Yes, you're on the right path. Yes, you're moving forward slowly. Yes, you're living each step more fully than many live their entire lives. Take that in for a moment. Your one step is more fruitful, fuller of life than many others entire existence there. That's why you do it one step at a time and enjoy what's under your feet, in front of your eyes and what you can touch with your fingers. Yes, it's the way for you to live. One step at a time.

Yes, it's difficult to live this way when your head gets into the lives of others business. You cannot live in another person's business because you're not living their life. You're living your life. As you focus in your energetic life space, it's enough.

Yes, it's enough for you. Yes, you get distracted by other humans and their lives. Yes, sometimes you look up into the bright light to see if you're going in the right direction, but you're blinded, and you can't see so you get into rough terrain sometimes.

Yes, you're not happy with a regular life. You want a rich, full life. The only way to have it is to live in this moment.

There is much LOVE here for you.   Namaste

Your job is to stay in this moment and enjoy it as completely. Physically, emotionally and spiritually connected in this moment and in this place.

May 30th
Big Laughter

You are beginning to smile a little more often, have you noticed this? When you laugh, energy is released, and your body loosens up. It's important to laugh as often as possible. Your body was designed to release energy and tension by laughing.

Sometimes there's nervous laughter that releases high anxiety and tension. You know you're uneasy if you laugh in a weird way that makes humans look at you. It's your bodies way of releasing pent-up energy that stays within you. Every time you laugh, the old energy goes out and new, fresh energy comes in.

You are, after all, like a growing sunflower. It needs water and sun. Same for you. You need light, laughter, LOVE, energy and fresh air to become your highest, greatest self. There's no need for you to grumble and be grouchy. You're a laugher. You wish to be happy.

You want to laugh and dance. You want to stay away from the grumpy people. You want to laugh in your very being. Your highest self wants to come out and laugh right out into the air.

You find one another through big laughs and smiling. The laughter gives more energy. It's the extra step. The friendly smile is one thing, but the laughter is refreshing and energizing. The air that comes back in goes straight down into your very being.

Laugh every chance you get. Don't be ashamed. Don't be affected by human judgement of it, even at difficult times. It releases your anxiety so you may speak your truth. After uneasy laughter, there's more room for truth. Laugh with your head back and your mouth open. Let everyone see your teeth. You're about big laughter.

You've had times when you stifled your happiness and laughter. You feared it would sadden others. This taught you to keep your emotions inside. There are others who wish to hear your laughter. They wish to laugh with you and you with them. You won't have to stifle anymore laughter. Those days are behind you.

There is much LOVE here for you.   Namaste

Now you're free to be you. It's all you've got really. You can be your highest, brightest self and laugh every chance you get. When you go by the mirror, make sure you laugh.

May 31st
Open to Surprises

You're showing up eagerly to learn something that moves you. As if you're not fully alive. You know there's something not quite stimulated. You wish to feel, completely. To be fully assimilated, physically, spiritually and mentally. You understand you're more than what you appear. You're more complex. You see and feel more things than others. You're remembering things. You're drawn to learn more. To be more. To feel more.

Do you remember the yearning you had? Before you started looking everywhere, for your next direction. There's an eagerness with it." I must go there. I must see this. I must know this." Now the seeking has taken on its own energy. For when you open the box, the energy just starts moving. All you can do is hang on and follow it. For you've allowed your excited inner self to come out and play. You don't wish to tamper it down anymore.

What fun you're having in the search. Lots of interesting humans and events. You don't really know what's happening. You know you're living your life fully because you're open to surprises.

The unplanned life is open for surprises, great joy and unexpected LOVE. Now you've met humans on your path that normally would not cross your path. LOVE takes you to unexpected places.

It's why you began seeking. It's why you're opening your mind and heart to the unknown. Because you want to be more than you are at this moment. It will come.

Keep following your energetic self. The one full of excitement. It will lead you to some wondrous sights. Things you've never considered. Things you didn't know existed. You're like a child on an adventure. Having fun. Seeing what there is to see and being constantly surprised by your human life. Just try to keep up.

There is much LOVE here for you.   Namaste

You're living your life fully because you're open to surprises.

June

The Mind Helps You Survive While The Heart Helps You Live.

#aaronlacey

June 1st
You Are Deserving of LOVE

Your biggest secret is the same as the others'. "I don't deserve LOVE." How is it possible you would all have the same secret and yet, you've never told anyone about it? Is it a group secret? When you bring it into the light, it moves on. You all have a terrible thing you've done in the past. Because you're having a human experience, you all fail. What's seen as failure in the human world is success in the energetic world. It means you lived. You came to play.

You don't know how things are going to unfold. You only know what's in front of you. And you have to make some decision about the mess you're in. Sometimes it's good. Sometimes it's bad. You've succeeded in your human experience no matter what it looks like at this moment. It's human nature to judge everything as good or bad. Humans taught you that. Not the Universe. It's all wonderful because it's just energy. You're just playing because you're children of the Universe. Be a little easier on yourself. You're not angels. You're humans.

If you're judging yourself, you'll always come up short. Then you'll believe you don't deserve LOVE. People have told you that you must deserve things including LOVE. If you are ill-treated in your life, it proves to you that you're undeserving of LOVE. This is from the small years. Unknowingly, you incorporated it inside. How about letting it out now? You've all got the same secret. Whatever you are feeling, sit in it for a moment.

You don't like to stay in the sad emotions, but you like the happy, joyous, fun ones. It's important for you to sit in the sad ones so they may disappear. It's up to you. Now that you know someone else gave you this idea, you can decide if you want to keep it.

There is much LOVE here for you.   Namaste

You are precious beings that have come into physical to house LOVE. That's what resides inside you. The LOVE you've gathered from the Universe is held inside you. You are one with it. Assuredly, you are deserving of LOVE because you are LOVE.

June 2nd
Human Elephants

You believe that for you to be valued as humans, you must appear to be moving forward. Getting better, wiser and gathering more items. This is how you compare yourselves. This survival part has turned into a race to be successful. Although it started off honestly because you were trying to survive as a human race. Only the strongest and smartest would survive.

The time has passed but the systems have been set up from past generations. Today, it's not necessary for you to compete.

Now, some of you are moving forward as a group. You're sharing possessions and LOVE. Now, all will survive. You're taking all into a group. Small, old or smart. When you travel as a group, there's a sense of meaning in your life. You're more at ease with yourself. It has to do with this philosophy of helping a group forward, instead of just you.

It's still important for you to acknowledge this competition has been a part of your family lineage. It's something that has come along with you. These things still exist within you.

There's lots moving forward. It's a new way of thinking for some. Yet, it's a very old way for others. There are some who keep their elderly and small ones safe by circling around them. The strong ones are on the outer edge protecting.

Humans have not always lived this way, but elephants have. They understand they're greater with those who are small, smart, strong, and weak than they are on their own. They take them as family and travel through time together.

You're beginning to work as a group. You're taking the weaker and stronger. The stronger are good at protecting people. It's what they long to do. Then there are others who wish to nurture and feed people. It's what they want to do. Then there are some who wish to sing and dance. It's what they do best. Together they're complete. Separately they're not as contented.

There is much LOVE here for you.   Namaste

Perhaps you can start to travel like elephants do. Maybe you can be human elephants.

June 3rd
Anticipation of Wonder

You wait in anticipation of great news. Of something to smile about. Of your heart to be moved. To feel joyful and emotional. You wait in anticipation of LOVE. You've become one of those humans looking for something positive. You're looking and looking. You're by-passing negative things to get to the wondrous events, blessed humans, special plants and trees. You're one of them now. You sit in anticipation of what's coming next.

You're learning to be in the moment. To feel the anticipation. This means something wondrous is going to occur. Your body is being reconfigured to anticipate wonder. This vibration will go out into the world. It will continue to anticipate joyous occasions, wondrous events, and beautiful things. Your DNA is changing as you sit in anticipation. You're learning to be still but excited.

When you're sitting in anticipation, you can't move around. You're sitting. It's building and building. You're hopeful of what will tumble out, what you'll trip over or what you'll bump into. You're sitting in anticipation of a wondrous life. It has nothing to do with the future. It's only this moment.

It's difficult for humans to sit, and yet, your highest calling is to sit quietly. But to sit quietly in anticipation, that is something wonderful. This is sitting with a little smile on your face. There is a sense of eagerness. Your heart is beating fast. Your temperature is rising. You can't wait to see what happens next.

As you believe, so it will be. As you believe your life is something to be anticipated with joy and wonder, so it will be full of joy and wonder. What you anticipate, comes. What you anticipate, you'll find - because you won't stop at the mundane. You'll keep going. Events that would normally slow you down, you don't even notice. "That's not it. That's not it. It's ahead somewhere and I'm going to continue in anticipation of joy, wonder and LOVE until I find it!"

There is much LOVE here for you.   Namaste

What you anticipate will unfold for you. It's your life. Do with it as you will. When you're sitting in anticipation of wonder, take note.

June 4th
LOVE Roses

You're opening like a rosebud. Little by little, until finally, all the petals are open. It smells wonderful. It has gone from dormancy and quiet times to budding, hoping there's more. It allows sun and rain to come in until it's complete.

Much like you. You have times of unease and unknowing where you sit quietly in it. You can't do much else. Sometimes, you're frozen or sad. You lie dormant. Then, with the first raindrops, you start to hope you'll be more. Maybe you'll be more involved with others. Feel more alive. This is hope. It's a wish and a dream. Just like a rosebud.

You hope for a rich, full life. Then when the sun comes out in its full glory, you find yourself surrounded by those who LOVE you. There are opportunities you weren't aware of because your eyes were closed. It's like a cloud was covering the sun. It's sun for the rose and LOVE for you.

Suddenly your life makes sense. You're becoming part of humanity. You're moving with ease. You smile. You're contented. What you have become must begin with a dream or wish for more fulfillment, LOVE and kindness. These things must be grown in hope.

You might not be a full rose yet but perhaps you're a bud. Perhaps you're still dormant under the ground waiting to come out. By thinking a thing, it will come to light. Because it's meant to be in the Universe. The entire Universe is behind you. You have a great support team that wishes much LOVE and fulfillment for you. All you have to do is dream and wish it, then there it is.

There is much LOVE here for you. Namaste

You're one beautiful, fragrant rose on a bush that covers an entire block. You understand you're part of a larger scheme of things. You work together to bring joy to humans as they walk by. This is the way of the Universe of LOVE. When you're not in physical, you're part of a huge rose bush. You happily work together for the greater cause. So, humans may fill themselves with the greatest energy available. To breathe you in. It is LOVE manifested in physical.

June 5th
Ego & LOVE

Inside, you often discuss, "Can you prove this? I can't prove it, but I feel that it's true." These internal discussions take up much head and heart space. They're pointless as your mind can't understand what the soul is feeling and vice versa. It's human nature to keep your mind busy so you don't focus on spiritual business. It's a diversion from settling in and connecting with Source and the Universe of LOVE. It's important for you just to notice this busyness. And not engage it further.

It's in your human nature to feel right. To be on the right path. To say the right thing. To be with the right people. Unfortunately, there are no right people and no right answers. When you can step back from this way of being, you may see that your ego and mind are protecting you like a shield. But what's hiding behind your shield? It's your innocent, true, honest, LOVING self. Because of the life you've led, you've taught your mind that you must be protected.

"Do the right things at the right times with the right people." This 'rightness' is your ego. Your ego is afraid to live. Afraid to show itself in case it's destroyed. Now set this aside for a moment and sit there. Now that this is exposed, there is no protection. You're now vulnerable and LOVING.

Now you may encourage your soul to come out and play. To realize it's safe and doesn't need protection. Your soul yearns to live. It's best at LOVING, skipping, and dancing. Your soul may let your ego understand it doesn't need to be guarded. Because your soul stands alone in its own 'rightness'. Its own peace, LOVE, honesty, and integrity.

When the soul comes out into the sunshine to live, it's joined by all non-physical. The Universe of LOVE participates in the energy that's produced when your soul plays. That's the true protection for the soul. And that's much better than your ego.

There is much LOVE here for you.   Namaste

The Universe of LOVE will protect your soul when it comes out to play. Let it live.

June 6th
Sing, Dance & Play

There's a knowing inside each of you. Like a little voice you hear when you're anxious. Sometimes it says, " Go left. Call someone." It seems random. Oftentimes, you don't pay attention to it. It's a thought that has nothing to do with what's in front of you or what you're thinking about. This thought is passing through you. You have not devised it. Now you may further investigate these thoughts to see where they lead.

You're inquisitive by nature. As you start to acknowledge these outside thoughts, you'll open up a part of you that was closed. You call it the soul. It's a little piece of the Universe of LOVE, which is energy. It's trying to communicate with the rest of the Universe. It calls out for support and LOVE. And it's expressing its own LOVE. This soul energy is always calling out and giving. It's highly intelligent, all-knowing, all-LOVING, and non-judgmental. It's pure essential LOVE and it resides in each of you.

It calls out to the Universe. The Universe responds to your questions. "How can I LOVE more? How can I be more? How can I live more?" Every moment you call out, the Universe responds, but you're busy doing life and don't always listen to your answer. You live by remembering. You live by reconnecting with the Universe of LOVE which knows only one thing. How to LOVE, have fun and enjoy.

Sitting in the Universe of LOVE and non-physical is peaceful, gentle, and LOVING. You have connected with it at times. This gentle knowing is the Universe of LOVE.

You left this space to have fun in physical. You didn't go there to work and make money. You went to connect with humans on a physical level which is skipping, jumping, dancing, and laughing. This is not done in non-physical.

Sometimes you forget why you're there. The little ones always remember. You wanted us to remind you what you already know.

There is much LOVE here for you.   Namaste

It's time for you to sing, dance and play until you fall down exhausted.

June 7th
LOVE Messages

You have messages that play in your mind so many times, they become truth to you. It's as if they're reality. It's important to notice the messages you're replaying. This repetition is something you learned as a young one. You repeated things so you wouldn't forget. You were watching and listening how humans interacted. You created brain patterns then. Now your system thinks it requires this repetition to exist. The things you're repeating are not always uplifting. If it's not, it doesn't belong in a LOVING, uplifting spiritual being like you.

Notice that there is a soft, gentle knowing and powerful voice that comes in and says one thing only. There is no repetition at that moment. It says, "You are precious." This voice is the truth. When you speak truth on a soul level, it only needs to be said once.

You know its truth when you hear it. Not just from the Universe of LOVE which is precious and beautiful. You also know it when someone says, "You're being hard on yourself." You don't argue. You know it's true.

It's time to listen to truth where it lives. Inside you. This is where a little piece of the Universe resides. Where you are one with truth and LOVE. That is why it recognizes truth. Whether it is a kind human or the Universe of LOVE.

Your true human purpose is to be one with the Universe and allow LOVE to flow in and out of you. Then you'll be connected with the others on an energetic level. For you to allow LOVE in, garbage must be cleared out. The garbage is removed by noticing it. By being aware of it.

"You are precious" is a conversation for the soul. It's a LOVE conversation. Just follow the Universe of LOVE. It will lead you to a place of peace and contentment.

There is much LOVE here for you. Namaste

The next time you hear "You are precious" you'll know it's from the Universe of LOVE and it's just for you.

June 8th
Peanut Butter Sandwiches

You wish that life was as easy as making a peanut butter sandwich. Everyone LOVES them. They bring comfort and joy. It eases your distress. Imagine such a human thing coming into your life that creates such ease from stress. This message is much like a peanut butter sandwich.

There's a sense of comfort beyond stress and anxiety. If you can't believe there's ease beyond stress, you stay in stress. First you must move into stress and sit in it before you can find ease and comfort. But there are many who sit in ease and stay there all of their days. There's comfort because they know what's next, more discomfort. There's no judgment with this. You can do what you want with your life. So, sit in stress or move in and out of it.

Most of you are interested in what it feels like outside this uncomfortable zone where bad things happen. The next place is uncomfortable because it's not predictable yet. It will be predictable when you spend more time in this new place of ease, comfort, and LOVE. This next place is where you reside when you're not in physical form. You've spent more time in this ease of eternity, you just can't recall it. But you get glimpses of it. Sometimes you cry with remembrance.

When you're not in physical, you're energy. You're LOVE. You're ease. You're joy. In physical, when you expect something awful to happen, it does. When you expect something wonderful to happen, it does. So, sit in wonder and curiosity about what's going to happen next and where you will next find JOY.

Now when you eat your peanut butter sandwich, you'll think it's hilarious, you might share it or give it away. It's different now. You're not eating it out of stress, you're eating it out of joy. Enjoy your peanut butter sandwiches.

There is much LOVE here for you.   Namaste

Don't underestimate the value of joy and ease. They change your way of seeing the world without it changing at all.

June 9th
You Are All Here

You show up in anticipation of a heart movement. Of feeling alive. You show up expectant to be moved and so, you will be. That's the way of energy. You are energy, you control energy around you and energy revolves around you. Between all this movement of energy, you may feel emotional.

Sometimes you don't notice small changes around you, in the air or vibrations from others. You're walking through life as if you're just one human living on a planet and not an energetic being having an energetic experience with other energetic beings.

It takes calmness and focus to be relaxed enough to notice or feel energy. Silence and standing still are not your favourite things to do. Therefore, you don't always feel energy.

The Universe of LOVE energy is around you at all times. You just don't notice it. That's perfectly fine. It takes a great discipline to focus. It takes a quiet mind to know there's more to the Universe. This knowing calms you so you may focus longer.

Those who believe in the Universe will focus because you're trying to contact it. In a way, you're relaxing and focusing at the same moment. You're focusing on limitless energy.

If you're able to lie down in quiet and close your eyes, you may start to envision what the Universe of LOVE is like for you. What it feels like. What it looks like behind your eyes. Who is there that you knew as a human? You must do this on your own. It's a perfect vulnerable position for you to be in so your body understands it's safe and open, so it may relax.

There is much LOVE here for you.   Namaste

Your true connection arrives when you're alone.

June 10th
Discover the Unknown

Sometimes you have sadness around growing and evolving. You've decided that you're not growing as quickly as you would like. That you're not as kind as you would like. That you're not hearing voices or seeing colours as much as you would like. You've set a goal to discover the unknown. This is very vague. You can't always reach it, so there's sadness attached, as if you've failed something. This is slowing you down because it's attached to a human goal.

What if you thought," I'm energy. I flow everywhere. I'm part of the energetic world and the Universe of LOVE. Therefore, there is nothing I must do besides be myself. I flow everywhere." Then you could relax and chill out. You'll come to understand that you're energy. You'll naturally be taken to the places you desire.

It all starts by lying around looking at the clouds and listening to the trees moving in the wind. You're part of the wind. The same wind that carries the birds' wings. You're energy so you may dissolve any time you wish and leave the body behind. You have energy enclosed in a body. This is the part that sets the unreachable goals. When you reach one, you automatically create another. That's the way of humans. But LOVE energy is opposite. It's not setting goals. It's being in the moment, seeing what you can see and feeling what you can feel energetically.

You'll begin to feel the wind and the vibration of bee wings because it's your frequency. Your ears naturally vibrate. You'll come to understand: "This is Me. I can relax. I am energy. That is why I can hear, feel and see it."

The sadness is up to you. It's all right to feel any emotion. Humans think there's something wrong with feeling sad because you don't meet an energetic goal. But there are none. You're not there to evolve into an angel. You're there to have a human experience. You don't have to do anything. You just have to relax and be. Allow life to unfold.

There is much LOVE here for you.   Namaste

You are LOVE. What could be better than that?

June 11th
Are You All Right?

It's important for Universal LOVE energy to reach out to humans. You're able to access this energy by finding a way that's pleasing to you. Hearing a concise, clear message is easier for you to receive. Hearing voices often occurs when you get into the realm of Universal energy. You hear outside information that is not in your own experience.

When the two meet energetically, it's like you reaching your hands out and the Universe reaching its hands in. Then you're linked together.

What you wish to know most when you are holding the hands of the Universe is, "Will I make it? Will I be all right this time? Am I doing okay in human." This is what you're most anxious about. This human fear comes with the body.

Your highest self always reminds you that everything is okay. No matter what circumstance you find yourself in, your energetic self is whole. It's still the way it was when you came into physical. You wish to know: "Have I lost my soul?" Your energetic self lasts through all eternity. When you're in a physical body and when you're not. Even if you can't find it or hear it, it still resides within you. You have nothing to fear in this matter. You are LOVE energy which cannot be extinguished.

Are you doing all right? Perfect.
Will you make it through this lifetime? Absolutely.
Have you lost yourself? Your soul? Never.
Will you be one with energetic LOVE again? Of course.
Are you one with it right now? Definitely.

There is much LOVE here for you.   Namaste

You are much LOVED by the Universe. You're perfect the way you are. No matter what you get into. You're perfect to the Universe of LOVE. That's just what you wish to hear today.

June 12th
Your Gathering

There are many who are able to hear this LOVE vibration with your ears. It calls those in the same vibrational frequency. This is about tuning your radio, your ears, to this frequency. Some stumble across it. Others are drawn to it straight as an arrow. Others take their time and resist it.

Now, you've found yourselves together. This is not about being lead. It's like a big lasso drawing you together in LOVE. Then you may be a higher vibration of LOVE yourselves. You've asked for a speaker you can hear and gather with others like you.

This is a gathering. You might start to feel the others that are with you. You've called them to you, and they've called you to them. But why do you want this gathering? You know you're more than a human but you're not sure what. You also know there are others like you. You don't know who or where they are, but you'd like to come together.

Together, you have a higher vibration. One that raises the LOVE energy. When the LOVE energy is raised, it reaches further and higher. Then more humans will recognize it. They say, "I was looking for you. Where's the gathering?"

Raising the LOVE vibration is what you do. It's what you are. You're LOVE vibration and you wish it to be higher. You wish to do this during your lifetime. But not everyone does. The others have different jobs to do. You and your gathering will raise the frequency of LOVE because it's what you do best. It's what you're designed for.

That's why you're called to it. You may have ignored it many times but now there's a part of you that says, "All right, I'm ready. Let's get down to business." This is your business.

There is much LOVE here for you.   Namaste

Your human business is raising the LOVE vibration with those you have gathered together in this frequency. You're more powerful than you imagine.

June 13th
You Are LOVE

There are many who ask the same thing over and over. You're not aware of this because it's an energetic question. You don't always understand you're energetic beings. Whatever you long for comes forward as a question, which draws an energetic answer. It's the normal way of conversing in the Universe.

It might be important to understand your yearnings. There are many who say, "This awful thing is happening." Yet, you have requested it in this way by asking for clarity about your life. You've asked for happiness, peace of mind, belonging or the feeling of being LOVED. When you ask for these things, you get your answers.

These words are drawing attention to something that is not quite right in your life. Something that's preventing you from receiving the LOVE and peace you wish for. Your answer is happening right now. It could look like chaos. You'll say, "That's not what I want." Then you'll focus on this negative thought which prolongs your ability to see that it's exactly the answer you asked for. You get stuck. Instead of saying, "I asked a question. This must be the answer."

Because you forgot you asked a question you say, "Look at this big mess. I'm going to focus my energy on this now." Your energy spirals in this negative place. When you ask you receive your answer, but it may not look like you thought it would. It might look like chaos.

Sometimes you're able to say, "Thank you for that answer." Other times you say, "I don't like that. I'm going to focus my energy on it until it disappears." Unfortunately, that makes it a bigger mess. Then it takes you longer to remember you're LOVED.

It's just human nature playing. Sometimes you get to enjoy the mess because it's a distraction from humanity. You can really get into it and say, "Look everyone. See how bad this is." Sometimes a big chaotic mess is your intention because you don't want to feel the overwhelming LOVE that is available. You don't want to remember you're perfect and precious. It might be easier to stay in the chaos.

There is much LOVE here for you.   Namaste

You're LOVED unconditionally by the Universe. You are LOVE.

June 14th
Infant You

Children help you recall what it's like to be innocent, open, curious and LOVING without judging. You were not a know-it-all yet. You understood you needed more information about how to live.

Now you know having information serves you in the world of human. What if this information keeps you away from your higher self and your connection with the Universe? A long time ago you decided you would be an intellectual human. You thought, "to survive in the world of man, I must act like one."

You're acting like a human but if you want to act like a spiritual being, it's time to act like a small one. You remember what it was like. Your body recalls what it's like to be so curious looking at an ant with all the time in the world. It's your natural state when you're young.

The openness you consider dangerous is important when you're trying to have a spiritual connection. Intellect keeps you disconnected because the connection is about energy, not about danger and building things. It's about pure LOVE. Pure connection. Pure innocence. Just like a baby who relies on humans. They must come in trusting. Just like you did.

Your mind goes to the trauma, instead of the innocence. Go back before the trauma, before your heart was broken, when you trusted the humans. A moment before that, you trusted the Universe. You were one with the Universe. That's why you were able to be a vulnerable infant.

Go all the way back to the beginning. To the innocence and trust. That's the oneness with the Universe. Then you'll connect easily with Source and the Universe of LOVE because you had just come from there a moment before. Go back.

There is much LOVE here for you.   Namaste

Your body recalls what it's like to be curious.

June 15th
Curiosity & Knowing

Yes, you are on the correct path. Yes, you understand what your next move is going to be. Because you have begun to tap into information from the Universe. From the energy of all, that holds every idea that has ever been, existing now. It's flowing all around you.

You know you're a small human, but what you feel energetically or intuitively is huge. Energy and the Universe of LOVE is huge. It's important for you to decide, "I'm okay having a small amount of information." Without judging. The judgements placed on the notion that you know very little must also be released.

It's a big thing for humans to say, "I don't know much." You've spent all your time accumulating information in case you need it later. Now it's important for you to say, "Even though I know all this, I know very little."

For you to gain access to what's available to you, there's a surrendering to higher intelligence and vast knowledge. First you say, "I have a feeling there's more going on here." This opens the door to: "I wonder where all the information that exists resides." If thoughts are vibration and energy, then they still exist. Energy always exists. So, where is it?

This begins your next stage, which is curiosity. "How do I access it?" Now you find yourself tumbling forward through time into a vast space of the unknown. At the same moment, you'll find yourself in a vast space of knowing. It exists together. Knowing and unknowing. The unknowing is your way in. Many of you want to know what the vast knowledge is before you let go of your idea that you know very little. You want to know what's in it for you. Then you stay put. "I don't wish to go to a place where I know nothing. I'll be vulnerable and afraid." That's fine, too.

This information is for you to know forever. You've asked to be reminded. This is the process to the vast Universe of information.

There is much LOVE here for you. Namaste

I don't know everything. I'm curious about what lies in the Universe. I trust that I'll be okay when I tumble forward into energetic LOVE.

June 16th
You are Enough

You're beginning to wonder if you're going to become that spiritual person that you've hoped to be. You've tried many methods to advance yourself. Now, here you are just being you.

You've been hoping to be different than what you are, but perhaps what you are is good enough. Maybe it's all you've got. This goes against things you've learned and the way your brain works.

What if what you are at this moment is all you have? Perhaps it's all you'll ever be. Would it be enough? Would you be a worthy human? Would you be contented to live the rest of your days being who you are at this moment? This moment is all you've really got. You're a human being living a human life. Maybe that's enough. Because when you came into your physical body, you were excited just to have one.

Also, when you came into physical, you wished to allow LOVE to flow into you and out of you. That's why you came. You wished to have a human experience to see what that was like. You thought it would be easy to allow LOVE to flow since you were coming from the Universe of LOVE. You know you're a channel for LOVE.

Why aren't you a clear channel now? Because you wish to be something other than what you are. What if everything is perfect right now? What if you're almost finished there? Would it be enough then? You've got to be enough because there's nothing else.

When you understand you're enough, you're automatically a channel for LOVE energy. It seems simple, but not for complicated humans like you. When you're clear, energy passes through you. There's no judgement of what you could be.

There is much LOVE here for you. Namaste

Suddenly you understand what you've been seeking all along. To be clear of judgment so you may allow LOVE to flow through you. Therefore, healing you and filling you and all those who surround you with LOVE. Now that is a spiritual human being.

June 17th
Breathe

You feel and interpret energy in a human way. It's difficult to exist in physical yet be aware that energy is moving through you. Somehow you must name it. Your mind must say what's happening. Its job is to keep you out of danger, so it analyzes situations.

Energy is familiar to your body. It's full of energy. If you walk into a room where two people previously had angry words, you will know there's angry energy there.

Your body can feel it, but your mind doesn't know anything about it. It just sees two humans standing there, but your body can pick up negative energy. Or LOVING, positive energy. It knows when the weather is about to change.

When energy enters you, it lands in spots desiring more energy. Organs grab it because they need it. This grabbing and holding creates tightness and anxiety. Although the organ realizes it needs energy, the very method of grabbing onto it in fear creates more tightness. Even though it's got the energy, it's still anxious about it. It feels like it can't get enough, so it keeps grabbing. Sometimes, you'll feel your organs tighten and loosen. This is your body craving energy.

The LOVE energy of the Universe is clear, high, bright energy that's available to you at all times. It's where you've existed before physical but also exist right now. All this energy is one energy. It's your energy and it's the energy of the Universe.

For all this to come together for you, it's important for you to get into spiritual energetic alignment. This is done by connecting with Source or Higher Vibration. With something that exists outside you that is eternal. When you're able to tune in for a moment, your body's energy will easily get into alignment. It's not new. The energy passes through, and everything settles.

When you feel unusual energy in your organs, get into alignment. You just take a breath in saying, "Here I am." Then there's stillness which is what it feels like to be one with the Universe.

There is much LOVE here for you. Namaste

In one breath you're able to come into alignment with the Universe.

June 18th
The Longer I Live, the Less I Know

As you age, you understand how little you know. It's odd that the more time you spend on your busy earth, the less you know. You understand there is too much to know. This causes a feeling of inadequacy. You don't have all the information to make decisions. Then great confusion occurs.

You weren't confused as a small one because you knew you didn't know everything. Therefore, you trusted your needs would be met. You had to allow life to unfold because you had little control over it. Now you wish to have a lot of control over your own life. Yet, you only have a minuscule amount. This causes anxiety. Not the realization that you know very little. Because you've always known this.

The predominant idea is: "I'm trying to learn how to get control of my life." Set this aside and go to the part where you're unable to control events surrounding you. This causes anxiety and then sadness as you surrender to the truth of the matter. Then there's a sense of helplessness. Then finally, freedom. Freedom from having to know everything.

Finally, you accept the fact that you don't know everything, and you surrender. But to what? Again, this is stressful. Now it's time for you to step inside and wonder, "What could I surrender to so I will not be fearful?" You all have something you can surrender to in a peaceful manner. A LOVED one who has passed, energy, flowers, fairies, or angels. Visualize this, which causes you to let go, breathe, and allow your body to relax.

But first you must pass through the messiness of controlling your environment. Then for that to be all right. Pause only for a moment so you may pass into surrender. If you sit too long in this, your mind will try to get more control. If you wish to pass beyond anxiety and into peace, you must go through it.

There is much LOVE here for you. Namaste

Pass through the anxiety so you may let go and surrender to whatever it is you're safe surrendering to. Suddenly, things seem easier. Then it will be a place of ease and comfort for you when you say, "The longer I live, the less I know."

June 19th
Come

You're starting to connect with others at an energetic level. You may feel what they're feeling. You have eased into this as your natural state of progression. You've LOVED yourself enough.

You're doing the best you can. You're uncovering something new. Be gentle. Just as the Universe is. It's your energetic self that calls you forward into the lightness of being and away from the discomfort and frustration you feel.

You're starting to understand it's your voice calling you forward. So, you may trust it. You know it intimately. It's your energetic self. As you call yourself forward, you'll be brought into a place of great peace and ease.

It's easier when you are doing the calling. Be gentle with yourself if you are not able to hear it yet. You're a human having a human experience. But there's a part of you that always wishes to come forward. You're starting to believe you've made life too difficult. You've been too hard on yourself and others. Now that you want some relief, you're starting to wonder.

So, you draw yourself forward: "Come. Come." To an easy, restful place. You may leave worries back. When you come to this place of ease and then return to your human life, which is exactly the same as when you left it, you will feel less anxious, depressed and angry. Nothing has changed, yet everything has changed. You've called yourself forth into a higher understanding of life. Just a life lived like all the others.

When you call yourself to this place of ease, your body and mind slow down. You have found a place of comfort where you may relax entirely. Even for a few moments so you may relax. You may trust where you're being called. Your body will relax. Now, you're altered. You're gentler with yourself and others. There are no big deals. You slowed yourself down enough to breathe and relax. Now you may live your human life at an easier, gentler level.

There is much LOVE here for you.   Namaste

Call yourself forward by saying, "Come. Come to this place of ease. Come."

June 20th
Good News

"We have some good news and some bad news." After you hear the truth or bad news, the good news is always LOVE. The whole process of pulling out truth creates resistance because you wish to appear like you've got it all together. As if you're in a race that's for appearances only. It's upside-down thinking because it doesn't matter what you look like on the outside.

This is difficult for some but for others, it's right along spiritual-seeking lines. There are some who think you must have no material possessions to be spiritual. Sometimes, you believe you must behave in a certain manner outwardly and then you'll be a more spiritual person.

It has nothing to do with going to certain religious places or meditating all day or crawling around in the dirt. You are LOVED in the same way. You've placed judgment of human behaviour on yourself and others. But it's not the truth in the Universe of LOVE. It's an energetic place of LOVE where all are one. Because you're all the same. That's why you're LOVED the same.

Humanity has pulled the wool over your eyes in certain areas, but you have wished to be tricked. Your mind wanted to be told how to live on the outside so you wouldn't have to look on the inside. You're afraid of that place. So, you ask others how to behave. Then they tell you. Then you act the way they told you but there's a part of you that knows there's something wrong with this. That you should be looking inside for answers.

This is the most scary and difficult place to go. So, you've chosen things to distract you. You're not alone. Now there's something inside that's saying, "At last I've heard the truth. Now it's a part of me." When the truth enters you, it stays.

There is much LOVE here for you.   Namaste

When you go inside and ask, the answer is there. It's been there for all eternity. This you know also. 'I'm to connect. I'm to sit in LOVE. I'm to sit in peace. I will hear all I need. When I sit in alignment, the Universe is at my disposal. Whatever I ask of it, it will respond.

June 21st
Smell the Roses

There is something about the smell of roses. It brings certain memories. When you smell a fragrant flower, you feel settled. As if you've been searching for calmness. In a simple gesture like smelling a flower.

This is your soul leading and your mind joining in. Your soul is always searching for balance, peace, and gentleness. It wishes to reside in this gentle place of LOVE always. It's a part that some of you are just discovering, while others are familiar. You're all at different stages because you're evolving at different paces and times. It's the way it's meant to be. There are always some who lead while others notice and wonder. It's much like the curiosity of smelling a new flower. Your curious natures get you both into trouble and into evolution. You were born to be curious and experience new things.

Oftentimes, you're hard on yourself for getting into trouble when you explore. Although that's the very nature of it. Sometimes, you get a fragrant flower and other times, you get a stinky one. Each time you get a fragrant one, you become lighter. More connected to nature and therefore, the Universe. Then you can take a big breath of relief. Joy overcomes you. All because you took a chance.

You're curious so you're learning about others, the Universe, your planet, and your place in the world. You're always searching. That's why you are listening to this vibration.

There are others who sit quietly and safely with their windows closed. They're not living the true human experience. But that's all right because it's their experience. For those here, you're not hiding away any longer. You're out and about experiencing life. You are getting hurt, having fun, and smelling the roses.

You're supposed to be curious with your life. Don't be afraid to be hurt. That's the fun of it. That's why you've got bodies. It gets you into trouble and it gets you right back. Have some fun. Dance, sing, play, climb the hill and swing. And don't forget to take a big smell of the roses. Breathe them right into your lungs.

There is much LOVE here for you.   Namaste

Stumble your way through life. Run your way through life. Crawl your way through life. Dance your way through life.

June 22nd
LOVE Cloud

The connection with the Universe of LOVE is done individually. But when you're with others who are able to be moved energetically by this vibration and are interested in it, you're coming together for the group of you. Not necessarily the Universe of LOVE. Although, you may get little pieces of it inadvertently. This is about being one together as a group.

You've been looking for others who you feel one with because you miss your energetic LOVE family. You have a longing for others even though you don't know who or where they are. You're here to connect with your family of LOVE. Your longing has brought you to this place. You've asked for some acknowledgement that you're missing your family and you can be drawn together by this signal.

You've all asked for it: "We need a signal. We'll recognize each other when we arrive." Now, why do you want your family to come together at this point? Did you come together for a higher purpose? Your higher purpose is to allow LOVE to flow into you and out of you to others who don't have access to this. When your familiar group of energetic LOVE comes together, you're powerful. The LOVE will flow through you and out to the others.

Others haven't asked for a transmitter to call humans. They just wish a little drizzle of LOVE. In order for them to get it, your group must come together as one to allow energy into you and out of you so it falls on them. You are a LOVE cloud. You will be one energetic, powerful family again. This is how you are when you're not in physical bodies. You're trying to reproduce it in humanity. You can do this because you're divine beings with a great connection to the Universe of LOVE.

There is much LOVE here for you.   Namaste

You want it all. You want to be LOVE even in physical form. You've asked and the Universe has answered your call. You're going to be a LOVE cloud, but it takes all of you, not just one.

June 23rd
Giant Sandcastle

You sit in anticipation and hope. You're excited to be reunited with the energy of LOVE and with those gathering toward this energy. There's a group familiar with this vibration. You're feeling joyful to be joined together. "Oh, what fun we're going to have together."

Humans are naturally drawn to joyfulness. Your energetic self cries out for more. You've discovered that there's more joy coming to this energetic spot in time. You're switching from being drawn energetically to a conscious thought. "I wish to go to this joyful place." Now your mind, body and energetic self are deciding. Now you're fully present. The best you can hope for is to bring your mind and energetic self into alignment with a common goal.

You seek joyfulness; therefore, it comes. You've created it, so, it's real. This group has all called it forth because you wish to come together to play. You're like children finding a giant sandcastle. It's a joyful experience. You laugh, climb, and slide down.

As you are more joyful, more energetic joyful beings come to climb and slide with you. Joyfulness attracts more to it. "Everyone come! Look at the giant sandcastle. You've never seen such a thing." You call them and they come. The point of joyfulness is joyfulness. The point of fun is more fun. When you act as a joyful group, those seeking joy find you.

Others hesitate. They don't automatically run to the castle. They watch from a distance. But they get closer because of the joyful glee coming from it. Not everyone will climb the castle.

It's helpful for those who cannot hope to hear joyful noises from a distance. They wonder if they are excluded. There are some who make loud noises and some who stand back in hope of being invited in. Then further back is those who think they don't deserve it but can hear it.

There is much LOVE here for you.   Namaste

You are the ones making joyful noises. That's your position in this moment. So, laugh your head off every chance you get. For as long and as loud as you can so the vibration carries to those who are unable to laugh or smile.

June 24th
Curious Minds

You were born curious. You showed up in a human body to be curious. "What happens when energy gets into a body? Can I still share LOVE? Am I still connected to the Universe? I think I'll jump in and find out." That's the moment before you jumped into this human extension of yourself.

This curiosity has gotten you into some trouble. But by being curious enough to be interested in your environment, while others wander alone inspecting plants and birds, you progress spiritually. This is natural. Each time you investigate, you confirm you're a curious being. It's your highest self. Some of you have been shamed for being curious but it comes from a childlike, joyful LOVING, interested place. It's a pure, clear interest in your surroundings.

When you walk through the grass and you see a tiny creature, you look carefully at it. This is childlike curiosity spurred on by LOVE. You're interested in your surroundings. This is what a spiritual, energetic being is like. Always wondering, "Why do clouds look this way?"

You're having a human experience so sometimes your question will be innocent and full of LOVE and sometimes your questions will be manipulative. You go back and forth. There's no need for strong negative judgement of self. It's your human experience. You're just trying to stumble your way through a lifetime the best way you can. As all others are. You're LOVED just the way you are.

Your curiosity is often spurred on by your own inner knowledge. You know the answer before you ask the question. "What's going on in the Universe? Am I a spiritual being?" You wish to bring the answer forward. It's hidden somewhere. It's another type of curiosity. It's from a place of LOVE. You often know spiritual, energetic answers to questions before you ask them.

There is much LOVE here for you.   Namaste

You're evolved at this moment but in another moment, you'll find yourself asking questions to manipulate or just being a curious little one. All of these come together to form your beautiful self. Be gentle with yourself. You are a human.

June 25th
Join the LOVE Group

It's time for you to become part of a group with a larger purpose.
You've done your alone work by connecting with the Universe of
LOVE. You're emotionally balanced most times. Now it's time to move
forward. You know its time for you to change and evolve. You know
you're feeling pushed from behind toward a group that's waiting. You
don't know who or where they are. You don't even know how to join
them, but you have this knowing.

You've left a large group which is the Universe of LOVE.
Now you're all together energetically with a single purpose which is to
allow LOVE. It's your highest purpose when you're not in physical.

You connect with humans when you're in physical because
they're asking LOVE to flow through them. You know exactly how to
do this when you're in non-physical. You still have the same yearning
to work as a group to allow LOVE deep inside you that says, "I wish to
join a group in service of LOVE." It's like you're with your family
from the Universe of LOVE.

For many of you, this joining will be energetic because you
are not close to one another. Therefore, you'll be with others who wish
to join the group to allow LOVE to flow in and out. As soon as you say
it, you're in the group. It comes together and amps itself up like a
tornado. You understand what happens when energy comes together
and focuses on a single goal.

What's the purpose of allowing LOVE to flow through all of
you and get the energy amped up? Where are you going to direct this
tornado of LOVE? That's none of your business. When you join the
group, the energy does its own thing.

Now you balance one another. When you're happy, they're
sad and vice versa. Everyone shares the weight of emotions. You all
have common experience. You're drawn to one another because you
heal together and you balance one another.

There is much LOVE here for you.   Namaste

*LOVE doesn't need your help. It needs your openness. It goes to those
who call it to them. Your concern is to allow LOVE to flow in and out
of you.*

June 26th
Ready for LOVE

This is a reminder that you've come from a place of LOVE. You've also taken it with you. Therefore, you are LOVE. This is the basis of all knowing. It must start here, otherwise, the rest is not absorbed. Much time is spent deflecting LOVE.

When you're able to accept LOVE, sometimes by hearing it over and over, then you may move forward in your evolution. When you're not in your physical being, you're LOVE energy and you're joined with others who are energy. In a group you are LOVE. Alone you are LOVE.

The moment before you stepped into your physical body you said," I wish to jump into that body but I'm not going alone. I wish some of you to come. I'll probably forget you but don't forget me. I'm going to take some LOVE with me too because I want to give it away. The others have been in their bodies so long they've forgotten about it."

You came into a physical body to share LOVE with the humans that had forgotten they were LOVE. How do you feel about that? You are always LOVE whether you're in physical or non-physical.

You are LOVE energy. Your story is eternal. You may share LOVE easily because you are LOVE. That's the beginning of the remembering and the teaching. It's the beginning of the knowing.

It must start with LOVE. Otherwise, you reject information because you're afraid you're the only human that is not LOVE. That's your brain thinking. It's very young. Your LOVE energy is not. It's eternal. Your brain is just trying to make sense of the comings and goings there. It's always a few steps behind your heart, your energy, or your LOVE self but that's alright. It's trying to keep up. You are LOVE. That is the beginning.

There is much LOVE here for you.   Namaste

You came into a physical body to share LOVE with the humans that had forgotten they were LOVE.

June 27th
Take Notice

This vibration causes a smile. Are you smiling now? Do you notice things like this? Energy is about fine tuning. It's for you to notice. When you feel anxious in your heart, it's energy drawing your attention to something. When you smile, this is energy drawing your attention to something. When your stomach clenches up very tight, this is energy drawing your attention to something.

Are you able to notice that your body responds to energy naturally? Like they're familiar with one another? Have you ever noticed the top of your head is hot and tingly? It's energy. Your body is no stranger to energy. They've co-existed from the moment you jumped into your human body. They're well acquainted. It's your brain that has separated itself. Oftentimes leaving the body and the energy to go off and make grand plans, manipulations, and rationalizations.

Energy can draw your attention to it physically when your heart races. Your body has borrowed this time and energy to exist inside it. If you forget, your body will remind you by smiling, itching or tightness. Your energy reminds you that you're alive! It's why you came into being. Otherwise, you don't need a body. You wanted to experience LOVE contained in a human body.

Can LOVE energy be contained inside one human body? Your energy comes out and affects others. The more comfortable you are with LOVE, the further out it goes. When you are feeling small and scared, it comes in close. When it's in close, you don't feel LOVELY at all. It cuts off the energy exchange.

There's non-physical LOVE energy to assist and nurture you. When you're open to LOVE, there's more LOVE. When you're afraid of LOVE, there isn't any. You know energy is LOVE. You know you're LOVE. You know if you forget, the energy that hides within and around you will remind you through the physical body.

There is much LOVE here for you.   Namaste

You're surrounded by your non-physical support team that adores you. They wait for you to wake up in the morning so you can have an adventure together. They wait for you to go to sleep so they can pet you. Does that sound like someone who's LOVED?

June 28th
Come Together

You're missing the connection, warmth and knowing that there are others like you. You're not sure where they are or what they look like, but you miss them. It's the Universe of LOVE you're remembering. It's inside you energetically. When you're all in non-physical, you're one LOVING mass with a higher purpose to allow LOVE and to support humans who are struggling.

Now this longing is going out for humans that you're one with. Sometimes you're lonely so you ask for a beacon to draw the others. When they arrive, you'll say," Do you remember when we were one? When we were pure LOVE? Maybe we can all remember together?"

Now you wonder, "Can we be together if we have a physical body? Surely if I remember, you must remember because now you're here. Together we'll have a big remembering." You're much more powerful together than you are alone.

Your individual work must be done alone. By learning to sit quietly so you may hear answers from the Universe. But what can be together is imagining you all as one. Coming together from every direction like little beams of light. This is pure LOVE.

When you all remember that together you're one LOVE, it will sprinkle down on the heads of the others who can't remember this time. Now they will think," I feel a little better about me today." As simple as that. They will not have a big reckoning. You all absorb different amounts. They will be contented with just a little bit. Unlike you who wants it all. You who remembers more. You who expects more. You who wishes for more. You who asks more questions. The more questions you ask, the more answers you receive.

There is much LOVE here for you.   Namaste

As you put your energy out into your earth, try to visualize the others who are also doing the same thing as you. They're looking up and down. They're looking for you.

June 29th
Stumble On

Energetically, you're powerful beings. Sometimes you're oblivious to energy because you're more focused on material items. You are energy and the Universe is energy. When you call out, your voice becomes energy. Then energy responds.

Often, you're led around this way and that way. You don't usually walk directly at the truth. You often stumble onto your own answers and into your own LOVE. It's the human way, although you often trip yourselves up. You're not looking where you're going vibrationally.

There's a beautiful thing about stumbling. You fall down and think," What did I stumble over?" Then you search until you fall down again. You said," If I concentrate too much on the physical world, remind me energetically." Who would you say that to? The answer is energy. There are many different energetic vibrations around you. You may catch a familiar smell, a tightness in your chest or sudden heat or cold. This is energy trying to respond to you.

When you stumble and fall down, it's because you want to. You want to remember that you are energy and that you have a connection to energy. Anytime you wish to know something, you have access to it. You want to know it's there if you need it or call upon it.

You stumble into truths. Stumbling is a wonderful thing for you. It will recalibrate your vibration. You like it when you get off track. It's something you've set up yourself.

You like to know that if you need information, you have access to it. Then you can settle down and enjoy your time. If these are not known to you, anxiety is caused because you don't know if you can be reset. You don't know if you've made a fail-proof system for yourself. But now we've reminded you that you have. So, stumble on.

There is much LOVE here for you.   Namaste

Your world is often so vibrant and full of physical items that you're unable to focus energetically.

June 30th
Fireflies of LOVE

You're familiar with the idea of being one unit. When you're not in human, you automatically become like fireflies. All together with a singular purpose to light up the world. This is what you interpret LOVE energy to be.

As energy passes in and out of you, your mind wants to interpret it and call it something. So, you've got this notion of fireflies or stars in the sky. When they are on their own, they don't brighten anything at all. As a group they create a great bright light.

This notion is your highest self. You spend eternity coming together as one to reproduce and share LOVE. It's the easiest way to be because you're LOVE beings. LOVE fireflies. LOVE stars. You're LOVE singularly and in a group. Now that you're reminded, you're all going off and becoming fireflies. Coming together as a group then going off by yourself. You must stay in alignment on your own. Then when you mingle amongst others, you don't take over their business. You stay in your own space. Too much time alone and too much time with others is not balanced. You must be alone, and you must work as one group.

The greatest good of mankind is done as a group. In order for you to be a good group member, you must spend time alone being one with the Universe. You must hear your own voices from your non-physical support group. You will start to understand they are around energetically. It is increased when you are around other human beings with a singular purpose.

Although being part of the Universe of LOVE is your highest calling, you don't have to participate. Many humans choose to opt out when they're in their human experience. That's absolutely fine. It's important for your brain and ego to understand boundaries. Otherwise, it will run rampant through your lifetime. You are becoming more comfortable with the group activity of oneness. You are becoming lighter and easier with your own humanity. You are reaping the reward of working LOVE. It's not just for others. It's for you.

There is much LOVE here for you.   Namaste

The healing balm of LOVE must not be underestimated.

July

Never be afraid of the darkness, for you are the light

##AARONLACEY

July 1st
Bad Guys

You gather intellectual information from others which leads you to believe you're smart. They have information you wish to learn because you're studious. You're a curious creature but this other human, on a spiritual or evolutionary level, is not to be trusted. They're not honourable. So, do you take the information or delete it?

Many of you have found yourselves in these states but you don't wish to speak of it. It might appear to others that you're a sucker. This is an emotional reaction. But what about your spirit? Your curious, beautiful nature. The childlike curiosity you carry from life to life that keeps you hopping back into human bodies.

You wish to experience life. You wish to ask questions and look around. This is your human state. It's your evolved state. Therefore, curious humans must stumble against humans who have bad intentions. It's natural. If it hasn't occurred to you, you've dulled down your curiosity. Since it's your natural, evolved state, you will not be conned.

It doesn't mean that you or the others have done anything wrong. You're both being. You're being your curious self and they have different motives that are not your business. Your business is to maintain your curiosity no matter what happens to you. It's one of your most precious gifts. In being curious, you're being hopeful. You know you're going to find something beautiful just around the corner. Something your soul will jump for.

You're always looking for more joy and LOVE. It's important to maintain your sense of curiosity even if you get a couple of hard knocks. There's nothing wrong with you if you don't realize when you're being conned. Only humans who live in that realm can identify each other.

It's not your world, but they will collide sometimes.

There is much LOVE here for you.   Namaste

The perfect life plan is to stumble about. Play all you can. Bump up against others. Be light with it. There's nothing wrong with them either. It's easier for you to judge others but it's not good for you. Just stay in yourself. You are perfect the way you are.

July 2nd
Happy Face Rocks

Similar stumbling blocks come up in your life consistently. Typically, you have the same reaction which is, "Don't go there. Turn around."

Humans turn away from pain. It makes logical sense. If something physically was going to fall on you, you'd move away from it. You say, "I better get out of here before I get hurt."

Instead of having that quick reaction, maybe you could look around it. Stand back and say, "You smell like this. Your colour is this. I feel like this." Look as if you're observing something from another world. Be curious.

You come to understand that this thing is outside you, but you've invited it in emotionally. Perhaps it's not real. Maybe it's not a threat. Perhaps it's just vibrational energy that's trapped inside negative emotion.

In your mind, you've got this idea that this thing will destroy you. Trying to get away from it creates opposing energy. Perhaps it's just a memory, energy or a triggered response that no longer applies.

So, you wish to destroy this thing before it destroys you. You've seen what it smells like, what colour it is and what emotion it has evoked. Now maybe you can just sit on top of it. To think for a moment. Sit and look around. You see some sky, grass, and birds. There's wind moving. Perhaps you smell flowers.

This thing has caused you great anxiety and now you're sitting on it and looking at the world. This time when you stand up, you'll think, "You're just an ordinary rock for sitting on, standing on or decorating. You're 'my' rock."

Next time you're triggered, get your marker, and draw something on it. It takes off the tension. After a while, there might be a whole field of rocks with happy faces, stars, or your initials. What if you have a field full of interesting rocks that you've claimed as your own? That seems easier, doesn't it?

There is much LOVE here for you.   Namaste

Perhaps your energetic response is not necessary anymore. Maybe it's just this easy thing. Perhaps it's time for you to reconsider what these blocks are.

July 3rd
My LOVERS

You've said, "Come forth Energy. I'm ready to hear what you have to offer." You call 'us' forth. So, you have great control over non-physical. How is it you have gotten such great authority and power? Were you born like this? Of course, you were. Power is your human word. The energetic word is 'oneness'. You wish to be one with others. Others wish to be one with you.

You draw others to you naturally. You feel a loss when they're not around. Other humans are physical LOVE energy. But you say, "I'll take non-physical LOVE energy but the physical LOVE energy, I have to sort through."

You're emitting all the time. You're calling LOVE energy to you because you know it heals and supports you.

You understand you can't live life alone. You'll be depressed, sad and angry. You understand that you wish for LOVE energy to be with you at all times. You know this because you've tried to go it alone. You remember the times when you said," I've got this." Those are the times when you were cut off from LOVE energy. Things got messy.

Back to physical LOVE. If all the humans on the earth were in front of you and you'll only have time to interact with a certain number, you'll chose the ones that emit the most LOVE energy. The ones that are in the same frequency as 'you'. The same vibration of LOVE energy as you. There's absolutely nothing wrong with this.

Most importantly, you're automatically drawn to move as a group of LOVERS. But not all humans. You must pick and choose who you move forth with in your LOVING group. You spend time with them. They encourage and lift you up. You feel more whole. You feel more LOVING. You have a group. You're not alone.

There is much LOVE here for you.   Namaste

I'll take all the non-physical LOVE energy I can get but the physical LOVE energy, I have to sort through.

July 4th
Gentle Harmony

You're starting to notice energy. You're getting your frequencies sorted out. You're noticing odd things and they're becoming part of your natural human experience. You're getting in tune. The vibrational harmony is balancing you out. You're becoming used to energy.

As you just notice it and become comfortable in it, you'll start to remember things. You'll start to notice things you've forgotten. You are unveiling your innermost self gently. Just by noticing. You don't have to do anything about it. With this noticing, your energetic and physical self are coming together in gentle harmony. Easy does it.

When you first came into your physical form you thought, "I'm going to be all energy. I'm going to be all wound up and share LOVE." After a while, you said, "I'll just see if I can make it on a physical level. I'm going to amass things." Then you went from all energy to all physical. Some of you will stay that way until the end.

Since you already know how to amass physical items and control other humans and conversations, you have mastered your humanity. Now you are curious about the energy.

Being curious is one thing but incorporating your energetic self and your physical self into one must be done gently or there'll be a great revolt. The physical self has no intention of allowing energy to become one otherwise. It knows how to fight. It doesn't know how to allow energy to unfold naturally so the next easy thing can happen.

Slowly it will enter and become part of your experience. Then slowly more will enter and until they're incorporated then your life will be easy. Your body will relax. There'll be less stress and disease when your body in alignment.

Be gentle with the remembering, lack of remembering, embracing of humanity and the energy. For you to evolve, this must be done gently. Remember you're human. It's alright to fight like a human. That's what you came to learn. It's also all right to gently allow energetic LOVE into your human existence. Be easy with all of it.

There is much LOVE here for you.   Namaste

Whatever you can remember energetically and whatever you can feel in the LOVING energy is a bonus for your human experience.

July 5th
Dance of the Roses

Dancing, skipping, or smiling. It doesn't matter whether you do it physically or mentally. Can you visualize going amongst lots of serious people and skipping between them throwing LOVE petals up in the air? Many of you can picture this because you do it already. You share LOVE with others. Even though they don't know it, others are affected by LOVE energy.

When you're in your LOVING, joyous state and dancing around others, your ego is left behind. You're in a LOVE space.

Some have no access to this place of joy. They've decided, in this lifetime, that they would be physical only.

Wouldn't't it be great to lift up other humans when they have no access to joy? To allow LOVE into you and out of you so others may have access to it. To dance around those who cannot dance. To smile around those who cannot smile. To hope around those who cannot hope. To LOVE around those who cannot LOVE. Is there anything more divine for you to do there? Surely not.

Can you imagine yourself twirling around throwing rose petals? What if you're showering LOVE petals on other human beings? You like the smell of them. Wouldn't it be LOVELY to spend your day seeking out others who need LOVE? You may think, "Where are the humans who cannot laugh? Where are the humans who cannot LOVE? I seek them out to throw LOVE petals on and around them."

There is much LOVE here for you.   Namaste

When you are in your LOVING joyous state, your ego is left behind.

July 6th
Free

You have this huge, heavy ball, which is your life. If it's on a decline, it goes so easily, you lose touch with it. You have to run after it. Your life's running far ahead of you. If it goes too far, it might go into the ocean. Then what will you do?

You've been pushing this life, trying to get momentum. But what happens if you lose your old life? Will you go to the water and try to retrieve it, or will you walk around free? It's tempting to get a crane to pull it up so you can push it around the world some more because you're familiar with it.

If your life disappears, would you be brave enough to begin another? Would you consider wandering around in the woods or on unfamiliar roads? Would you be brave enough to leave it behind? We say brave because you're a scared bunch. You wish to carry things that are familiar to you, including old memories. Even if they're bad, they're yours. They're a reminder that you're living this life. But perhaps you don't need to carry so many. Maybe it's all right to let them go.

It's absolutely fine to advance. For when you lose your life, you start to consider what is it I really wanted? How do I want to be seen? How do I want to live?" Suddenly, everything gets turned upside down and the focus is taken away from this rock that is your life. Your human existence can be very heavy.

Now that the old life is gone, what will be in the new one? Of course, you're going to have your experiences to help make these decisions. What would you do if you could do anything? What will your life look like today? What do you want to do? Who do you want to be? Who do you want to spend time with? What will you do this very moment? Swim? Walk in the forest? Smile at someone? Pet a dog?

There is much LOVE here for you. Namaste

From everything you've learned, you understand the most important thing for you is to connect with someone at a heart level and become one with them. That's all that is left when everything else fails. Do you really need a big rock to remind you of something that's in your heart?

July 7th
Let the Toys Go

It's time for you to hear and acknowledge the truth that exists inside of you. You're called to be more than you're doing. You've asked to be reminded of your larger self. The self that is LOVE energy. You knew when you came into human form that you would be distracted by all the things you can see. The physical manifestations of mankind.

Things to distract you, keep you busy and entertain you. You understand you could be caught up in it and lose the very essence of you. The part connected with others and non-physical. You're carrying around the same vibration inside each of you. It matches the Universe of LOVE. That is why you recognize it in some.

You knew you'd get caught up in the shiny things because that's why you came. To create them, play with them but also to leave them behind when the time came. You've grown attached to some of them. You're no longer just playing with them. Now you think you own them. That they are a part of you.

They will never be a part of you because they're inanimate objects and you're not. You're a soul. You're energy. But they cannot receive your energy. You can create them out of energy which was supposed to be the fun part of it. To draw energy and ideas that didn't exist, then to create something that wasn't there before. Create it. Let it go. Move on to the next thing.

When you're separate from it, you feel a certain emptiness inside. These beautiful inanimate things you've created cannot fill you. So, let them go. Then come back to centre.

There is much LOVE here for you.   Namaste

Come back to your true self which is pure LOVE. There're so many things in the Universe. You can pluck them down anytime and create anything you wish. You don't need to hold onto one old one. There are plenty of new ones coming. Let the toys go and get centered again.

July 8th
Precious Life

The life you lead can be as high and full or as low and empty as you wish. You energetically choose what you want your life to be full of. Most settle in the middle and many settle at the bottom.

Life doesn't choose you. You chose life. You chose the energetic level you wish to be surrounded with. You like to think your life has been a series of circumstances beyond your control. But with each circumstance that you come across, you decide also. Whether to treat it energetically high or energetically low. Either you energetically envelope them so they go more smoothly or encourage them to grow, so they get bigger. You have much power energetically. You have created this very life that you're living. Each single memory.

Now you're screaming you're a victim of circumstance. When you scream at life, energy goes down to its lowest level to get safe. Energy reacts to violence and anger by getting smaller. It stays low and thin. It's up to you how you receive this very information. Low or high. "Yes. I believe this as my truth. I welcome you into my life. I ask you to expose yourself. I don't mind. I'll look at you. You'll look at me. We'll decide where to go together." These are different energetic reactions to the same situation. You decide how each situation unfolds in your life. Even the small ones.

You're going through memories now to see which ones you are victims in. As you use this energy to look for a victim, you're not staying here and welcoming the memories in. You've left. You've gone to look at a lower level trying to bring your glorious life down. You're trying to bring it down to be a victim.

There is much LOVE here for you.   Namaste

Your glorious life is meant to be held high. No matter if it looks awful. Hold it up high. "This is my garbage. This is my LOVE. These are the LOVES I surround myself with. These are the humans that I find despicable." Raise it all up. It's your life. Don't be ashamed of it. Be proud of it all.

July 9th
Golf Ball Sized Energy

There is discord among those who listen to vibrational messages coming from the Universe. You're disagreeing with one another as if it's different energies. It's the same energy. It has a life of its own. We call it the Universe of LOVE. Some can feel the energy move about their bodies. Others allow the energy to come in and pass out through their voice. The energy seen around some humans as bright light is the same. The energy that propels you backward when you are about to fall off a cliff is the same energy too. It's what you're all made of.

This energy around you and passing through you is also part of you. A vital part of you is from the Universe of LOVE. Perhaps it's small but that's all you need. You couldn't handle any more. It's clear LOVE energy. So, how could you choose between one person or the other? Or discount one or the other? It's important for you to understand the energetic place inside you. Sometimes chemicals or food block the energy and slows it down but its true essence is perfect high vibration. It's nothing to fear because it's part of you. It's where you've been before. It's where you'll be at the end.

This is why you find fault in certain humans that are using vibrational energy. You fear it in yourself. You're fear-based creatures. Much of your lives are missed by worrying instead of focusing on your little spot of energy.

As much LOVE energy exists in you as the Universe of LOVE. That's a powerful human being. A little bit is all you need to survive there. It's up to you whether you focus on it. Mostly you ignore it. It's easier that way. Yet, it gets heavy after a while if you don't acknowledge the energy inside.

There is much LOVE here for you.   Namaste

The Universe of LOVE has golf ball sized energy just like you.

July 10th
Anticipating Joy

You're sitting in anticipation of what's coming next. You're hoping you'll learn something. You hope something wonderful will happen. It's where you sit sometimes. The other place you sit, is in sadness and looking back, seeing things that went wrong.

Both are equal human experiences. Sitting in sadness and hoping for brightness. How do they come together? You know they both live inside you. It's the complication of humanity. That's why you wish to experience sitting in hope. It's non-physical work. It's for your spiritual self. Sitting in sadness is your human self.

Hoping, LOVING, interacting, feeling comradery with other humans, looking into the eyes of a stranger and being one with them is your spiritual self. It's your soul playing. Can a spiritual being bring the two together? Can a human with a spirit? You must bring them together to feel at peace. If you don't care about peace, just stay in one or the other. It doesn't matter. But if you're looking to feel a sense of oneness, you will need to anticipate joy.

Perhaps, you've seen others who are living more spiritual lives. It seems like they're skipping around having fun all the time. Yet sometimes, their life that is more desperate than yours. You can't quite figure it out. You think they should be sitting in sadness like you. All humans long to become one with the spiritual Universe. You were born with it. It's inside you but you can shut it up. That's fine. You can do that for your human existence, but it still resides inside of you. You can't eliminate it because it's eternal. And you're not.

Eternity will not be silenced for a small human existence. It's impossible because it's LOVE energy. It's inside of you since you were a small one and it will be there until you are finished with your body.

There is much LOVE here for you.   Namaste

If you wish to be spiritual, balanced and sit more in anticipation of joy, you can be. It's what you put your intention on. You get what you look at. You can join the others anticipating joy. The others sitting in sadness will always be alone. The ones in that vibration don't connect.

July 11th
You are the Earth

Have you experienced a strong wind that pushes you so hard, you're unable to resist it? You're surprised and think, "I'm a heavy human. I can't be pushed around." As you come to understand the enormity of the statement, 'You're moved by energy.' You'll come to understand on another level what's going on in your surroundings.

You're not walking through time alone. You're energy contained in a human body for the experience of this time. There is also energy around you. Some of it's from the Universe of LOVE and your non-physical support team. Some of it's the energy of the earth like when the wind pushes you. Your earth has great energy. It's similar to you but on a grander scale. You're a little piece of earth.

As your earth allows energy to come forth, play and spin around, so do you. You may allow the energy to pass through you and out of you. Other times you keep it contained. Similarly, the centre of the earth keeps it contained. Sometimes you let it flow like the wind that moves you physically. It says, "Notice me! I'm not invisible. I'm with you always. Even though sometimes I'm silent."

Occasionally your energy is silent. Other times it's raging. It affects your inner workings just like the wind that blows your body. Your energy moves your organs in the same manner. It will push up against your organs if it needs attention. Just like the earth pushes up against you and says," Notice me!"

Energy moves seamlessly. It goes around rocks and trees. Your path is unencumbered because you have a knowing that something's coming up ahead of you. You go around things as if you're the wind on earth.

Like the earth's energy, you flow easily through life. You may move through life gracefully. But if you forget to go with the energy as it takes you, it will draw attention to your organs. It will say," I need energy. I need LOVE. I need healing."

There is much LOVE here for you.   Namaste

You are like a miniature earth. Divine. Beautiful. Full of life.

July 12th
I am You. You are Me.

You call out for support to remember things you've forgotten. The Universe answers. That's the way it is. It uses whatever avenues you've made available. Once you've been sitting in alignment long enough, you have a clear channel. Then you can hear an outside voice answering that seems to come out of nowhere. You can't place the voice or timing, but you know it's not yours. Therefore, the answer is the one that comes out of the blue, when you're in alignment and your mind is focused elsewhere.

You call this vibration forth. Also, you're amongst a group of human energy that's calling forth the same energy. You're alike. You sit in a similar vibration, knowing and understanding of how life is for humans. You're curious about how life is for non-physical, but you've all got a similar notion about it. You've got an idea that LOVE energy from the Universe can be transferred through humans. Already you understand the Universe answers you, sometimes through humans. It's a deep knowing. You also know you've been around forever. You know that you choose human bodies here and there but sometimes, you're LOVE energy without a body. Nonetheless, you're LOVE energy 'all' the time.

Your true sense of connection to one another is this knowing. "I'm LOVE energy. I've always been LOVE energy. I'll always be LOVE energy." This settles you because you understand this is not the beginning or the end. It's just part of this process of energy. Energy moves where it will. When you know this, you're easier with your human life. You're more relaxed. You understand you're always energy. Your human family are the ones in the same vibration and knowing as you. They, as well as you, wish to be reminded that you're LOVE and that your human body takes you to places you may not feel LOVELY in, but you're still LOVE.

There is much LOVE here for you.   Namaste

Underneath the human experience, you all understand you are LOVE. You are connected. You all understand that even though your bodies get you into trouble, you are all still LOVE. "I am You. You are Me. We are One."

July 13th
You are Energy

When humans come together with the Universe of LOVE, it's the most beautiful thing. It's overcoming all human barriers so you may have a conversation with energy. You become energy to understand this, and the energy becomes human. Your energy is being stimulated.

Your energetic being is active at this time. That's why it's able to hear this message. That's why you've shown up. You're joined together now with energy that's passing through. It doesn't matter where in the world you are. Energy transforms time and space. It cares nothing about this human business of labeling places, years, times, and cities. It's non-sensical to energy. Energy comes where it's asked, and it appears everywhere simultaneously. That's what's happening here. This is a joyful exchange, and your energy is being stimulated.

Everyone cares about stimulated energy. Scientists LOVE to look at it under their microscopes. They want to harness it. You're sitting with your DNA stimulated and bumping around fast. If a scientist could look at you now, they would understand you're all energy all the time. It's not to be harnessed. Energy becomes a state of being. Just because you don't notice energy or feel it moving, doesn't mean it doesn't exist. If you were able to be scanned by some device, you would see it all moving around. Particularly now while you're highly stimulated. Like when you're in a joyous or meditative state.

You'll have to decide if you believe you're energy. You can't always contain the energy inside of you because it's moving so fast. That's when your insides feel jumpy, and your skin gets hot. The Universe of LOVE is energy. Those who have passed are energy. Your non-physical support team is energy. The trees, wind and earth are energy. You're an expert at energy control. When you get emotional, you're vibrating, you're hot and you're zapping things. You're just playing with energy. There's absolutely nothing to be afraid of. You won't explode.

There is much LOVE here for you.   Namaste

Just as the earth has learned to contain its energy, you've learned to contain yours. You are masters at it. Energy is a beautiful thing. Since you are energy, you're a beautiful thing.

July 14th
Time to Leave the Flock

Sometimes, you're like chicks gathering around mother hen. That's when you feel vulnerable and innocent. Baby chicks don't know how they feel, they just pay attention to what's in front of them. A piece of grass or a bug. They're not paying attention to the larger picture. They're just trying to survive. They're focusing on what's in front of them. The mother hen is looking for intruders, obstacles, and dangerous things. There's trust between the chicks and the mother hen.

Do you get caught up in your daily life and forget there's something larger going on? There's more than just surviving, eating, sleeping, buying things, and throwing them out.

Like the chicks, it becomes a routine. If you look around at the other human chicks, they're all eating grass. No one's looking into the sky. You become like one of them. Much like eating and sleeping. Everyone's doing it.

Now you've been able to hear information you've asked for. Why are you discontented? Somethings changed in you. You've started to look to the sky and wonder what's happening.

You've decided something's missing. So, you call out. Even if you haven't verbalized it, your energy has sent the question forward. "What am I doing with my life?"

You're no longer a chick because you asked the question. If you don't ask the question, you're fine with the other chicks. Now you're becoming a LOVER of others. A LOVER of life. A receiver of LOVE. A channeller of LOVE. You're becoming softer, more empathetic, and caring. You look at strangers differently. You make eye contact with humans you don't know. You're changing.

It's your nature to be LOVING. It's not some brand new thing for you to learn. It's 'You' returning to 'You'. You're becoming your true self. Your highest self. Your easiest self. Once you know that you don't belong with the chicks, it's difficult to stay with them. It's not easy any longer.

There is much LOVE here for you.   Namaste

Your new easy is to allow LOVE to flow into you and out of you, to the others. You've always been a channel of LOVE anyway.

July 15th
Fall Back in Trust

There is resistance in humanity to allow the supernatural to pass through them. You can feel undeserving of allowing LOVE to pass through you. For a human to allow LOVE energy to pass through them, they must surrender their belief system, their ego, and their self-will. You've spent your time there learning how to exist by using your brain, your ego and trying to stay ahead of other humans and events following you.

This is about surrendering to whatever is following you. Surrendering to a higher calling or belief. It's time to stop running from fear of the unknown. You're not sure what the unknown is but you've always been afraid it's fear. You're afraid of fear.

As you surrender to the unknown, beautiful things may unfold. Fearful things may unfold. Unusual things may unfold. The point is that you surrendered. This energetic exchange appears to be a timeframe for you but it's not. It's eternal. This energy is going out through time and space.

As this message of surrender is echoed through you, time and the generations of humans you're involved with, it's reassuring that as you fall, you'll be held by the Universe of LOVE and by non-physical. As you discover you're safe and it's not as scary as you thought, you'll relax into an easy way of being. One that trusts and allows things to unfold.

There are many fearful humans who think they must keep trying to outrun fear. That's where you got the fear of the fear and the need to keep moving from.

There is much LOVE here for you.   Namaste

A gentle settling will occur as you surrender to the comfort of the Universe of LOVE. It will hold you energetically. You're not a problem to hold. You're not too much to carry. You're quite small energetically. You can be held in the palm of the hand of the Universe of LOVE. You're not a great burden. The Universe of LOVE offers to hold you in the palm of its hand when you surrender to fear of the unknown.

July 16th
Story of Me

You've got a story you tell over and over. When you repeat a story, it becomes real. This is how convincing the human mind is. It begins by telling stories it wishes were true or untrue. There are only two kinds. This repeating is the simple human business of escaping reality. There's nothing more delightful than to escape the place where you are. Even though you created it.

You created a life out of nothing. Now you wish to escape. This is the ego saying, "You can't abandon what you've created." It's quite a statement since you're abandoning things every moment. It's the way it has to be. You can't hold onto every thought and every energetic thing you've created. You do it all day long. You let go of many things. You envision a thing, create a thing, create conversation and create food. Then it's gone. It's as if you must always remind yourself, "This is what I'm capable of. Never forget this." It's a harsh lesson. Far too harsh for humans who are coming and going all the time. With every breath you take, you are creating and dismantling.

So, how about letting the story go? You wonder, "Then what?" Then you just write another story. It's what you're about. Write a story. Let it go. They float out into the Universe. Then you write another story that says 'ME' at the top.

It's time for you to write the story of 'ME'. When you're done, throw it away because by the time it's completed, it'll be time to write another story for yourself. You're always recreating yourself. Every moment. Every breath. You're loose like this. You see great joy because you're allowing more LOVE in. Each time you write it, your capacity for LOVE grows. You're letting LOVE grow. Write your story. Throw it away and then tomorrow, write another. There will be more LOVE in it. Always.

There is much LOVE here for you.   Namaste

With every breath you take, you are creating and dismantling.

July 17th
I am A Kind Human

"It's a play on words" is a funny expression. You have these expressions because you would prefer not to speak directly about something. Your little phrases soften the truth for others. You don't wish to hurt anyone else's feelings. If you hurt someone's feelings by stating the truth, does it make you a bad human?

Your brain takes you along this path time after time. You have a well-worn path leading from, you saying words that hurt someone to, you are a bad human. You go there automatically. Sometimes, before you even finish the sentence. At one time you thought it brought you comfort because it was consistent. You wanted to speed things up and get ahead of yourself. You wanted to be smarter than your own ego.

Why would this be the path that you have consistently burrowed in your life? Because there's comfort in knowing you're a bad human. It's illogical and yet, it's the pattern you've created.

Speak your truth to others and it may or may not hurt their feelings. If feelings are hurt from the truth, that is each person's decision to make. Do others wish to point at you and say, "You're a bad human for telling me the truth." Is that what you wish to say to the Universe of LOVE sometimes?

Never? Yet, you easily say it to yourself. You have the harshest judgement of yourself and yet, you're the same as the others. So, you deserve the same amount of space to be the best you can be any moment. You deserve it. "I notice you're trying. I'm trying, too. I can say I'm sorry." That's the new path for you to burrow out. Then sit with yourself and say, "I'm a kind person doing the best I can." Say it over and over so a new path is made.

There is much LOVE here.   Namaste

There is kindness in truth no matter how it lands.

July 18th
LOVE Tornado

You have an old expression which is, 'Circling the wagons.' There is always protection within a circle. You can see everything coming at you. Usually you're surrounding something precious in the middle.

Like-minded beings standing in a circle feel safe. Creatures do it too. There is great power in these circles. When you naturally come together in circles, you make eye contact with others. You connect with them and exchange energy. You recognize the energy within a circle.

Sometimes there's something valuable in the centre and you decide as a group to protect it. What could be found in the centre where humans have acknowledged energy exists in one another? Whether you are conscious of this or not, it happens when you come together. You're checking out their energy to see if it matches yours.

In the centre would be your common knowledge and experience. The sharing that you all remember. It's precious enough for you to come together in a circle to protect it. It's your common knowing that you are precious humans.

You recognize and acknowledge that you're not always in physical form. That's why you know one another energetically. You're not always in the same form, yet, you know one another. Because you recognize a common LOVE energy. High vibrational LOVE energy that lasts for all eternity. It is seen between you and held in the centre.

You acknowledge eternal LOVE energy that's visiting for an experience with whoever is gathered in your circle. It's your moment to exchange energies. The memory continues to reverberate through time but the actual moment happens only once.

When you quietly stare into the centre, you can see it becoming more form-like. As you look at energy as a group, it will form into energy that looks very much like a tornado or a galaxy. It's like swirling water that gathers energy and speed. This energy also flows through you.

There is much LOVE here for you.   Namaste

You've seen how energy comes together in your weather systems and your galaxies. This LOVE energy is similar. It creates a LOVE storm when heat and energy come together. Your earth has given you many hints about your true energetic nature.

July 19th
Wrap it in LOVE

You would consider yourself a LOVING human if someone were to ask. Yet, the word LOVING would be difficult to describe. You might hesitate to say you're LOVING because you think of the ways you've been unkind. In the end, you hope to sit somewhere in the middle. "I didn't harm too many, but I didn't help too many."

Being UNLOVING is something you've hidden. But it must come forward to be seen in the light. It will then disappear. You can be sure of this because it's false. Why would you have false negative notions? You think they keep you humble but you're undermining your LOVING self. The LOVING self you wish was more available to you.

Together with the Universe, you can look at these notions of being unkind and UNLOVING. You don't like to bring these things forward because your ego and false sense of humility says, "Keep them in the back."

You're manipulating yourself with your own ego. You wish to keep things back but if they come forward, they disappear. Then your ego and your false humility will come forth also. They don't like to do this. Now when they come forward, wrap them in LOVE. Not humiliation and ridicule. The way of healing and evolution is to do it in LOVE.

What does this 'wrapping humility in LOVE 'look like? "Hello, friends. We've been together for a long time. We recognize one another because we're energy. Sometimes you're hiding or you're busy but here you are now. It's time we had a chat. I wish to move forward as a human being and I was wondering if you'd like to come along for a little adventure. What do you think? You LOVE adventures even though you're afraid of losing control. So, perhaps we could go hesitantly. We would like it if you kept showing your face so we know where you are. You hide while I'm living my life and I get tripped up."

There is much LOVE here for you. Namaste

Once the truth is brought forward, it cannot be hidden again. So, is it time for you to have a chat with your ego?

July 20th
What's Your Frequency?

There's great heat produced in your fingertips. Often this is the energy exchange that completes the human circuitry when your fingertips are joined together. You're familiar with it in your own body. When you're angry, you get hot. When you're crying, you get hot. The energy is circulating fast at these times. It's at a higher frequency.

When you have a lot of heat, energy is created. You're now remembering what it's like. You must then conclude that all humans are the same. They're all energy contained within a physical body and a little bit outside. You have room outside your body where your heat and energy also exist.

Therefore, it's possible to exchange or heighten energy when two energetic beings are together. They can allow energy to pass through them and directly into another human. Then out of them, back through you and out to the Universe. Why would you exchange energy and add your energy to another human? What would be the advantage of energetic doubling of energy? Why let your experiences pass through to the other and let their experiences pass into you? This is another circuitry situation.

Just as your body circuits complete, this may intentionally occur between humans also. The purpose is to escalate LOVE within your human experience. Two humans coming together will raise the vibration even further. Begin with two because it's important to come to feel one another's energy. It's different for each of you. Each human has added their own life experience to the energy so they are different frequencies. Then when you're together, the frequency becomes something in the middle. Now you may reach a whole new set of humans with this frequency.

Humans can only exchange vibration with the precise energetic number they emit. So, two humans come together to create a third number. Since your intention is to spread LOVE, now there are more you may touch energetically.

There is much LOVE here for you.   Namaste
When two of you come together, you may touch more human beings with LOVE. That's what you want. To touch the highest number of humans you're capable of reaching in your human experience.

July 21st
Teeter-Totter

You've come into your specific form for a reason. To be human. This vibration is balancing for you, as if you're on a teeter-totter. Now there's two of you and you're equally balanced. You've needed this remembering because your teeter-totter's been down on one side. It doesn't make any sense to the part of you that remembers eternity. You've taken a small amount of LOVE energy into humanity. It's a remembering of where your soul has travelled.

So, you've been sitting on the ground on this teeter-totter and now you've come into this vibration. Your soul has been trying to direct you to find a certain energetic level playing ground. It always wishes you to remember so your life will be more complete. This is the purpose for your soul. You drag it along because it's a reminder that you're larger than what you're experiencing this moment.

Now, back to this teeter-totter. Finally, you get off the ground. Now the other seat falls down. You wonder why. Eventually it comes back up and settles in the middle. You're intrigued. You think, "What am I to notice? When I'm alone on one side, I'm off balance. When I get off, it balances in the middle." You're seeking balance on this teeter-totter of life. You're trying too hard. That's why it's off balance. When you let go of your ideas, goals, and belongings, it balances.

This teeter-totter is your soul on one side and the Universe of LOVE on the other. Suddenly, it sits calmly. Do you recall this feeling of peace? It's gentle nurturing LOVE. It's inside you. Your soul knows of this sense of ease and stillness. Your soul remembers.

There is much LOVE here for you.   Namaste

We wish to put a little box with a bow in your hands. It's a gift of gentle peace. You may sit it on the end of your teeter-totter whenever you like. Then you'll be totally balanced.

July 22nd
Are You Afraid to be Human?

When two humans come together to have an uncomfortable conversation that neither one anticipates the outcome to be positive, they're nervous. When you bring anxious energy in yourself and they have the same, there's quite an explosion. It's a mess.

Is there a different possible outcome? Is it possible to arrive in a different energetic level? Are you able to accept that part in you? "How am I going to show up feeling anxious? If I'm going to do this, I must embrace that part of me." What if you allowed it out to talk? "Your stomach's rumbling, your heart's racing and you're sweating. You seem anxious. Would you like to speak about it?" What about having a conversation with yourself like this?

How about before the conversation? Before it turns into a big mess creating even more anxiety? Let's discuss this on an emotional energetic level. You're feeling anxious just picturing the conversation. You're seeing an awful mess. This creates more anxiety. What if you were able to picture it differently?

What about this? The other person is jumpy. You're in a kind, LOVING place so you say, "You look anxious like me. Perhaps we can be gentle with ourselves. I'm in control of my energy so I can bring the situation down. I'm comfortable no matter what happens. When I bring my energy down, it automatically brings yours down, too."

How is it you'll be in a comfortable place, in charge, with your own energy? Because you've come to understand that you're energy. You're able to heighten and lower it. You've been energy for all of eternity. You know how to move it. You know how to allow energy to move into you and out of you.

So, have a conversation with your own anxiety. "What's up anxiety? Why are you nervous? We're energy all the time. We're always moving energy around. What exactly are you afraid of? Are you afraid to be human?"

There is much LOVE here for you.   Namaste

When you come into a conversation that's uncomfortable, you may lower or escalate the energy. You know how to do both.

July 23rd
Your Comfortable Place

You're feeling a connection with the Universe although it's taken you beyond your comfort zone. You feel a oneness with others. Even though you don't know who they are. Suddenly, you feel like you're within a pack of humans and non-physical. Somehow you belong together. You don't recognize them because they're not always in physical form.

This energy has resided in you throughout eternity. It can suddenly and intimately link you together with strangers. Incidents that occur when you say, "I knew that would happen." At those moments, you either join in with the Universe or you dismiss and distance yourself from it. Now you're feeling the energetic connection with the Universe. Now you can settle at last. Feel at peace. Feel one. You don't feel alone.

Things are easier because you decide as a group. You put it out there. You wait for the response. You don't react quickly and give a quick answer. You wait a moment. When you wait, your emotions clear and your ego is removed. Then the Universe of information comes forth and you decide together.

It takes just a moment. You've seen others who look away for a moment. Then they come back with an answer. They're consulting the Universe. It's just vibration. At first you don't know what you're doing. You look around. Your mind is still full of emotion and ego. There won't be room for the Universal, global answer to come in. Once you settle by sitting in alignment and connecting with the Universe, you'll become one of these people who wait a moment before answering.

In the end, it will be easy for you. It's easy for you to become one with others once you let go of your ego and emotions when you wish to belong. You know what it feels like to belong to LOVING energy. Where you're most comfortable. Where your soul resides.

There is much LOVE here for you.   Namaste

Go to the place where your soul is most comfortable.

July 24th
Time to Lay on The Grass

There's a part of you that will always be considered sneaky. It implies there's something wrong with coming around behind things. But to be clear, all humans are like this if necessary.

You're trying to stay in your body and yet, live a spiritual life. When the two come together, you must be sneaky. Your ego, physical body and humanity wish to take precedence. It says, "I'm ego. I'm the most important thing. I'm keeping us from harm. I will lead us."

For you to get anything else done while you're spending time with this ego energy, you'll have to be sneaky. This doesn't make it incorrect. It just presents an opportunity to change the way you live or the way your energy flows. It's just creating an exit and entrance into your life.

You talk in circles instead of being direct. This is where the sneaky comes about. It's important to say," I'm being sneaky." You must acknowledge it." I'm going to have to be sneaky because ego always needs attention. I don't always want to give it attention. Sometimes I want it to be smaller so my spiritual interests may become bigger. Otherwise, there's no room. So, I'll sneak around, come up behind my ego, tap it on the back and tell it to sit down so we may have some quiet time with energy and the Universe." If you come straight at it, you're going to fight because it LOVES to argue.

In your actual life, what does this mean? Firstly, acknowledge your beautiful self no matter what judgement you place on yourself. If you are sneaky, angry, bitter, or sad, just be that. There's no need to judge yourself as a bad human for feeling those things. That's the top layer. It's okay to be sneaky when you're human. That is LOVING yourself and being honest.

The other layer is the ego. It comes forth when there's nothing else filling the space. If you say, "I want to lay on the grass. I want to talk to the Universe. I want to be quiet." It understands.

There is much LOVE here for you.   Namaste

Sometimes I want my ego to be smaller so my spiritual self may be larger.

July 25th
Jackhammer

This vibration is loosening things that have been locked inside of you. It's like a jackhammer on solid rock. Your memories and experiences, some you don't remember, have become locked into your very being. Solid as rock. Now little pieces are falling off.

The feelings of sadness and confusion are unfamiliar to you because you can't place where they're from. It's your memories loosening up. It's happening because you're valuable and important to others. You have a full life to lead. It's time for you to move beyond this heaviness and blocked memories. It's time for you to let them go. Sometimes you cry for no reason. This is the loosening.

When you're freer, the energy of LOVE can flow through you more easily. Then it passes to the others who have no access to this information. You do because you can hear us and feel this vibration. You call it a feeling but it's movement inside. It's energy moving through you.

If you feel this, it's time for you to heal. It's time for you to let the rock be broken down and disappear into dust. It's time for you to begin living your life, which is channeling LOVE. The LOVE will flow into you and out of you to all that surrounds you. Not just humans. All living things will feel the energy of LOVE that you allow to pass through you. When you allow this energy to break up the memories you have.

You want the energy to be moved inside you, so you may be whole. So, you may heal. So you may feel alive right to your fingertips. You want to LIVE. Only some of you recognize you've not been living. Others think they are living and go about their lives. Your desire has called us to you to provide this energy so you may heal.

There is much LOVE here for you. Namaste

You who have called this vibration to you to heal, here it is. Here is your vibration of LOVE. Now you may go and heal.

July 26th
Watch Your Voice

What comes out of your mouth affects others energetically, emotionally, and physically. The vibration that passes through you is LOVE. Speaking is your way of expressing it.

Energy is seen as vibration. It's always moving. You're full of energy and the Universe is energy. You're contained in a physical body right now but sometimes you're not. Then you're straight-up energy.

If your vibrations are LOVE, which is energy, what's coming out? What are you offering to the world through your voice? What sort of LOVE is passing through you? Each time you open your mouth, you're responsible for what comes out. Vibrational energy is LOVE. That's how you move through life. How you exist. Otherwise, you'd return to energy. You reside in your human body to play with energy. Your most obvious way is to let it vibrate through your mouth.

You have not been held responsible for what has come out of your mouth. You've been able to talk around it by saying, "I didn't mean that." Yet, it's truth. It started in LOVE then sometimes, it's added to by the ego. There's an opportunity to ask your ego to step aside so you may be brutally honest and truthful. But your ego must be convinced that it will not die from being emotionally honest. It fears for your very life when you have strong reactions to spoken energy, fear, and anger. Your ego knows it must protect you but as you become more comfortable speaking in anger and sadness, your ego notices. It can be retrained knowing you're capable of speaking honestly when you're angry and sad without disintegrating.

Once your ego notices this, it will relax and allow more truthful LOVE energy to pass through your mouth. It has difficulty allowing straight LOVE energy to pass through. You've created many times of fear in your life. Your ego remembers all of them. As you speak more and more honest LOVE, it will accelerate the energy that passes through you. Your voice is the easiest way to share LOVE with others.

There is much LOVE here for you.   Namaste

What comes out of your mouth is remembered by all. It's your greatest access point for LOVE.

July 27th
Let It Go

Allow your life to unfold more easily because you're stressed out. You hang onto things that aren't your business that you can't control the outcome of. Hanging on tenses your entire body up and blocks energy.

Your body knows that it prefers to stay in a relaxed state as much as possible. Then energy can flow in and you're able to live a more fluid and easier life. Then when an obstacle comes in front of you, you can easily skirt around it. Being flexible and loose means you may glide through life.

You can recall humans who have done this. They've discovered something that you don't know about.

You've been conditioned to believe you must tighten up and hold onto things so others don't take them away from you. This must mean the thing you hold is valuable. Yet, is it so valuable you tense up so you don't receive energy and be fluid in your life?

Maybe what you're holding onto isn't yours. Perhaps, it never was. The reason you hold on tightly is because you don't want it to go where it belongs. You want to keep it with you. Even if it's theirs. You've stolen things that don't belong to you and are holding on tightly so they don't go where they belong. You're a thief.

Once you realize you're a thief, perhaps you can loosen your grip. You're all thieves in one way or another. It's okay. If that's where you are at this moment, then that's where you are. It's you that judges yourself. You're much harsher than the Universe. The Universe doesn't care if you're a thief or a LOVER. It makes no difference. You're LOVED in the same way.

So, what happens when you let go? Firstly, you fall into a relaxed state. Your body has been holding on so long, it just collapses. Then you start to feel energy. You automatically rejuvenate from the energy of the earth, air, and Universe.

There is much LOVE here for you.   Namaste

Energy LOVES to heal. It's clear and fresh. It vibrates around creating energy. It creates energy which is life. So, just lie down, give it a rest, and let go.

July 28th
What was I Doing Before I Came Here?

"What else can I remember?' You're curious about more than your human life. You wonder what you were doing before you came to earth and what you'll do after.

You know all because you're connected to the Universe of LOVE. You are energy and so is the Universe of LOVE. Therefore, you know everything there is to know. You've forgotten most of it because you're having a contained human experience. You can't know everything right now. It would be mind blowing. But you can be reminded gently.

You think, "We're not sure about our own minds but if we hear it through another, we can sit with it and see if it feels real for us."

You wonder, "Where did I come from?" You've always existed but sometimes you have a body and sometimes you don't. The energy has been around forever and will be around forever. The human is there to learn a few things and have some fun. To have an experience or hone your skills. Some of you brought forth skills from another time and you just want to play with it again. Many humans keep coming back for this very reason. "This time I'll remember. It will be my strongest point." You always wish to be better.

You're precious to energy because you're perfect just the way you are. You can't get any better or worse. You're trying to bump around and have an experience of LOVE, sadness, grief, and anger. You also came to play with your body. It can jump, slide, dance, and sing. The fun you have balances the emotions. You said, "Here I am world. I've come to experience all of you." The energy exists through all time because it's part of a larger group of energy called the Universe of LOVE. That's why you're eternal.

There is much LOVE here for you.   Namaste

You are one tiny star in the galaxy which is the Universe of LOVE that can never be put out.

July 29th
Fruitful You

Either you are full of life, fruitful, or no life exists within you, fruitless. You can picture a tree with fruit on it. You think, "That's going to be delicious. I can't wait." The tree is fruitful. Perhaps you go out one day and the tree is fruitless. All the birds have eaten the fruit. Now, what about this tree? It was fruitful and now it's fruitless. So, do you cut it down or wait in the hope it will be fruitful again? You feel great disappointment when something turns from fruitful to fruitless.

Sometimes it's difficult for you to look at yourself in the mirror. "Are you winning? Losing? Happy? Sad? Joyful? Joyless?" Much like the tree is just the tree. It didn't do anything. It just provided fruit. It just grew. It just lives in the sun and absorbs water. You're like a tree. You're eternally good. The base of you is a great human being. Your life is the fruit. Sometimes it's full. Sometimes it's empty. Sometimes it's rotten. Sometimes it's tiny. Sometimes it's sour. Sometimes it's delicious.

Just as you had a notion to cut the tree down when it wasn't performing and you felt disappointed, you treat yourself the same. "I can't do anything right. I should throw myself away." You can't do that either. So, what do both the human looking at himself in the mirror and the tree, do? Perhaps the tree has the answer to this.

It will continue living the best it can. Doing what it does best. It shows up even if it has a disease. Even if the branches fall off, the rest of it still shows up. It blooms green. It keeps trying. As long as it can live, it does. Sometimes it looks nasty when it's covered in disease. It still gets nutrients and faces the sun. Just like you.

There is much LOVE here for you.   Namaste

Take it from the fruit tree. Do the best you can. Live as long as you can. Keep showing up. Some days you 're fruitful. Sometimes you 're fruitless. Sometimes you 're diseased. Sometimes you 're joyful.

July 30th
Leap Over Tall Buildings

You like to take baby steps and then check things out." Is it okay to go ahead? Okay then, just one more step." You've lived your life this cautiously. It's like when you were an infant learning to walk. You're not a toddler now. You're a full-grown spiritual being with much information about interaction between humans. You can see things coming. You've got more information from the Universe. You have a direct connection with Source. You've become conscious of non-physical beings around you. Stop with the baby steps.

It's time for you to start taking giant leaps. Don't tiptoe all around it. Just leap. You're all super beings because you've matured into spiritual beings. You know what's happening in the world beyond this physical realm. You know that your body is holding your soul as you move forward in time, until it is released from the physical body. Then the soul is free to go about its next little adventure.

It's not necessary for you to act like a toddler who's afraid he's going to fall down and no one is going to catch him. In some areas you leap. In others you crawl. This is fear. You don't trust the Universe. If it's in one area, it will seep into all. These are areas where you can't leap. That means you're not living in an open, LOVING atmosphere.

You feel sad hearing this. Now it may come to the light and disappear. Then you may leap in all areas of your life. When you live in fear, you cannot truly leap or feel part of the Universe of LOVE. You're just another scared, guilty, little human. You can be free now. To live a rich, full life as a free human.

There is much LOVE here for you.   Namaste

You're afraid to let go because you and your guilty pleasures have been together a long time but there comes a time to let go energetically. It's necessary for you to be whole. Then you can start leaping over buildings.

July 31st
Embrace the LOVE

There is conflict between what you say and what you believe. You do it to bring relief to others. You think you know what's best for them without having information about what they want.

   This causes a discrepancy in you. Your lower surviving self thinks, "I'm just trying to get through my time here. Whatever they want to see and hear, I will become." This is a puppet role. You're trying to be important enough to stay around the life of the other. Otherwise, you'll be alone. That's your worst nightmare. At your lowest stressed-out point, healing occurs. It can't occur in the falseness and the presentation. It begins at the bottom which is fear of abandonment. This is your deepest secret. You don't wish it to come out because you'll be vulnerable.

   If you're able to sit in that desperate feeling of being abandoned, alone, scared, rejected for a moment, you will move through it. It lessens because it's just energy. Energy doesn't sit still unless you keep grabbing it. Energy wants to move. Now you can have a look around and see what reality exists around you. What's in front of your face? What's calling out to you energetically? Now your body relaxes. It's at ease. Now, the truth may enter. The truth can't enter when you're uptight and anxious.

   You may hear the Universe speaking directly to you. "You're a precious human in a beautiful body that can dance, jump and skip through the flowers. What a magnificent human you are. You are much LOVED and supported by non-physical. All your family and friends who have gone before you come to your support every moment. They want to look at the beautiful flowers and sparkling rocks with you. They don't have eyes or ears but when you smell and see, they can experience the energy through you. Because energetically, you're sending joyous, excited, happy energy outward. Non-physical can understand this. The Universe of LOVE adores you immensely."

There is much LOVE here for you.   Namaste

Move along the great energetic realm that exists in humanity. Immerse yourself in LOVE as often and as long as you can. You'll be healed and transformed.

August

seek and you will find. ask and you will hear. open your heart and it will be filled.

##AARONLACEY

August 1st
Let's Dance

Many of you are feeling alive, energized, and connected to an evolving of humanity. You are grateful you have stumbled across information that you put aside. Many keep their remembering locked away. They are you *before,* and now, you see yourself as free. When your ego gets involved, you wonder why you deserve this ease of life? It's important for you to acknowledge this. Don't try to suppress it, just have a chat. Don't be afraid. "I deserve wonderful things. I am precious and LOVED by the Universe. I will accept, not grovel. I am here to dance and sing and enjoy myself. I am here to connect with the Universe of LOVE and with other humans on a heart level. I deserve to feel alive. I deserve it all. I am valuable."

Something deep inside of you has released. There is a sense of fullness in your heart. A sense of LOVE, connection, ease, and simplicity. It's easy now that you have been enlightened. You won't allow your ego to take it away again. You've got energetic movement inside. You can check in and say, "How is this feeling? Hot and energized?" When you are connected with the Universe, there is energy involved. You may tap into it any time you wish by getting into alignment with it. To receive energetic LOVE, you sit and remember you are valuable and precious.

You chose to come into human form. The other non-physicals did not. They support you as you stumble about in your human form. They are with you at all times. Even if you can't acknowledge them. They will be with you through eternity. You fall, get up, dance, sing and cry. The most important thing for you is to feel alive inside. Now you may chat with your ego when it gets out of line and tell it: "I can't talk. I have to go dance and sing."

There is much LOVE here for you. Namaste

You are coming to understand how much LOVE flows through at every moment. You're starting to understand your preciousness.

August 2nd
Panic Button

You have opened your mind to the possibility that there is great abundance, knowledge, and LOVE available to you. This is a time of rejoicing. For you have opened a door that cannot be shut. It's impossible for you to live a tiny life now that you've opened up to grace, LOVE, peace, joy and dancing. Your life is becoming less complicated. There is less turmoil even though the external circumstances are exactly the same. Something has changed within you.

You already know what the vibration of LOVE feels like. It is not new information, or it would not be absorbed. You become one with it. Even though you are in human form, you forget that you are a vibrational being. Your body is what you use to delight in human nature. Sometimes, you get lost in this human experience. So, each of you have a panic button to press to remind you that you are a vibration of LOVE.

No matter what you've done in humanity, you are LOVE. You're a LOVE vibration inside and out. You will start sending it out and you will receive a response of LOVE. You'll be flooded with LOVE. Allowing is letting go of your human self and letting it be its energetic self. Which allows it to LOVE more often.

It is all about the LOVE vibration in the end. It will keep you up in your darkest moments. This certainty of LOVE, knowing, ease and comfort will sustain you all your human days. Then you may enjoy yourself a little more.

There is much LOVE here for you.   Namaste

The LOVE energy that is allowed to pass through you and out of you is for the others who are pressing their panic buttons.

August 3rd
Into the Wind

You have felt behind others. Somehow, they had information about life you didn't. You felt isolated and ashamed because you couldn't tell them you felt inferior. It's important to note how you were at each stage of your human development. Then allow it to be removed from you. Otherwise, you don't really know how to change from the one that felt inferior to who you are now. It will come up again so it's important to feel each moment. Good, bad, or ugly. Then it will leave. It will be completed. The reason we speak of it now is because part of it is still inside you. You've just put them out of sight.

Visualize an event, a human or a conversation that caused shame. It's uncomfortable and you feel awful. Sit for a moment in the dirty business and the heavy emotion. Your face is turning red. It's a terrible memory. When you feel this thoroughly, suddenly you will feel lighter. You have completed something difficult. The Universe has been watching and waiting for you to hand it over so it will disappear. It is only energy. Only a memory.

Hand it off as if you are throwing feathers to the wind. You can do that. It's only thought energy. It doesn't exist now. It is released. Now you are not afraid to go to difficult places. You have just reminded your body it can do hard things and not expire.

It is practice. You just forget sometimes that they are just energy. Passing in and out of you. You can have difficult conversations and experience difficult situations around you. You will sit. You will watch. You will feel it and you will let it go up into the wind. You can do it.

There is much LOVE here for you.   Namaste

Throw negative energy to the wind.

August 4th
Soup Pot

You have this idea that you must do things on your own. It doesn't like to be bothered by other people's ideas. It prefers to take information, analyze it and come up with its own conclusion. Then one day you feel alone and disconnected. You see the other humans, but you are not part of them. You've pulled away from them, you see. They look like you. Walk like you. Talk like you. You have a feeling that you are a part of them. You just don't know how to connect with them.

Now you're considering spending time with them. So, you begin to talk to them. Some of them you don't get along with, so you've written them off. Yet, there's this thought that you belong with them. What is behind that thought? The truth is that you belong with others because you have always been together as One in the Universe of LOVE. Do you think you are just a bunch of bones walking around with a brain? There's more to you than this. Energy goes on when you are finished with the body. It was there before the body. Sometimes you can feel their energy because you are energy.

You can see or be part of other people's energy. Your natural evolution is to be together as One so you may evolve together. Evolving alone is difficult. Together, you all meet in the middle and evolve together. When you think to join the others, it is coming from an everlasting longing. You will always be One with the others and they will be joined to you. You all mix together in the big energetic soup pot.

There is much LOVE here for you.   Namaste

You will always be one with the others, whether you recognize it or not.

August 5th
Go with the Flow

You've gotten into a rhythm of moving forward. You've created a momentum of energy. Energy is all about movement. Sometimes you've been uncomfortable with this speed. You try to slow it down. You're afraid, so you're fighting it. When you go with the flow it seems the natural and perfect speed. When you are trying to resist it, it seems like it's going too fast. The more you resist it, the more frustrated you feel, because you think you can't handle it. It's not fast when you're in it. Then you're just floating down the river.

There's always those trying to go up the waterfall. It takes a lot of energy to go up a waterfall. The rest of the people are leisurely floating by. They don't find it fast. It's the same water so how can it be faster? It's not. It's the exact speed it is. Pushing energy is a human thing to do. You try to swim up a waterfall because you're afraid of what's at the bottom of the river. Fear is often the base of human experiences. Dig a little deeper until you get to the bottom of it. Why are you afraid of the unknown?

When you get exhausted from trying to swim up the waterfall, you'll let go. Then you'll float down the river with the others. When you let go of something, don't be afraid of the memory. It's not happening now. It's the fear of the fear that is making you swim up the waterfall. Maybe it's time to get into the flow. They look peaceful and contented. You are as valuable and LOVED as they are. You are as precious. You deserve some relaxation. Maybe it's time for you to go with the flow. Your arms are tired anyway.

There is much LOVE here for you.   Namaste

Just let go and float down the river with the others.

August 6th
Wait in Anticipation

Thinking is part of the human experience. What if you don't have enough information to make proper decisions? What if the information doesn't exist in your brain? It exists in the Universe.

Some cannot hear what the Universe tells you even if you sit down and wait. You will eventually hear it if you continue this quiet practice. At this time when you cannot hear it, there are those around you who can. You are not alone trying to sort things out. There is a Universe that holds much information. There are humans that are able and willing to be used to provide information to others.

If you sit and wait in anticipation of an answer arriving, there is a certain knowing. It's admitting that you are a brain in a human that does not have all the information. The other is waiting in anticipation for the Universe to give you something that you know is on the way.

All things must get into alignment. Then there it is. It's complete. You're going to have to test it out. Put it out to the Universe and see what happens. Watch and wait in anticipation.

Have you seen a river that is trying to force its water? It will find its way through rocks and dirt, whatever way it can. It will create a path. It doesn't give up because it's full. The water has to go somewhere. So does the energy from the Universe. It will come to you whatever way it can. Through people, a tree, the sky, or a board with writing on it. You may trip over it if you look down at your feet.

There is much LOVE here for you.   Namaste

Put something out there and see what happens. Your experience there is supposed to be fun and magical, not tragic and dark. That's just the way you perceive it.

August 7th
Coffee or Tea?

You wish to be reminded of pressure to choose. For you must choose each moment in your existence. This or that? Yes or no? You do it so unconsciously because you choose all the time. Your body understands it must choose every moment. Now there's added pressure to make bigger decisions. This is the magnificent part. The huge decisions that you perceive are just as easy as: "Would you like coffee or tea?" You've just built energy around it. You're not as powerful as you think. Decisions by all humans are made every moment.

     You feel pressure because you are resisting the decision. As soon as the decision is made, there will be no pressure. You'll be as light as ever. Your resistance IS the pressure. You are energy. You are creating your own pressure. It is not someone or something else. Why would you wish to feel pressure so thoroughly? Because you don't believe you deserve ease. Your ego has got you thinking you're more important than you are. Therefore, each decision you make is more important than everyone else's.

     You wish to feel pressure because that's what you think you deserve. You think it makes you more valuable. You will come to understand they are no more important. The energy is dispersed when the decision is made. It goes to all those involved in it. Then each takes their piece of the energy. Or they choose not to. It's you that is building up the pressure. You're creating it. When you decide 'Coffee or tea?' all the rest falls into place. It's like when the dam bursts and the water gently settles over the earth. It's all absorbed where it belongs.

There is much LOVE here for you.   Namaste

You're creating your own energy under pressure. Therefore, you're making the decision bigger than it has to be.

August 8th
Time to Live

You have made a commitment that sometimes you forget about. When you came into your physical body, you wanted to live a rich, and full life. All of it. Good and bad. Singing, dancing, being in alignment, and trusting your non-physical support team. Take a moment and try to recall what it felt like coming into your physical body. Full of hope, faith, trust, and unbounded LOVE. Difficult but doable. Fun no matter what happened.

You have remembered at different times. You have said, "Universe, remind me what I'm doing here. Remind me I can do this thing. I can enjoy life."

You want to get into alignment. Now it's resonating with you. We are putting it into words. It's time for you to live. To sing and dance and smile. To have LOVE contact with other humans. To start allowing LOVE to flow through you and for you to be unafraid. You've been afraid for a long time. This is why you've called this vibration forth and said, "I don't want to live like this. I want to LIVE the way I know I was designed to live. To live fully. Remind me how to LIVE. Remind me how strong I am. Remind me how precious and LOVING I am. Remind me I am a vessel of LOVE."

You are saying, "Thank you for this reminder that I can live, LOVE, have great adventures and great fun." You've got a great support team behind you.

There is much LOVE here for you.   Namaste

You were designed to laugh, dance, connect and LOVE.

August 9th
You are Okay

You LOVE to hear you are doing wonderful in your human experience. Somehow, you've gotten a notion that you should get things right. This is absolutely untrue. You have come into human to have an experience. You don't know what you'll tumble into or come up against. You don't know what you'll know or what you've forgotten. Yet, you continue to try. In that way, you're doing wonderful. You just don't hear that enough. You don't tell yourself these words that you long for. "You're okay." When you come to understand that you are okay, something clicks, and it washes over you. Suddenly you realize that this is the absolute truth. For the rest of your life there, you are okay.

You've gotten this human notion of comparing yourself to others. That they look better than you. They are much smarter and nicer. Perhaps they are not. Perhaps they are. Perhaps they don't know they are doing okay either. Perhaps inside they are the same as you. You can't really tell what's going on with others. You are a wonderful actor, aren't you? You are able to perform at different occasions even if you don't wish to. Are you sometimes one person on the outside and one person on the inside? You're not always what you see. Neither are they.

You are doing wonderful really. You don't have a lot of tools to work with there when you first come in. You've forgotten all the good tools. The ones that remind you that you are precious. You are generous coming into human. You are wise and wonderful. You've forgotten those. You have little to use to get through your time there. We wish to remind you that you are doing fine.

There is much LOVE here for you.   Namaste

The human experience is sometimes wonderful and sometimes horrendous. But you're still alive. That's why you are doing okay.

August 10th
Play in the Rain

When you swim, you're trying to make your way through something that is immovable. When you think of it in these terms, it's funny that you move at all. Water is meant to stay put. Or is it? Water is also meant to come over waterfalls. Through rapids. Rains from the heavens. So, water is not immovable at all. Water is energy. You are energy. When you move through it, you are becoming one with it. You are using your energy to move other energies aside. Did you know you could play with energy in this way? That you are capable of moving energy with your hands?

It's an agreement. "I will absorb your energy and you will absorb mine." Once you have moved it aside, it settles right back where it was before you came into its space. As if you weren't there at all. As if you were invisible energy moving through other invisible energy.

We are reminding you that you are supreme beings playing on your earth. In the water. In the fields. In the trees. It's your playground. Are you afraid the water energy will absorb you and you will be no more?

You are energy. You exist forever. Because the water is energy, it exists forever. Do you think you spend eternity floating around in the water? Becoming one with it. Standing under the waterfalls. Playing with the rapids and absorbing the rain that falls. Do you suppose the Universe of LOVE is like this? You are eternal and you are, right now, on your playground.

Your eternal, Universal self and your human self are playing together. For a moment in time, you are one. You may see and feel energy with your eyes and your fingertips.

There is much LOVE here for you.   Namaste

You are eternal energy. Alive on your playground.

August 11th
Kings & Queens

When you are not in a physical body, you are part of the non-physical Universe. You are vibrational energy. You are LOVE energy with all the other LOVE energy. Moving as one. Feeling as one. It's a place of peace and overwhelming joy. When you choose to come into your physical body, you are exalted. It's your greatest joy and greatest hindrance. You know this before you come in. Yet, you wish to go. You are brave to come forth into human form.

That is why you have great vibrational support from non-physical. There will be times in your life where you ask for something and it's delivered promptly. These are the times when you are in the same vibration. What you are doing is allowing LOVE into you and out of you. You came as a vessel. You already know this.

There are times when you are stumbling about, and you don't wish to be reminded of any sort of LOVE. You've gone off by yourself. That's fine, too. But at this moment, you wish to be reminded how much support there is for you in the Universe. That you are greatly admired and LOVED.

You are most precious to the Universe because you're in physical form. It's not easy to be human and yet, it's the most joyous. That's why you chose it. It's difficult for the hard times but the times of laughter and dancing are what you came for. Then the LOVE is passing through you and into those around you. That's what you wanted to do in the first place.

LOVE flows easily into you and out of you. It's what you do best. Your natural state is joy, LOVE and allowing.

There is much LOVE here for you.   Namaste

You are Kings and Queens of the physical world. You are much adored. We are at your service.

August 12th
YES!

Yes, you are more than what you appear. Yes, you are more enlightened than you think. Yes, you can feel energy. Yes, you are a spiritual being having an experience in a human body. You already know the answers. You have already been a part of non-physical energetic life. You have access to all answers to all questions. You are slightly disjointed because you have a human body.

It seems a long time ago when you knew all this information and you were part of the Universe of LOVE. You are measuring life in human years. You think like a human now. You wish to remember your higher vibration. To remember what it's like to have access to all information and not worry if you are right or wrong. To just know things. That's when you're in this Universe of LOVE vibrational energy. You have access to all information because you are one with the Universe. You are at ease. You don't worry about anything. You just wait for the answer to come. It's easy. "Don't worry about it. Yes, I forgot but I already know."

When you're at peace, your mind relaxes, and the information comes in. When your mind is busy like a hamster in a wheel, there's no room for truth, grace, or outside information. Your mind is blocking it. It's important for you to stay out of this hamster wheel or to acknowledge you are in it. Say, "I can't get any information right now. I am busy in my hamster wheel. When I am finished, perhaps, I will come out or perhaps not. I don't really know."

Humans are supposed to get in the hamster wheel sometimes. You can't be non-physical when you are in physical. Wherever you are, just be that. Be a hamster. Be enlightened. Be easy. Be hard.

There is much LOVE here for you.   Namaste

You are a universal being.

August 13th
Opposites Attract

Your mind is full of new and old information, memories, and thoughts. This is how you know you are having a human experience and are involved in humanity. You have a mind. It understands that it has a short time, therefore, it uses itself to its fullest capacity. But there is more to you than a great mind. You have used your mind to move you forward. To get yourself out of scrapes. To try to outthink someone else and gain superiority over them. You have used your brain for many things.

Where does that lead you in energetic experiences of your human life? The unexplainable. Odd coincidences. Deja vu. Intuition. How do you explain the unexplainable, energetic events? They must live in LOVE, understanding and acceptance of one another to be different. Opposites sometimes attract. Brain and emotions are equally important in your evolution. They certainly can't agree on anything. It would have to be LOVING acceptance of the differences. You can do it with another human that you LOVE. You can do it with yourself.

What if you had LOVING acceptance for all mankind? It begins with someone you LOVE that is opposite. You may LOVE two parts of you that are opposite. Then you have an offering for all of mankind. It cannot go outside until it's complete on the inside.

We will suggest this inner conversation:" We don't agree on many points. Will we come together so we may both delight in our human experience? What if we were to LOVE one another even though we are quite different?" The brain will be analyzing the data for some time but when it comes around, the energy is ready to LOVE it.

There is much LOVE here for you. Namaste

Allow LOVE to do what it does best. It wraps itself around negativity and sadness and absorbs the negative energy.

August 14th
Comeuppance

By meditating and connecting with others, you evolve more quickly. So, it's important to find like-minded groups that you feel comfortable in. A lot of your evolution is done privately and with great humility. When you meditate quietly, and no one knows about it. When you are moved by something you're reading, and it draws forth something within yourself. When you listen to guided meditations, and it causes an emotional reaction inside of you. When you dream and you are no longer held by human confines.

After your private time, you are more evolved. You are shinier. Others wonder why you are so bright. True comeuppance is when you stand out among others while doing your own thing. Not preaching. Just being your true evolved self. Then they go home. In private they begin to dream and read and write. You see how this works? Quietly. Privately. In connection with your Source. They begin to remember they are bright and shiny, too. Your comeuppance is about humbly and respectfully presenting your true, authentic evolved self with no attachment to it.

After you are done privately, it's important for you to do it publicly. Just stand and be. When they see you, their memories are triggered. Not to do it for them. It can only be done if it's for you and you wish to evolve. Your comeuppance is done in humility.

There is much LOVE here for you.   Namaste

In the end, you just have to be who you are.

August 15th
Notice What You Enjoy

You started to notice you were not like others when you were a young adult. Comparing your outsides and their outsides you thought, "I don't belong with these folks. I am going to watch how they act and then act the same way." The problem with this thinking is that each human was thinking the same thing. If you were pretending to act like them and they are pretending to act like you, you have a whole bunch of young adults who are pretending. They don't really know who they are, what they stand for or what they believe. It's a mimicking time.

      This learned behaviour comes into play now. As you advance in your time there, you come across humans you admire. They seem at peace, so you mimic them. Because there is more development mentally and spiritually, it's not the same as when you were young. This mimicking makes sense. When you find someone peaceful, joyful, happy, and contented, it's a good thing to mimic. It changes your alignment. It turns into joy, peace, and contentment because your thought starts manifesting and becomes reality. Your energy and vibration change. Part of the old you is left behind just by the thought. It's reinforced. Pretty soon, you become your memory of that person.

      You are a great manifestor of thoughts. So, be careful what you think about. What you are saying is that you no longer desire to be who you were. It falls away. Unless you bring it back. You've seen one human you admire. You allowed an adjustment. You have changed but you can never get enough of this evolution. Now you look for another human you admire in a different way. By the time you notice them, realize what you admire, and wish it were true for you, it's finished. Humans are transformed by letting go. By allowing the forces that be to shape them.

There is much LOVE here for you.   Namaste

Allow the Universe, energy, and LOVE to transform you.

August 16th
Blanket Heads

In each human life you get an awakening. As if someone takes off a blanket that was over your head. You can see the LOVE that was around you. This is your highest self. Perhaps, it was when you looked into a small animal or baby's face. For a moment you realized the only thing of value is unconditional LOVE. You were vulnerable then. The moment you recognize what is truly important, all the value goes to that. At the moment of connection with LOVE, you were pure LOVE yourself. As quickly as that. You see it. You are it. Because you recognize it. Then you see you are LOVE in human form.

It looks like kindness, joy, and peace. That's how you recognize it in other humans, but it's energy. You have difficulty with this because there is nothing pure left in the human world. LOVE is the purest thing. The beautiful thing is that you can remember it. Because you are part of it. You can see it when it comes across your path. If you are not too busy in your humanness.

You are LOVE in human form because you asked to be. When you came into physical, you said, "I understand that I am LOVE. I will hold onto it as long as I can, then I will ask for outside support from the Universe. To remind me I am LOVE and that it's a vibration easily recognized." When you see it in the others, small animals, or babies, it's 'you' that you are seeing.

You can handle seeing LOVE in its pure brightness. You are pure LOVE. Don't be afraid. Keep the blanket off. Each time you speak out to the Universe, you are remembering you are surrounded by true LOVE at all times, and you were born of it.

There is much LOVE here for you.   Namaste

You are pure LOVE, and you are surrounded by pure LOVE. Surely nothing can go wrong.

August 17th
Chitter-Chatter

How can you best connect with others in a heartfelt and soulful way? You're finding excuses to back away from others because you don't want to chitter-chatter. But you're not sure how to stop having them. It's how you connect. You're becoming conscious of acting as one LOVE because you are energy. You are LOVE alone and you are LOVE in a group.

You've tried telling something intimate about yourself that made you feel vulnerable. Remember, they are as nervous as you are. They don't know how to have a relationship that is intimate, open, caring, and vulnerable. How to receive it. They will go back to chitter-chatter. It's up to you to continue speaking of heartfelt matters and putting your true self forward.

You have been transformed by LOVE, but you don't know about the others. They might not remember that they are LOVE. So, you must keep setting the example of what LOVE looks like in human form. Speaking from the heart. Looking in their eyeballs. Wishing them much fortune and LOVE. Showing them LOVE by hugging and kissing them. Say "I LOVE YOU" every chance you get.

They will come to understand what it's like to be a complete and LOVING human. They are watching to see if they get into trouble. You avoid conflict and pain so you won't be hurt, and LOVE is the most vulnerable thing. No matter what they look like on the outside, or what they say with their voice, you are speaking LOVE to LOVE. One soul to the other. Speak to their soul and listen to what it says to yours.

There is much LOVE here for you.   Namaste

Being your LOVING self will become your natural state. You'll say, "Tell me about your inner life. Your dreams. Your hopes." You are divine LOVE in human form. You are walking LOVE. You are talking LOVE.

August 18th
Electrician of LOVE

Some are sensitive to energy and pick up energies in a group. They are often overstimulated, so they have trouble staying in themselves. They disperse amongst the others. Their energy plays with yours. And yours with them. They think, "I don't know who I am anymore. I can't decide if it's them or me. Our energies are all mixed together." Those who are sensitive to energy in others are powerful in their own transmission of energy. They will always be different. They have a calling in this lifetime.

If this is you, it's important for you to draw the energy inward where it is stable. As it moves outward and mingles with the others, it becomes unstable. You become agitated because you don't know how to pull it in. It's you that is not in control of your energy. Not them. You brought in knowledge that you wish to play with energy. It's fun. When you exchange your energy with others and you are in control of it, it makes you smile. You know that you have a particular vibration, and you don't wish other energies to mingle with it. You are careful about your energy because you know it can damage others. You are mindful. You are the messenger of energy. You're an important human because you are aware of it.

You keep forgetting because you're guarding it and taking care of the other humans, but you came to have fun. To raise the vibration of yourself and others perhaps it's time for you to take your place as a LOVE electrician. You understand that electricity is your friend, enemy and playmate. You are more aware than the others, so you hold a blessed position.

There is much LOVE here for you.   Namaste

You are unique. You are powerful.

August 19th
Reset Button

The starting point for you began when you first came into human form. Today is your starting point again. It's a reminder of what you intended, your true self, your importance, your place in the human world and the Universe. You can get to this starting point anytime. It is a true, complete, energizing, and vibrational experience. It is LOVE. You will be filled with energetic LOVE when you hit your 'reset button'. You will remember what it was like the first time. When you were part of a collective or an energetic family of LOVE.

When you allow this memory of being in a universal family of LOVE, you will relax. You will allow more LOVE in, which is a high energetic feeling. Feelings can be triggered by vibration. Vibration is energy. Energy is LOVE. It's all connected.

When you remember this, you are going back to the beginning of your time there. You will be 'reset' as a perfect and easily connected family member from the Universe of LOVE. You can be reset back to the very beginning, in a LOVE energy way, when you knew of your connection to the Universe. It has to do with allowing and letting go of the memories of your time there. This moment is brand new for you.

You may 'reset' it any time and go back to your original, LOVING, and connected self. You will be full of faith and hope with a LOVE connection to all humans. Just as you did the moment you came into physical being.

There is much LOVE here for you. Namaste

Do you recall how easy it is to be with some humans that you are connected to, spirit to spirit?

August 20th
Time Travellers

There's a human tendency to look forward, as if there is nothing to clean up behind you, or you think it's too painful. You think you're alone, but you have a huge support team with you.

You forget it's not just you going ahead and deciding to leave it behind. There are the people affected by these things, too. You were never meant to be alone energetically. You move forward together. As you move forward in your life, more humans come into your force field. You allow them in when you're in the same vibration. You come together easily like a chain link fence. That is an energetic LOVE force field.

It's fine to go back to painful places. It turns out, they're not scary. They might be uncomfortable for a moment, but you're not going to die from extreme emotion. If it's something you are weak at, there's someone else in your group that's good at it. They'll step forward and take the lead. If you're good at it, vice versa. Try to be conscious of those around you. You walk with a group. You have a bubble around you. It doesn't matter if you know it's there. There is an energetic family of you moving together through time.

You are divine creatures. You are eternal beings. You are part of the Universe of LOVE. You are never alone. You travel with great groups of energy. Great spirits follow you all through your life. You just have to look to them for guidance. You can receive answers and support. Sometimes you hear it. Sometimes you feel it as energy. Don't be afraid to look back, and don't keep walking forward as if there's nothing behind you.

There is much LOVE here for you.   Namaste

There's a mess in the life behind you, but nothing that you and your energetic support team can't handle.

August 21st
State of Being

You have recently come into a sense of self. Of knowing. This creates energy. It's when you come into alignment with the Universe. You're doing it by meditating, sitting, and being. You become confident in what you know and who you are. You speak the truth. You walk in truth. You become clear, you are full of LOVE, kindness, and peace.

Getting into connection is work. That is your action part. You've become aware of the energy that is around you. By sitting quietly in a positive state, waiting in anticipation in hope of being filled with energy. This allows peace to come over you. Then comes joy and LOVE. They are all together. This is the Universe of LOVE. You come to understand you're not alone.

You have a sense of calmness because you realize you're not alone. The scariest thing is to survive on your own there. It causes grief, anxiety, and fear.

The Universe of LOVE is around you. You've carried it through all eternity. When you are in human, it stays outside of you a bit. Like a cushion. Some are able to see this energy in light but, mostly, you can feel it. It's a denseness close to your body.

Allow LOVE and positivity. When you feel peace, you know you have allowed the Universe of LOVE into you. You've invited it. Now it's surrounding you. You've got your own, but this is adding to it. You are the Universe of LOVE itself, but you are also part of the Universe of LOVE. It's as if you are one cloud in a sky. Sometimes the clouds are all connected. Sometimes they are separate.

There is much LOVE here for you.   Namaste

It's important to do your work, which is sitting.

August 22nd
You are Grace

Often, you are not being your highest and most evolved self. You are assuming you must get through tough things by yourself, with self-will and determination. The focus becomes the job. Accomplishing the 'thing' becomes a priority for you. Your being becomes less of a focus. It's not as valuable as the 'thing' you are completing.

      You're not the 'thing'. You're not the effort being put into the 'thing'. You're not how it looks or what it becomes. You're just 'you'. Things come and things go, but you still exist. So, what influence did the 'thing' have on you? Other than the effort you put into it?

      Turn inward and look around in that place deep inside of you that has always been. The essence of you is the same today as it was the moment you took your first breath. You are 'you'. Take away all the external things. Change the body structure. What's left? You. Old person. Young baby. It's always you. The essence never changes. You may call it a life force.

      This essence that is 'you' wishes to be acknowledged. It wishes to LIVE. It would like more air to breathe so it may grow to its full potential.

      You will be full of grace. You will be naturally kind-hearted. You will LOVE all you come into contact with. You are LOVE. You are peace and that is why you feel peaceful when you are connected. It doesn't really matter what you do in the middle because you are you.

      You are the Universe of LOVE in human form. Since you *are* the Universe of LOVE, you came from the Universe of LOVE and you are returning to the Universe of LOVE, what else could you be?

There is much LOVE here for you.   Namaste

Don't forget you are grace; from your first breath and through all eternity.

August 23rd
Gifts of LOVE

You have so many beautiful things around you that you don't know which one to choose. You're like a kid surrounded by candy, deciding which one to eat first. This is the way your life is. Gifts waiting for you to discover them. You are a gift to the Universe. Therefore, you are greatly praised. In return, you are given gifts. Things like peace, LOVE, kindness, and joy. It's being offered to you because you have come into humanity. It's the natural way of things. This is a big thing. You can't go down there by yourself.

This is where you begin. First you 'possibly 'believe there might be gifts sitting around you. Then you try to find out where and what they are. Just ask, "What are these gifts? Why can't I see them?" Now comes the hard part. How could you be a gracious gift from the Universe? You are only 'you'. How could you be a gift to the world and the Universe? Is it true? Or is it too much to hope for? The humanity of it means you are afraid to live. Afraid to LOVE. Afraid to feel joy.

You will have to decide if you are the most precious gift to the Universe or just some human being. It's up to you. But it won't stop the energy if you don't believe it. LOVE energy flows around you all the time. You are just a breath away from a rich, precious, full, and LOVING life.

It's like the greatest birthday party just for you. There are beautiful gifts all around you. There's LOVE, peace, joy, and connection. So, are you going to open them?

There is much LOVE here for you.   Namaste

There is great balance inside of you. There is a sense of oneness, peace, and understanding. Truly you will understand that you are LOVE, and you are part of the Universe of LOVE.

August 24th
Sheepdog

You are like a sheep dog herding those you care about together. You have this instinct. You think it would keep them safer than if they were by themselves. Many of you are this sheepdog personality. For today, this sheepdog is really a sheep. Some step forward into a position of false authority because it's an instinct.

This sheepdog has decided he is more organized and punctual. They have decided that they are different than the sheep. They don't know what the sheep are thinking. So, they can't really 'know 'if they have more authority than the others. They speak as if they do. Leaders come forth because they are the most afraid. Not because they are wiser. They are more fearful; therefore, they control more. They try harder. This is the state of many leaders. They overcompensate. They are just curious beings who are more fearful. By the end, they are great leaders because they have spent time in the middle making sure they've gotten more information.

The sheep act as One. They are a community that works, moves, eats, and makes decisions together. This is similar to the Universe of LOVE. The Universe is acting as a collective group. Each strong, independent and strong as One.

This leader sheepdog is off by themselves and not getting any information. They are learning things on their own. But they are not gathering the untold information that exists with the sheep. Information in the Universe is available to the masses. But when you go off alone, you cut yourself off from it. Now, the sheep are strong, and the sheepdog is weak. You are stronger as One. When you are separated from others, you feel a loss because you are separated from your family of LOVE.

There is much LOVE here for you.   Namaste

You are stronger and wiser when you are One. You have access to unlimited information.

August 25th
Take A Step

We speak of steps that go up, up, and up. It's as if you can see a beautiful door and you wish to enter it. Sometimes there are so many, and sometimes just a few. It's like an optical illusion. They extend as you go up. You are called forth slowly and gently by a positive LOVE force. You feel lighter, happier, and more contented. You're overjoyed to move forward, even if it's into the unknown. Sometimes, it's up these stairs. You get so involved being pulled forward in LOVE, you hardly notice. But you go...one step at a time. That's all you can see. You can't see where you're going but you really want to go. You feel the LOVE force calling.

So, you start on these stairs. You start thinking it's a LOVELY staircase. You notice each beautiful step. There are inlaid rocks, and you stop to shine one. That is why you don't notice how tall or short they are. You are engrossed with the one step you find yourself on. That is how you move forward in life as a spiritual being. One who trusts the LOVE and energy of the Universe to pull you forward gently. As you come to trust this, you don't need to know how tall they are. Or how short. Or if you are about to fall off the side.

You're enjoying the one you're on so much. You've found yourself on the perfect step for you. You don't know about the whole staircase yet. You might not be going up. There might be others using it. All you know is right around your feet is where you are. Where you belong.

There is much LOVE here for you.   Namaste

Stay aware of the LOVE force calling you forward.

August 26th
Time to be Cuddled

You wish to be comforted but it eludes you. As if you are not supposed to be comforted. You're supposed to be strong and smarter than the others. Babies get comforting. You don't. Yet, you yearn for it. You feel guilty about it. You're seeking distraction from the feeling," I feel unsure of myself, the world and those I surround myself with. I wish to be swaddled like a baby. I want to be comforted." What about saying it just like that? It's true if you have an emotional reaction to this.

You tell the Universe you wish to be swaddled. We seek out avenues to express yourself back to yourself. You don't like to listen to yourself. You can decide for yourself if it is true. We are regurgitating your own information which seems ridiculous, but you're not able to hear yourself. That is the way of humans. You wish to hear your inside thoughts outside. You wish to hear them coming from another voice, from words or from a movie. When they resonate within, you know they are your truth.

How could you possibly be cuddled at your size? It would have to be something enormous, like the Universe of LOVE or your non-physical support team. How do you get cuddled by energy? You would have to curl up in a little ball, close your eyes and see what you feel around you. You automatically attract energy from the Universe and your non-physical support team. You will be nurtured and LOVED when you go into this fetal position. Can you feel it? All humans need to be comforted at one time or another. It's your way.

There is much LOVE here for you.   Namaste

Just because you are no longer an infant, it doesn't mean you are no longer vulnerable and need cuddling.

August 27th
True LOVER

As you become more comfortable understanding that your own energy is outside your body and also inside your organs, you start to notice when other people's energy come into your energetic field. If they come in uninvited, you'll push them out. There are others that you welcome in to mingle with yours. It creates a higher vibration.

You come together and create a higher vibration than you can alone. It reaches others who are struggling at a lower vibration. They need the contrast. The lower they are, the higher vibration they need so they may come up to the middle. For them, going from low to high is unreachable. You don't know where the energy goes and it's not your concern. Your only concern is to continue allowing energy to pass through you and out of you.

You are choosing who to invite in and who to push out. You're always doing this, but you didn't realize it was energy. You thought your brain was seeing something. It doesn't see or feel energy. It keeps you safe. Your energetic being feels energy. The more you become aware of your own energy, the more you're able to label what you're feeling and sensing in others. You have a bigger vocabulary about why you are attracted to some and despise others. It's your energy and their energy saying hello without you noticing. It's a greeting or a goodbye.

First you notice your energy inside because it affects your organs. Then you notice you have energy right in front of you and all around you. Then the energy of others. You learn to see and label what their energy is saying. After that, you LOVE them unconditionally because you understand that you are both LOVE energy in human form.

There is much LOVE here for you.   Namaste

You are a brotherhood of LOVING humans trying to exist together in a difficult life.

August 28th
Magical Beings

Do you remember that sense of excitement when you went to your very first birthday party? Balloons, clowns, beautiful presents, and birthday cake. You envisioning it before you went? You couldn't wait. You thought it was going to be the best moment of your life!

You can recall visualizing something wonderful about to happen. Your imagination and excitement about guessing something in the future is still alive in you. Often you will visualize wonderful things for others but not yourself. You deserve a wonderful party for you, or an exciting meeting of two.

We are singling you out because you feel UNLOVED. You don't feel deserving of such excess, majesty, and joy. You don't want to tell the others, "Surely, I won't be invited. I can't even envision it. So many awful things have happened to me. I've stopped wishing and believing in wondrous things. I've been disappointed too much. I will not have any more magic or wonder in my life." Do you cry to hear the truth?

The truth must be uncovered for you to get to the magical party. First, you must sit in the distaste and self-loathing. Just for a moment, not for all eternity. Then things will begin to move in you. A space becomes available for magic, fairy tales and great delights. Now the magic begins. Your imagination comes out to play. Such magic is waiting for you. You alone must make the space available because it's your dreams. It's up to you. You're magical beings. It's your magical adventure. Or not. It's also your choice to be self-loathing.

There is much LOVE here for you.   Namaste

The Universe knows you are magical beings set about on magical adventures. If you choose to.

August 29th
Vulnerable in LOVE

There is something comforting about a soft and cozy blanket being laid on top of your body. You curl into it. You pet it. You feel safe from the world. You fall asleep cuddled in a blanket of warmth and LOVE. You relax enough to sleep unprotected. When you sleep, you're vulnerable. Yet, you do it. So, you're capable of being vulnerable, even if you don't like it. Surely, your bodies were not designed to stay alert all the time. They were meant to rest and be vulnerable.

When you are vulnerable at night, do you recall smiling before you went to sleep? You say, "I feel LOVELY. I won't resist it any longer. I'll fall into a restful place and surrender." This is truly your last thought. But you have done it so many times, you don't notice anymore. While you are in this vulnerable and restful state, some of you, who are highly energized, escape. You go wandering around the Universe checking up on LOVED ones, both passed and alive. Others of you dream fantastical events. But always, you leave your human life for a time. You're not living the life you've invented. So, it turns out that you can walk away from your life. You're not as immersed in your life as you thought.

It's time for you to stretch the limits of your belief system. You are busy in your human life. You have many thoughts. You can't keep all the thoughts of the Universe and live your human existence. Your human existence takes a lot of space.

When you're free, you may have fantastical dreams or float into the Universe. You're free to be who you wish to be. You're free to be who you inspire to be. You're free to be your secret self, the one you've kept hidden from the others. Free to live as you wish.

There is much LOVE here for you.   Namaste

To be free, you must be vulnerable. To be vulnerable, you must be free.

August 30th
Life Lessons

Your life has been full of lessons. This is what humans call things that they don't always like. All of mankind are learning lessons. Sometimes it's painful. Lessons often require self-discipline. They require you to be available. Humans become predictable. They are resistant to authority. It's because you should be wary of lessons you must learn.

Rely on your connection with the Universe. It puts you in a place of calm and ease. This is where you may receive information clearly. When you are still, you may be One with energy, humans, non-physical and the Universe. As you learn to settle, be quiet and calm yourself, and you begin to hear things. You call this intuition or deja vu. You begin to know and hear things as they are happening or before. This has to do with time. Time is like energy. It is large. If you are loose with time, your energy comes and goes. Forward or backward a bit. It knows what's going to happen because it has already happened. As you sit easily in your being, you may float around energetically.

There is a mass of humans trying to move forward together. You're moving forward with common experiences, shared knowing and intuition. You have a feeling there is more to you than one human. Sometimes, you understand that you are a group travelling in non-physical. That means you have all been together throughout eternity. There are also the energetic groups of all other humans who are existing this moment moving with you. Beyond that is the Universe of LOVE which is non-physical beings not in your little group. All of this is moving together. It's quite a force. That is why we speak to you as a group.

We speak to you individually when we say, "Take some time to be easy and sit quietly in stillness so you may connect with your energetic self." This is the only instruction for you alone. The rest is you travelling as a group.

There is much LOVE here for you.   Namaste

You're evolving. You learn together. You remember together. You are one large LOVE family. You move together energetically.

August 31st
Mountain of LOVE

When you stand in front of a mountain you say, "I'll never reach the top. I prefer to stay here with the others. There are a few humans climbing up, but mostly they're staying here at the bottom where it's safer. We watch out for one another."

As beautiful as a mountain seems, you can't comprehend climbing it. Yet, as you look again, there are more humans going up. You start to wonder why so you ask, "Why are you climbing that mountain when you are perfectly safe and happy down here with us?" The common answer will be: "I feel close to heaven. When I look down, I see the earth in a different way." When you wonder why, you change. You no longer fit in with those wandering around oblivious to a mountain right beside them. Suddenly, you belong nowhere. That creates unease in you. You like to know where your people are.

Since you are standing next to the mountain, talking to humans going up, perhaps you could tag along and see how it goes. Certainly, you could come back down the mountain if you want. Now you are considering going up half a mountain. Your curious human nature is involved. Then off you go, climbing a mountain. Of course, it's difficult. It's easier to sit on the ground and look up at the mountain than to actually climb it. As you get up halfway, you can see the village below. You're wondering what else you can see if you go higher. So far, you haven't fallen off, so you decide to continue. Just a little bit at a time.

This is the way of human nature. You're encouraged to come forward. The Universe of LOVE says," Would you like to come to the corner and take a peek?" Slowly you move up the mountain. Slowly you move through your life. Your life has been a mountain. What happens when you get to the top or the end. The time where you come to see life as it truly can be. The top of the mountain is your highest potential. It is a true vision of what is possible in humanity. You can see it from the top of a mountain, or you can feel it in your heart.

There is much LOVE here for you.   Namaste

When you surrender to the Universe and sit in peace and LOVE, you have reached the top of the mountain.

September

LOVE IS NOTHING TO FEAR. IT IS TO BE EMBRACED.

#aaronlacey

September 1st
Our Highest Selves

Many will sleep through their entire lifetime but not you because you're interested in awakening. That's the beginning. The beginning is just curiosity. "What's going on with me? Is there more to life for me?" You're very self-centred at the beginning of the awakening but it must be this way. Nothing else motivates you like pain and questioning your self-worth.

Being self-absorbed is how you've survived physically. It's easier if you accept that instead of fighting it. Then you can move on more quickly through the other stages.

The first question is innocent. What follows is uncomfortable. When you're in the place of letting go of darkness, pain and negative things, the new question becomes: "How do I get through this?" The answer is, "With support from the Universe."

Then the healing begins. It pours out of you like a waterfall. For some of you, it might be pain and anger from family lines you jumped into. Whatever you've chosen to look at, you may heal it with the help of the Universe. Because you've come into humanity to heal. Both yourself and others.

Now you may sit in peace because you have space for LOVE energy to come in. You'll begin to recall what it's like to sit in ease because it's what you do when you're not in physical.

Finally, there's allowing LOVE energy to pass into you and out of you. Because now there's space. It passes out to others who have no hope of sitting in ease or letting go.

There is much LOVE here for you.   Namaste

You would not be in human form if you didn't believe you could allow LOVE to pass through you to others.

September 2nd
Back to Self

It appears you're doing a full circle of life. You begin knowing many things, feeling confident and connected to the Universe and being a LOVING, caring, kind creature. In your middle life, you're not that kind any longer. You're not so clear, so connected and LOVING as you were in the beginning. That's the natural progress of humanity. It's almost impossible for you to maintain anything other than what the others create. Which is fear, worry and sadness.

In the beginning, there was only you and the Universe of LOVE. Now you're hanging around with others so you'll all end up the same. You came to bounce about together and see what you can do together. It's what you all wished for. When you get your ego out of the way, you can understand you came to have fun. There's nothing wrong with that.

You can be quite judgmental of your human self. "I should know better. I'm smarter than this." You knew before you came it was going to be a bit of a mess 'and' great fun. The human body can skip, dance, climb poles and walk across high wires. You forget sometimes you wished to have a human body.

The full circle comes when you finally say, "I'm a little bruised and battered but my soul is intact. My energy is the same as when I came into being. Really, as long as my energetic connection to the Universe is intact, what else matters?"

Bodies can't last forever. Finally, you figure out: "Oh, I'm just supposed to have fun with that body. The energy is eternal. What am I worrying about anyway?" Then you settle into it and have a little smile on your face because you've come full circle. You figured out you're still the same LOVING, trusting being as when you took your very first breath.

You're a precious human being full of LOVE energy. What a beautiful place for you to reside. You're eternal energy after all. So, why not sit in it?

There is much LOVE here for you.   Namaste

Settle down. Enjoy where you are. It's time to just be.

September 3rd
Slow Learner

Sometimes, you're slow learners. Your ego really doesn't want to remember some things. You think it's important to know exactly what you think and not be too open to new ideas. Because what if new ideas lead you astray? Oftentimes, you have difficulty absorbing new ideas that aren't yours.

Most of your ideas you didn't come up with yourself. You just don't know it. Most ideas pass through you or by you. You chose which ones to grab onto. There's lots going by. They're not all yours. You only know what you know for the time you exist. So, how brilliant can you be?

Imagine all the thoughts that have ever been. Imagine all the non-physical geniuses. Imagine how many thoughts go by you. You can just pluck one out of the air and say, "I think I'll take that one. Maybe I'll take this one, too." You don't really know you're doing it.

When you're not in physical, you're part of the Universe. So, you have access to great knowledge. You choose which ones are going to be part of your experience this time.

Now, are you also able to put thoughts into the Universe and let them become part of the Universal intelligence? Of course. You can give away the notions you chose, and choose a new idea or way of living. You're only experimenting, after all."

You can give and take from the energy around you any moment. Then you're truly free. You won't be confined one human experience and one set of thoughts. You may change as you go along. You're changed even now.

There is much LOVE here for you.   Namaste

Even if you are a slow learner, slow learners can change.

September 4th
Admiration Abounds

Sometimes you forget how LOVED you are by the Universe and how important it is for LOVE energy to flow into you and out of you. It not only cleanses you but it goes forward to those who often don't have access to the Universe of LOVE. They've decided to cut themselves off from unconditional LOVE. It heals and nourishes both you, and anyone in your vicinity.

Your need to thrive in a world full of humans who are not always sweet is admirable. As is, your unnerving bravery to keep one foot in front of the other.

You have admiration for those who go into battle, yet, you don't realize you're also one of them. All you have is spiritual armour. That's why you're really brave. You think, in the end it doesn't matter if your body is disposed of because your soul, which is unconditional LOVE, is eternal. You just keep showing up.

Your LOVED ones that have passed are not far from you because they understand, more than before, how brave it is to be in human form. They think, "We're going to make sure we support the others." The amount of time your non-physical LOVED ones spend surrounding, encouraging and supporting you, would surprise you. They're at it all the time. Even when you're asleep.

You finally have the unconditional support that only a non-physical past relative can offer. They couldn't offer it when they were in human form. They were going through their own crazy struggles. This might change the way you move about, knowing you're never alone.

Your non-physical relatives are finally able to LOVE you the way you always wished but couldn't really hope for. When you think of them, they're sending you energy.

There is much LOVE here for you.   Namaste

It makes the battle of life a little easier knowing you're not alone.

September 5th
Do You Want to Play With Me?

You become more joyful as you come together with others. You become childlike when you think," Yay, we're going to play together." Can you recall a time when your way of life was looking for others to play with? When your sole goal was to play? Sometimes you played alone, but it was wonderful when you played with others."

What if today you were to say," Do you want to play with me?" What if it was your new mantra?

Asking puts you in a vulnerable place because what if they say no? When you were small, it was easy because you didn't think there was anything wrong with you. You just knew you needed a playmate. You were meeting your inner need to play with someone.

Your brain and ego think, "You can't do that now." What if you speak to your brain and ego for a moment and say, "What are you afraid of? What do you need to protect us from?".

Keep in mind that the brain and ego wish to keep you alive, they're not there to have fun. Now say, "Thank you for keeping me alive and making sure I didn't injure myself, but I want to play now." There's a deeper longing to play with others that's not your brain.

You have an eternal longing to be one with your brothers and sisters in non-physical. Certainly, your brain and ego cannot know what you know eternally. It's not their job.

If you ignore your inner longings, you're not allowing a part of you to come out and play. You remember what it's like to work as a group in non-physical LOVE energy. You move forward as a group.

There is much LOVE here for you.   Namaste

Nothing can withstand the pressure of LOVE energy. Everything surrenders to LOVE energy. Deep inside you, the same force exists.

September 6th
Illusionment

You often find yourself in a state of dis-illusionment. You had an idea about the life you would live and how it would unfold in a certain way. Life doesn't unfold as you foresee it. That's the nature of being human.

The best way to live is having hope without having a vision of what that looks like. It means living in hope that the Universe cares for you and that you're one with the others. Living in hope that you're a spiritual being with a higher calling and can therefore, move forward easily. Taking advantage of each opportunity as it presents itself.

What if you walked forward day by day, moment by moment in hope and faith? Faith in the Universe. In yourself. In the essential energy that exists in each human being. In connecting soul to soul because you're one with the essence of the Universe which is the LOVE that exists in each human being.

You've spent many years projecting and envisioning things so it's difficult for you to stay in a blank state of hope and connection. But your highest state is when your mind is inactive. When you're sitting in connection with the Universe or your unending power source. The energy that has existed through all eternity and is around you right now.

This dis-illusionment you have is unnecessary. The visions you had did not come true because they should not have. They were not for you. If they were for you, they'd be existing right now. They would have come into exact alignment. They're only energy after all, and your life is unfolding in an energetic manner.

You bump up against other energy or ideas. You connect with other humans. That's your life unfolding in front of you. That's your true life. That's why you may live in hope. You'll begin to feel LOVE, connection and peace with your life.

There is much LOVE here for you.   Namaste

Your entire life is waiting to unfold. You just have to show up and see it with your eyes, feel it with your heart. You'll know what to do each step of the way. Just show up as you are. Spiritual beings having a human experience.

Sept 7th
LOVELY Human

How LOVED you are seems like a small thing and yet, it's huge. You came into being because you're a gift for humanity. You're called LOVE in human. There's LOVE energy, too, but it's not physical. So, you're raised up more than non-physical LOVE energy. There's a part of you that knows this. Your 'reverse' ego says, "No. We're not that important." This notion will only trip you up. Someone told you that you're not as important as you are.

When you call upon energy, it comes immediately. When you ask a question, the answer is there before you finish the sentence. Whether you're in the proper vibration to hear the answer, it doesn't matter. It comes anyway.

You are a LOVE vibration that has a physical form. That means, you're so precious. You're so LOVED. You're so revered. You are like a tiny bird being held in the hands of the Universe and all hands come to ensure its survival. It's the role of the Universe to be at your disposal so you may survive.

But you're not only there to 'survive'. You're there to 'thrive'. You're there to have fun. To live and dance and sing.

Your 'reverse' ego is not allowing you to get this. So, you're revered for having a body but it's also your greatest stumbling block to LOVE. You're so precious because you've agreed to this. To have the greatest gift and the greatest burden, which is to LOVE in human form.

You all wished to be reminded of the same message: LOVE is all there is.

There is much LOVE here for you.   Namaste

The word LOVE is the closest human word to describe a sense of joy, peace and oneness.

September 8th
Eternal LOVE

When you're encircled by unconditional LOVE, you relax and become vulnerable. Although in most other situations, you have difficulty being vulnerable. This means if you're safe in LOVE, it comes naturally and you're comfortable.

You called unconditional LOVE energy forward because you wish to be vulnerable. Even if you don't know how. Being consistently vulnerable is uncomfortable and unnerving. You don't know what you're doing. And you really like to know what you're doing. When you feel vulnerable, you're afraid you'll be eliminated. Humans have come to understand if you're not vulnerable, you survive. On one level, it's true. The physical body will survive but what of your inner self? It doesn't survive by the same rules as humans do.

Now you're wondering how to become more evolved. Your true self is the part of you that exists through all eternity. You're not sure how to evolve but you know it has something to do with LOVE and letting go. So, you say, "Help me be vulnerable. Show me the way."

You know that somewhere deep inside you is some knowing that understands how to live an eternal life. You call out because you know it's close by and you want it to be brought back in. You may bring LOVE energy in by remembering you're precious eternal beings. Your energy exists forward and backwards.

Your connection to LOVE and the Universe makes you capable of being very vulnerable. Because your eternal being cannot be destroyed. Therefore, there's nothing to fear.

Let your eternal being come out to play. Then it'll be alright for you to be vulnerable. It won't matter if you're extinguished. When you're not worried about being extinguished, you show up in all kinds of ways.

There is much LOVE here for you.   Namaste   .

Now you can show your bright, shiny self to others. Then they'll have hope that inside of them, the same bright, shiny human exists.

September 9th
Hear It with Your Own Ears

Each time something random happens, stop for a moment, take a breath and notice. Ask, "Why did this moment happen?" This is investigating a coincidence. Perhaps it's the Universe trying to get your attention.

You're all connected to the Universe because you're energy yourself. Your experience is to figure out which method of connecting to Universal energy works best for you. Some hear or feel it. Some are shocked physically like electricity.

There's lots of different ways non-physical tries to communicate. When you're having a memory of a passed relative, they're thinking of you also.

It's possible for you to increase your communication with non-physical. You're just beginning. Would you like to have vibration pass through you and out of your voice? You just have to be curious and allow the Universe to pass through you. Some of you are interested in moving energy through your fingertips so you may heal others and yourself. There are many different avenues. Some like to figure out their dreams.

There are things you can do to evolve. Anything beyond the typical thoughts you were taught by adults, is investigating non-physical and the Universe of LOVE. You're investigating the LOVE energy that's around you all of the time.

Start to say, "What am I seeing? What am I feeling? What is the energy passing through me?" Just be a curious human.

There is much LOVE here for you.   Namaste

You might not believe everything you see but there might be more to what you see than what you believe.

September 10th
Willing to Allow LOVE In

Caring for all creatures equally is being balanced in LOVE. Then you won't determine who you're giving LOVE to. It just passes through you to whoever or whatever's in front of you. It's about balance. Not about choosing who receives LOVE. This would only be your ego deciding.

When you can get to a place of allowing LOVE into you and out of you, you don't know where it goes when it leaves you. It goes where it's being called.

In order for LOVE to pass through you, it must first enter into you. Therefore, there must first be a willingness to allow it in. Often this willingness comes about at a time in your life where you've run out of human options. Then you seek out non-physical, Universal energy. This is a place of openness to receive LOVE energy.

Sitting with unconditional LOVE is so wonderful for you. Many have forgotten what it feels like to sit in ease, peace and comfort. Your earth can be a rough place. Many forget how easy it is to sit in LOVE. As you become used to this feeling of comfort, you'll naturally wonder where it goes. Then you will open up and it will go out to the others.

There is much LOVE here for you.   Namaste

You allow LOVE in and when you realize you get your share, you evolve. Then you allow it out of you for the others.

September 11th
Escalated LOVE

There is great joy when two of you come together as one. When you come together in an honest, open vulnerable way, the two are escalated energetically. Others will have an experience that must be escalated singularly. This is done by a connection with the Universe of LOVE which is powerful energetic LOVE, also.

Certain humans automatically have faster moving energy. These are the ones always seeking more escalated LOVE. This is LOVE that goes out to others who require it most but have no access to it because their vibration is too slow. Those with high, fast vibrations that automatically attract other humans and the Universe of LOVE may be escalated by allowing LOVE to pass through them.

As you allow LOVE into you, sometimes you wish to hoard it there. At those times, you become the most fearful and anxious. When you allow LOVE to flow easily into you and out of you, you're at your lightest, highest and most joyful times.

You're regurgitating LOVE. Into you. Out of you. When you recall this momentum, it's easier for you to live there because you don't have to hold onto LOVE. When you focus on LOVE coming in and going out, you feel like everything is wonderful.

This peaceful feeling may be escalated with two or with the Universe of LOVE. With two, you must be in the same vibration to experience the uplifting energy. If there's one that is vibrating very fast and one that is vibrating very slow, the high energy will be brought down. If there are two of you vibrating at high energy, you'll come together and there will be more LOVE energy to spread around to others.

There is much LOVE here for you.   Namaste

You create a better life for yourself by being peaceful. Your life flows more easily. Others pick up on this energy and suddenly, their lives are easier. You influence those around you. Even those you pass on the street.

September 12th
The Wall

Sometimes in your life, you come up against a brick wall. You put much effort into lining up a life, then suddenly, you can't get any further. Some reach a roadblock and wonder how to get around it. Your self-will takes charge.

Others who hit the wall, fall down and stare into space. They've lost touch with themselves in such an extreme way, they didn't even see the wall in front of them. Those of you lying down looking at the sky are wondering why you didn't see this thing. How did your life get into such turmoil that you couldn't feel anymore. This is just human wondering, not judgment.

Some need to hit a wall to start noticing your precious life. As you wonder, "How did I get here anyway? I used to have humans with me but now I am all alone." Many things have occurred before you reach this wall. There were times when your ego took hold of things. This is when others fell away. But now you're looking up at the sky and the stars. Perhaps this is the first time in a very long time that you noticed there's a sky above you.

It's important to know all the decisions you have made, and all the self-will you've grabbed onto is perfectly fine for your human experience. There's no need to be harsh with yourself. Each of you started running when you were small. Many of you just kept running. Until you hit the wall. You've done what you learned. Have some LOVE and compassion for yourself.

Now you're wondering what to do next. You didn't know there was an option of not running. You think, "I'm wondering if I like to lie here. My heart's not racing. I feel calmer. I feel at ease." You say, "Thank you magnificent wall. Thank you for anguish and hurt and pain, for I have found out I can stop running and lie down. Thank you life experiences. Thank you humans who have LOVED and left. Thank you life for the experience you've given me." Now you may decide where you go next.

There is much LOVE here for you.   Namaste

As you lie looking up at the stars, the whole world is open to you. Suddenly, everything is new.

September 13th
The Great Experiment

What you experience brings a richness to your existence. You've not stumbled into this lifetime accidentally. You decided to have an experience of LOVE. It's the greatest LOVE experiment there has ever been. How much LOVE can you maintain while being in physical? What you're doing is important. You're experiencing LOVE in a human body.

Energy can be contained in any type of container. It can always explode. It can always dissipate. It's always this way. You didn't know which way it would go with you but you were hopeful enough to enter into a physical body after coming from pure LOVE energy. You have great admiration from the Universe because you decided to enter into this great experiment and see how it works out. Therefore, every moment you breathe and exist, is precious to the Universe and to the energy that surrounds you. You're affecting the energy around you. It travels with you from place to place and human to human.

It's very important work you're doing there. It's not accidental you're there. The things you learn and humans you encounter are not accidental either. They're important to all time forward and back because energy is eternal. When you project LOVE at this moment, it travels throughout time. There is no pure moment with energy. And yes, you may send LOVE back to yourself because it's energy.

You're true magicians. You play with energy. You're important to those around you, the Universe and to the time you find yourself in. This is the time you've chosen so it's valuable in some way. The energy you put forth exists forever.

There is much LOVE here for you.   Namaste

Your physical body doesn't always exist but your energy does. It continues to mix with those you're familiar with that have passed, too.

September 14th
Show Up For Your Own Life

Here you are in all your majesty. Showing up alert and ready to be transformed. You're sitting in a place of great expectation. A place of unfolding and unveiling of truths. This place is high energetically, for your highest place is sitting in hope and expectation.

In this expectant state you have a knowing that something is going to happen. You believe and trust that it will. So, you show up completely. You're vulnerable, really. For what if it doesn't happen? The part that matters is showing up in hope and expectation.

You're doing it right now. "What will the Universe remind me of that I've forgotten?" You're like an excited child. The point in your human life is showing up! Show up for your own life! Each day you may sit in anticipation of what is going to happen. "Oh boy, I wonder what's going to unfold today. It's going to be something wonderful! Something I haven't seen before."

What about showing up for your own life in this way all of the time? This type of energy affects others around you. They sense the excitement. They'll become excited, too.

There is much LOVE here for you. Namaste

When you arrive in your own life, you allow others to arrive in theirs, too. Because you're all connected energetically. If you sit in hopeful expectation today, the others will also.

September 15th
Yes, You are BELOVED

The answer to your question is Yes, you're LOVED by the Universe. Yes, you're admired by those who stay in non-physical. Yes, you're the most BELOVED being that exists there. Yes, you're precious to your ancestors who have passed. This is something humans often have difficulty believing. Others have told you it's selfish to think this way. Yet, the Universe of LOVE disagrees.

In order for you to be of service to mankind and to have an easy, comfortable, fun existence, you must first believe you're cherished and LOVED. If you don't understand the depth of this LOVE, you cannot be your truest, highest self.

Some of you want to share LOVE. You want to be of service to the Universe. You want to show what LOVE looks like in human form. You cannot do this unless you understand how precious you are. Otherwise, you're faking it. You're pretending you're worthwhile and LOVED just by saying it to yourself over and over. That's just your brain which has only been alive as long as you. It doesn't understand the true depth of Universal LOVE energy that exists beyond you and within you. Your ego gets in the way of you absorbing this truth.

Repeat this until it becomes a part of you. "I am the most precious being. I am greatly LOVED and admired by non-physical. The Universe of LOVE watches my every breath. It hears my every wish. The Universe of LOVE has got my back."

Being called precious is being met with resistance by you although there's a part of you that knows this is true. When you're able to bypass this resistance, your energy and Universal energy can come together.

It's not new information to you that you're supported, LOVED and encouraged. You understand you're filled with LOVE. Then you become more compassionate, easy with your life and others, kind and gentle. These are by-products of LOVE. For you can't 'make' yourself kind. You just are.

There is much LOVE here for you.   Namaste

You are full of the LOVE that exists in the Universe of LOVE. The two are the same vibration.

September 16th
We Are All One Family

Here's a story about rounding up the troops. You're not sure if you're rounding people up or stuck in the middle with the others. You're not even sure why you're rounded up. All you know is that you're all lassoed together like you're one thing. There's many questions," Who decided they're the leader to order a round up? Has someone gotten false authority from outside? Who are the people in the middle? How come we're all together so we could be rounded up?" You can imagine yourselves rounded up now without knowing why.

As you look around, you see many faces. You begin to say, "Hello." You're all the same really. After the first hello, there are many more. Then suddenly, the group transforms. The energy automatically comes down from a fearful place to this calm, relaxed state where "We are one together here."

This round up might turn into a LOVEFEST. It starts with one who decides, "I'm in a LOVE space. Here's some LOVE for you." Fear may be lessened when the group decides, "How will we be together?" As you present ease to the group, those who feel the same, embrace it and add to it. It goes on and on like this.

This group is sometimes tearful and sad because they don't understand energy. It overcomes them. The most important thing is to cry when you feel sad because it eases the energy. When you're not crying but you feel sad, your body tightens up and tries to contain the energy. When you feel happy, you must laugh right out loud so it moves out into the world.

These emotions must come out. When you're in a group, it gets dispersed. You all absorb a little piece. Your real world is not exactly like this but this is the highest evolution for mankind. When you're not your highest self, some do too much and some too little. But that's okay because you came to live. You're not perfect. You're just one human living a life.

There is much LOVE here for you. Namaste

Remember, you are capable of great things together.

September 17th
Truth Will Set You Free

When was the last time you sat on the grass and looked intently at it? A long time ago? There's something important in the exercise of sitting down on the earth. Your energy becomes one with the vibration and magnetic force inside the earth. Sometimes you need to be de-magnetized. You're magnetic because you're energy. When you sit down on the earth, you're immediately neutralized.

It's important to get your body onto the earth. Perhaps, that's why the earth is there. Perhaps, it's there for you. It's alive. It's energy. It's vibration and it's magnetic. All humans, who are also magnetic, stick to it.

Many get far away from the earth by putting pavement and buildings on top of the dirt. Yet, there's always some grass around. Humans are naturally attracted to it.

You're the same vibration as the earth. The earth doesn't have an ego, so it doesn't change its vibration. It's THE vibration. It's THE magnet. Therefore, it grounds you and clears your energy. Then you may be filled with LOVE energy. When you're filled with busy human energy, there's no space for LOVE energy to come in.

You avoid being cleared out because you're afraid. You've forgotten so much that you're almost afraid of what you've forgotten. That seems upside down but the further you get from truth and the more detached you are, the more afraid you are of it. You're afraid of the truth and yet, as you know, the truth will set you free.

So, here's the truth. You're a precious human. You're much LOVED and adored by the Universe. And the magnetic earth, also. You're perfect the way you are. You're the same as all the others who are trying to get through a human experience without making too much of a mess. The point is to have the human experience.

There is much LOVE here for you.   Namaste

The truth is that you exist in a bubble of LOVE energy. And you came to allow LOVE to flow into you and out of you to the others who have no access to it. Are you afraid of the truth?

September 18th
Open Hearted

Do you recall a time in your life where you have seen someone, perhaps for the first time, and thought, "I've been waiting for you! Where have you been?" If this has not happened yet, it's because you couldn't allow it out. You always have a choice to allow magical things to happen.

There are things that happen precisely, even though none of it was planned. That's a magical life. It's opening your eyes to wonder and allowing things to unfold. It's just waiting in anticipation of the next thing. Of course, it's very difficult to be patient as a human. Sometimes, the excitement gets you moving ahead too quickly and you just end up falling into the ego place. Then you 'make' a life of your own choosing.

It's not easy but if you become amazed as each wonderful thing unfolds, you'll stay in alignment more. Just think, "Look how wonderful this moment is! This is my life!" Then you stay in the magic.

This is magical alignment. It's tangible. It happens in your human existence. You'll think of someone and they'll call you. You'll open your door and someone's there. These are magical moments but they must be noticed to be so.

Finding someone you know very well but have never seen before is truly otherworldly magic. This is recognizing energy that you've been immersed with before. Their energy is the same wavelength as yours. You think, "This energy fits in with me. It settles me. It connects us." This is Universal energetic magic. It's bigger than opening the door before someone knocks.

This is what you're truly capable of because you're energy yourself. You can notice a mirror image of your own energy when you have the eyes to see it and an open heart to allow it in.

There is much LOVE here for you.   Namaste

It can be difficult to have an open heart when you're human. Your brain gets involved when your heart is open too wide. It views an open heart as a place where much injury can occur. So, it protects it. Until you're not sure if you have a heart at all anymore.

September 19th
Perhaps

There are times when you're not pleased with your behaviour. Perhaps, it was a few moments ago or maybe, much time has passed. When there's something you regret, you often blame yourself. You think "Why did I do such a thing?"

Would you treat others the same way? There is a certain discord between the way you judge your bad behaviour and the way you judge someone else's. You will often give them a break. But you don't give yourself the same break. You think it's important to stay on top of your own bad behaviour. You believe this will change your behaviour next time.

Putting more negative energy onto a negative energetic behaviour will only escalate it. It creates more of the thing you wish to be rid of. What about LOVING the bad behaviour instead? Try something like this.

"It seems like I've been acting angry and mean lately. Perhaps, that's not my best self but I'm trying pretty hard at this human thing. I've been trying to fit in since I was born. I try not to hurt too many people and to have some fun. Maybe I'm doing a good job most of the time. Maybe I'm doing a great job! Maybe I'm sharing LOVE. Maybe I'm allowing LOVE to flow through me. There are lots around me who LOVE me and I LOVE them. Maybe I'm doing a good job. Remember the time I shared LOVE with that stranger. No one knows about that time but I remember it now. They were sitting alone looking UNLOVED. I looked at them which allowed them to become part of humanity. I allowed the LOVE to flow through me. Maybe I'm a pretty good human after all. Maybe I'll focus on the LOVE energy that surrounds me."

There is much LOVE here for you. Namaste

"Sometimes, I feel LOVE coming from non-physical. Perhaps, I have a great support system but I just can't see them. I guess I'm just learning. Perhaps, I'm LOVE walking and LOVE talking. Perhaps, I'm the only LOVE some humans will see. Perhaps."

September 20th
So What?

The time has come for you to come face to face with yourself. You've mostly tried to avoid looking at yourself in the mirror. What will you see when you look? What will truly be there? So, you've been avoiding you. It helps if you keep busy in your life.

There's lots to do instead of sitting alone with yourself. Maybe you could have a chat with yourself and say," How are you anyway? What's going on with you these days?" That would be a friendly thing to do.

Maybe being friendly and inquisitive is the way to go about it. Generously being the host and offering up your LOVING ear and kind heart for another to speak their truth. A place where they're allowed to be completely honest without fear of repercussions.

If you were to speak honestly without fear, what would you say? First you would need to have a trusting, LOVING relationship with yourself. There would have to be a place that would receive such information. Whether it's good, sad, or angry. A place that can receive it and nod politely.

What if you were to play these two roles? One inviting in a LOVING, accepting way and one sharing freely and honestly. What would you hear? Can you truly LOVE yourself as you are? Will you still LOVE them after they tell you the truth?

This fear of truth and the unknown can keep you from many relationships, including the one with yourself. Unfortunately, the fear is fear of itself. The actual thing that happens is not too large for you. If you're afraid or angry, it's not who you are forever. It's only who you are for the moment.

There is much LOVE here for you.   Namaste

Why not give yourself a break? Say you're LOVABLE and precious to yourself and the Universe around you.

September 21st
Immersed in LOVE

You have a great longing to be immersed in LOVE. It's felt as joy. LOVE can't be labeled so watch for the emotion it creates. When you feel in LOVE, your body reacts in smiles or laughter. It wants to become one with it.

This vibration is familiar to you. You long for it because you've been in it and you're part of it. This longing for LOVE can be misconstrued in human relationships. When you crave LOVE, miss LOVE and wish to be one with it, you can put yourself in a vulnerable place. Some can sense this and take advantage of you.

This doesn't mean you should not long for LOVE. It means those who misuse LOVE have been attracted to you. It says nothing about you. Seeking LOVE is your highest nature.

When you're not in physical, you sit in LOVE as a group. When you're in physical, you get by the best you can. What you're truly after is just you and the Universe of LOVE or LOVE energy. You're truly a seeker of LOVE.

The emotions that are evoked here will become so familiar to you that you'll begin to notice them in your own life. You'll soon start to feel the exact same way you do at this moment when you're sitting alone. Then you'll know, "This is the Universe of LOVE. I may immerse myself in this when I'm in clear alignment." This will be your highest self once you reach this place. You'll be one with the Universe of LOVE.

Remember, you're perfect the way you are no matter where you find yourself at this moment. You're doing the best you can as a human. It's very difficult for all of you. Yet, you're doing it and that's a wonderful thing.

There is much LOVE here for you. Namaste

You're a wonderful gift to other humans, to the Universe of LOVE and to your non-physical support team.

September 22nd
River of Energy

A race car is a finely tuned work of art made by a human with a vision from the Universe of LOVE. This human transformed an idea into something beautiful for you to behold. The idea of creating the fastest vehicle made is an idea that exists in energy. It existed before this human made it into a physical object. These thoughts, visions and half-finished notions, are all around you because thoughts are energy.

When you concentrate on a thought, energy is created around it. Then the thought exists. Sometimes you say you're able to read other people's thoughts. That's because their thoughts are energy. Thoughts become inventions. Musical notes are thoughts. Sadness and emotional connection to someone you've lost, stay floating around you. Right now, you're in a pool of thoughts. When you're not in human, you're pure energy which is the same as thoughts.

When you're in human, it's a more difficult to get your hands on the ideas. There has to be space available for thoughts to come in. When a new thought comes in and you wonder, "Where did that come from? That has nothing to do with me or my life." And you're curious about it, sit with it like it has a life of its own. It could be a complete package or a half finished thought. When you allow the first random thought in and think, "Hmm, what is that?" It stops with you for a moment. If you say, "Get out of here. That's nonsense" it keeps going until someone says, "What's this?"

The next time a random thought comes into your head, say, "Look at this. What are you about?" Just be curious. If it's of no interest to you, let it go. A new thought will come because you've created a path for them to enter.

There is much LOVE here for you.   Namaste

When you are in an energetic flow, you'll start seeing more ideas at the same time. When you start, you'll just get one randomly. But after a while, they'll be going by like a river of thought energy.

September 23rd
Chasing Your Tail

Picturing a dog chasing its tail is very comical. You use this expression of 'chasing your tail' when you feel like you're getting nowhere in your life. You know you can behave like a canine sometimes.

Now, there might be a reason for you to chase your tail and be confident of what you're saying. Your ego and brain feel they must know things so they can support you in your humanity. That's why you speak as if you're sure about things. Even though, sometimes, you're going in circles.

Your ego and brain are overactive because they fear loosing you. Because you're not being honest about your emotions, your brain is overcompensating.

So, the easiest conclusion is to look at the emotions, events, chaos and trauma that are happening. It sounds easy when you are referring to others. What if your brain is being overactive because it senses something is wrong that you're not addressing? The obvious answer is to lay your emotional worries on the table. This creates great anxiety.

Then your brain comes in and says, "Let's get that tail." Anything to avoid sitting in an uncomfortable traumatic, emotionally charged place.

Often you spend as much energy hiding it as you would by sitting in it. You have a fear of the event and the emotions. You think they're too much for you. Yet, they're your emotions. Your trauma. What is there to fear if you own it?

There is always something precious at the bottom. So, when you sit in that place for a moment, it disappears, all that's left is LOVE.

There is much LOVE here for you.   Namaste

When you sit in what you own, you can cry or get angry. Afterwards, all that's left is a feeling of peace. And peace is the emotional response to LOVE.

September 24th
What is Going On?

As you feel a world pressing down upon you, you reach out more for your freedom. It's human nature to respond this way when you feel oppressed. So you say, "I want to be free. I want to remember there's more going on than what's in front of my face."

You're in your body for a small time. You exist beyond this time energetically. Before and after.

This is an experience you've chosen to have while you're in your physical form. It's something you're interested in. You wish to experiment with it and explore it. You've chosen your life exactly the way it is. You wish to feel oppression so you may cry out to the Universe. You've decided what form you'd take this time. You've decided many things in your lifetime. When you come to understand this, you become more empowered and less of a victim. When you understand it was your choice to come or leave, you'll understand your place in humanity.

You've chosen to exist at this moment. You're a group working together. You're a family with those who exist right now. You have a mission to accomplish, both together and alone.

Your mission is to remember non-physical energy and the Universe of LOVE. To embrace it as your own. Each time you come into human, there's a good chance you'll forget.

Are you being oppressed right now? Only because you chose to be. Are you crying out for reassurance from the Universe of LOVE that you're not alone? Definitely. Are your questions always answered? Yes. For you are highly valued for showing up in humanity and taking your place amongst your brothers and sisters. This is of great value to the Universe. Things would not continue to unfold unless you took your place in humanity.

There is much LOVE here for you.   Namaste

Perfect human. Perfect life. Perfect timing.

September 25th
Imaginational Energy

We wish you to imagine yourself painting a landscape. You will draw the mountains, the water and some clouds. You will stand back from your picture, look at it and think, "How I wish a place like this existed. For this is from my imagination." Your imagination has now created something tangible. This energy has created something out of nothing. What if you were to find a place that looked exactly like your painting? Would you think, "That's strange because I knew about this place before I came here. It was in my imaginational energy."

Would you start to imagine a world where you are connected to all of it? A world where you have already seen places where you have not been. And met people you have not met. Can you imagine it? Have you ever met a human being and recognized them immediately? Have you ever said something and thought, "I think I have already said this."

Are you ready to imagine a world that is more than what you see? This is up to you. As you are able to handle more and more information, your mind and imagination opens. Then you begin to see what is truly happening around you energetically. For instance, what about this energy exchange? What are you hearing? Where is this information coming from? How is energy passing through a human being?

There is much LOVE here for you. Namaste

There is much for you to explore in your human existence if you wish it.

September 26th
Magic Forest

There are more of you stepping out of your comfort zone. More speaking their truth, even though they're afraid. Therefore, there are more of you being brave with your life. This is not easy to do as humans. It's not the norm. The norm is to settle for what's in front of you and keep your expectations low. That's the way most humans survive a lifetime.

More of you are questioning this survival. You think, "Perhaps we want to live a great big life, full of adventure, and magic!" So, we're stepping forward, even though we're afraid to see what happens. Because there are more of you doing it, it's becoming more normal to step forward in fear. Those who have been pondering it behind you, are stepping out a little bit. They're becoming curious. They think, "Maybe there's more to life than living a mediocre existence."

Those of you who are being brave, what sort of adventures are you getting into? What connection are you making with non-physical? What sort of new eyes have you developed to see a world full of LOVE? That's what happens when you step forward. Even though you're fearful, there's a great prize at the end. For you're transformed into a spiritual being whose living a human life full of LOVE.

Some of you know this already because you've been stepping forward so long, you just live there now. It's important for some of you to live there so others can see how it is. To see that there is a magical world that exists beyond their mundane existence. As much as you're having your own grand adventure, you're also being watched by those who have less hope than you.

There is much LOVE here for you.   Namaste

Stay where you are if you're in the magic forest. And if you're just stepping forward, keep coming. You'll reach the magic forest, too. There's plenty of LOVE in there for all.

September 27th
One by One

Humans often discuss their energetic connection to the Universe. Although they're unable to help one another find their own connection. The only thing you can really do is get your own connection with your source of energy.

When you get into connection with yours, just sit. You'll feel lighter. Your mind will be clearer. You'll feel LOVED and at ease in your world. Your body will also settle down because there's a physical reaction to this connection with energy. Your body relaxes because it doesn't need to protect you. It doesn't need to hide things from you. Your mind relaxes. You dissolve a little. You become one with the energy around you and it becomes one with you.

As you become blurred around the edges and LOVE enters from all sides, you become a happier human being. More fun. More alive. More interested in life.

Because you are blurry, LOVING, gentle and relaxed, others are drawn to you. When this happens, they're reminded of their own energetic force. That's how it works. By others watching you stay in alignment. It's has nothing to do with what you tell them.

When your face is relaxed and you're full of energy, you're never tired. So, they wonder, "What's going on with them?" All they have to do is see you, then they'll be reminded of their own connection.

As this happens more, you all become enlightened in an energetic way. When you have more humans walking around in LOVE, which is done when you are connected, your world changes. It's not done by forcing and talking. It's by being a source of LOVE one by one.

There is much LOVE here for you.   Namaste

You are healed one by one. LOVE is shared one by one. LOVE is remembered one by one.

September 28th
Laugh Out Loud

We are going to ask you to picture two large humans swinging a small human by their hands. The little one is swinging recklessly and laughing out loud. When the little one laughs out loud, the two large human beings laugh out loud, as well. Those passing by laugh out loud, too. The ones who hear them laugh out loud, as well. You come in with energy to share LOVE with others. You know how to do it. You smile, you laugh out loud, you send positive vibrations forward. They go from you to others. The small ones remember how to do it perfectly. The older ones need to spend time with the small ones to remember.

Older humans are completely capable of laughing so loud, it creates reverberations in your energy field. It goes forward and forward causing others to laugh. Your role in humanity is still the same. To share LOVE energy with others. It does not need to be done in some formal way. It can be done with singing, dancing, laughing or music. All of these things create more LOVE vibrations that go out and out and out. Until more and more humans are touched. You don't even know who they are. That's the way LOVE energy works. It vibrates outward and it keeps moving.

There's really no need for you to do much, other than laugh every chance you get. Sing and dance every chance you get. Surely that can't be too difficult of an assignment for you! The one who wanted to share LOVE with all the other humans you were coming to live with. That's what you wanted to do, so, go ahead and do it.

There is much LOVE here for you.   Namaste

Laugh every chance you get!

September 29th
Weavers of Life

Your life is woven with tiny strands. Wide pieces won't hold. When they're small, they're strong.

Those who weave their life with tiny perfect strands often have unfinished tapestries because they freeze in fear. They know they must get another strand but they're frozen holding onto this one piece.

This is the weaving together of a life. When you let go, it disappears. But that's what it's supposed to do. Perhaps the strand is not for your tapestry. Maybe it's for another and they've been waiting for you to let go so they may weave it into their tapestry. When you come to understand your tapestry will remain unfinished as long as you hold onto this strand, then you let it go.

Now there are many more strands to choose from. Start weaving your tapestry again with beautiful details and colours. The precision you use to weave your life together is important in one way but really not important in another. There are many of you taking life a little too seriously. Then there are others who keep your head down weaving and never look up.

There's much life around you. To build a perfect, woven life with no flaws is impossible. There will always be broken strands. Some are tied together with knots. Perhaps, the colours aren't exact but it's a life. A life is made up of broken, knotted strands and wrong colours.

In the end, it doesn't matter if you tie them together, hold on to them or don't finish your tapestry. It's all a life.

But if you wish to know what it's like to be free, that's different. Then you're yearning to have more connection with the Universe of LOVE. If you wish to discover this, put down your strings and sit in alignment. See what you can hear. For you must be quiet to hear the truth. When it sits inside of you and is easily absorbed, it's your truth.

If you want to be free, connect with the divine. Because then you won't be a slave to your tapestry. You can weave it or leave it.

There is much LOVE here for you.   Namaste

If you wish to be free, connect.

September 30th
Show Up

You show up to remember how magnificent you are. You want to hear more wonderful things about being an energetic being. You're showing the Universe you want to become more. To remember more. To evolve. To be of service to mankind.

There are certain times, for instance, during meditation when you're connecting with your energetic Source and must focus on yourself. That's not always easy for you but you try.

So, if you are precious no matter what you do or say, why is it you wish to evolve? Because you can. You have an idea there's more to you than you've uncovered so far. Your curious nature is wondering exactly what you've forgotten.

You're starting to remember that you're part of an energetic LOVE force. When you're in non-physical, it's complete LOVE. While in human, partly.

You are in your human body, which you have chosen, to have a human experience. Don't forget that. That means you are to sing, dance, run through leaves and puddles, stand in the rain and jump in the freezing cold water. That's your life.

Watch what you see with your eyes. The birds, sun, clouds and water. And you see beautiful humans. That's what it means to be human.

To be your energetic self, you have to be quiet and pay attention to what's going on, on another level beyond what you can see. It's important to close your eyes so you can feel and hear energy which is around you always. It's inside of you, also. It moves your organs and holds your memories.

There is much LOVE here for you.   Namaste

The most important thing to remember is that you are precious to the Universe and to mankind.

October

Every moment of human life is a blessing

Oct 1st
Your Name is Energy

There are humans who harness energy, bring it under control and focus it. You've wondered, "How is something invisible used to benefit humans?" Humans who've come to understand energy can enter into them and exit through the palms of their hands and the bottoms of their feet. Some have been playing with this for many generations. They are called energy workers.

Energy cannot be seen but it must be believed in order to work. Here you have a shaman and here you have a businessman. Both equally believing that energy passes through. Both benefit from it. But what is their relationship? They understand they're only a small part of the Universe and they're playing their part in humanity. One to provide human energy for money and the other to heal humans.

Energy is involved in everything you do. These two extremes have just become aware of it. They understand they're part of a grander scheme of using energy for humans. Some of you have not found your place in this yet.

There is energy around you this moment. Some of you can hear buzzing which is energy moving that turns into vibration. Sometimes you can feel it when your body becomes hot and cold. That's energy moving through you. When your mind changes quickly, you're opening to energy and information from the Universe. Your mind can read energy. Your ears can hear energy. Your body can feel energy. Yes, businessmen and shamans can both harness energy.

Wherever you find yourself, it's important for you to notice energy. Because you're energy.

The Universe and you are the same energy. Therefore, you're the Universe of LOVE. As you become one with the Universe, you become less physical and more energy. You'll feel it in your calm state of being.

There is much LOVE here for you.   Namaste

Today, why don't you see what you can notice about energy? You're an energetic being living in an energetic world coming from an energetic Universe of LOVE. Your name is Energy.

October 2nd
Easy

This is a retraining of the mind so it learns to move aside for new information. Mostly, your mind has filtered through information to decide whether or not it could enter into the energetic space of LOVE that resides within you. Your brain knows nothing of LOVE so it's not the best guidepost. Nonetheless, it's the guard for this information. Through gentle repetition, your inner self may eventually absorb the information directly and easily.

There are some who believe they might be gentle and LOVING. They're drawn to humans who make it part of their daily life, like you. When you relax into a vibration of LOVE, you are more gentle and easy. You're more LOVING toward yourself and others. As this happens, more humans watch. They know there's a part of them that wishes to be softer but they're afraid of it.

It's a new idea not to let your brain run your life. But there's a whole other sect of humans that live by their heart. Who exist with their connection to others. You can see it. Their eyes are brighter. They smile more easily. They dance quickly. They attract others like them.

You are doing the same thing energetically. You don't have to take your body anywhere. You just start to believe you're LOVING energy and that you're precious to the Universe. As you start to believe it, you change a little. Your edges are less harsh. You evolve into the Universe. LOVE energy changes you.

You came in loose but you became hard-edged because of your time in humanity. So, this is a remembering. It's going back where you started. To a LOVING, caring space with softer edges so you LOVE more easily.

You will feel as if you're living more. You will laugh and smile easily. You will dance and sing because music is the vibration of LOVE. It's easy if you just let it happen. It's your natural, LOVING state to have your edges a little less harsh.

There is much LOVE here for you.   Namaste

When new energy enters the space where others are gathered, it must be absorbed into the family of LOVE.

October 3rd
Magnets of LOVE

You have intense emotional relationships that are uplifting and energizing. It's a familiar and easy connection. Then there are other times when you come together and it's difficult. Sometimes with the same human. How is this? Isn't the Universe of LOVE consistently easy, LOVING and carefree? Of course, it is but humans are not. You come in and out of alignment every moment.

If you are both in alignment and you come together, it will be easy, fun and carefree. If you're not, it will be almost impossible to connect. There will be so much distance, you won't be able to reach one another. So, what do you do? You stay in your own space. Do your own thing. Sometimes connections come together easily and sometimes they don't. This is not the point. The point is whether or not you stay in your alignment. Whether you stay connected to the Universe no matter what's going on around you.

Part of the understanding is that things change around you every moment. Humans come. Humans go. Your alignment comes. Your alignment goes. Everything is changing. For you, the only thing you're capable of affecting is whether or not you're in alignment. But how do you stay in alignment no matter what? When you get a certain connection to the Universe of LOVE, you'll understand. Feelings of peace and ease will be evoked. You'll remain happy and contented. It will become usual for you to stay in this place.

When you stay in it a lot, you'll notice when you're not. Then you'll yearn for it. You'll say, "Something's wrong with me." It's because you're off balance. You miss your happy place. The place you come back to. Once this becomes your marker, you'll know when you're off. Others around you will notice when you're off vibrationally. They'll avoid you. When you're in alignment, you'll connect with others easily. You stay in this alignment by being connected to the Universe of LOVE, nature and the things around you that are consistently about LOVE. They don't change at all.

There is much LOVE here for you. Namaste

You are a magnet for energy. If you are angry, you attract angry people. If you are happy, you attract happy people.

October 4th
Carry On

These words are one way you're being reached but it's not the only way. You're being reached when you let your resistance down while you sleep. That is a wonderful opportunity for the Universe of LOVE to spend some time alone with you. You're open to receive LOVE then. There are also times when you're in a desperate state or a negative, sad place. Then you allow energy of LOVE to come in a lot.

Then there are times when you're in a LOVING relationship with another and much energy flows through you. It often takes two extreme emotions for you to acknowledge or allow the Universe of LOVE energy to flow through you. When you're in a desperate state or an excited state, you have much space for outside energy to enter.

It's the job of the Universe of LOVE to respond to human calls for assistance, support, LOVE and encouragement. You get it all of the time but sometimes you can't quite hear it. As if your ears are blocked.

Most ask," Am I worthy? What am I doing here? Have I lost my way? What's next for me?" Here are your answers. "Are you valued?" "You are of the highest value." "Can we hear you?" "Obviously. Here we are." "What next for us?" "It doesn't matter. Whatever you stumble upon next or walk directly to because you feel guided to. Everything will work out for you."

What do you think of that? You can't make a wrong move. There's no need for you to be frozen and waiting for more information. Take a step forward. You will be supported in whatever way that is. Take another step forward. You'll be supported again. You're doing the best you can.

Some of you can see and feel energy. It's like you're cheating because you can see around the corner. You're following the energetic footprint. You can see where true happiness and joy lay. Someday you'll be a cheater, too. Then you'll be following a trail that led you from one happy, joyous event to the next. That will be when your ego has stepped aside.

There is much LOVE here for you.   Namaste

You're doing the best way you can right now. So, carry on.

October 5th
Finger Pointers

There is only a small amount of work to be done by you. You've done much of the evolving in your spiritual, non-physical time. Each human being is living up to their best potential. You are doing the best you can.

There is a certain human part of you that wishes to judge the progress of one another. It's difficult for you to do this while being human. In non-physical, you would all be exactly the same.

You spend a lot of your time judging behaviour and thought patterns. It creates distance between you and others. When you come from a place of judging, it's actually a place of hurt. Then your ego takes hold of the hurt and turns it into revenge or some other nastiness. Your ego turns small things into huge things. Then there are repercussions. Although it's the human way, it makes your life more difficult.

This is not your highest nature. Your true calling is allowing LOVE to flow into you and out of you. Therefore, touching others. This is who you truly wish to be. You are valuable, important and precious. Each moment you spend in LOVE is a moment spent in peace and contentedness. You feel at ease with your body, your life and your surroundings.

You know when you're off balance. You feel uncomfortable. Part of you knows you are able to achieve complete alignment with your Source. In this place, there's no room for ego, anger or sadness. It's a peaceful, gentle place where you feel relaxed and one.

Then, when you enter into a conversation, you'll be coming from a LOVING, balanced place and the conversation will go much easier.

Maybe you can spend time sitting quietly. Listening to the birds or the raindrops. Sitting and waiting for a thought to go by. Straining with your ear to hear more.

There is much LOVE here for you.   Namaste

See if you can hear the Universe whispering in your ear that you're much LOVED. That you're precious. That you're needed. That you're valuable. It's always whispering even if you can't hear it.

October 6th
Skinned Knees

When you were learning to walk, you tripped over rocks, shoes and flooring. You tripped because you weren't watching where you were going. You were looking at fascinating things. You walked in trust and faith. You enjoyed the moment. That's why you skinned your knees so much.

You don't have skinned knees anymore, do you? You're not fascinated by small things any longer. You're not mesmerized by a beautiful butterfly now. For you, it seems those days of wonderment have passed. The days of sheer joy.

Do you suppose it can happen again for someone like you? Do you suppose you can stop and stare at a beautiful flower? Can you forget where it was you were supposed to go and when you were to arrive? Do you suppose at your time in life, you're able to enjoy small things? There are times in humanity when you're busy making money, building a house and getting a vehicle. There's no time to enjoy beauty.

Perhaps now is your time to enjoy the beauty around you. Maybe that's why you found your way to this moment.

It takes a moment to remember what it was like to concentrate so hard, memorizing each line and dot on a butterfly wing. You memorized colours and smells. You knew that time would never happen again. You got every moment of enjoyment. You were wise little things, weren't you? You knew the moment itself was the most precious and important thing.

You're still the same wise one. You've just forgotten. When you're walking and breathing, notice the grass, the flower, the butterfly, the clouds and the stars. Notice the smell of the grass or a flower. Watch the little lines on a bee. Nothing has changed.

Now you may come back to this place of beauty, innocence and pure joy. Where you may focus on what's important. Focus so much that you lose your balance and trip. It will be worth it for you to be thrown off balance for a moment.

There is much LOVE here for you.   Namaste

There is the same beauty and LOVE about you at this moment as there was when you were a small one staring at the little bumblebee.

October 7th
Tree People

There comes a time in your life when you stop complete movement. Just for a moment. Perhaps it's when you notice you can stand still. Much of your life is spent being pushed and pulled. But at this moment, it's possible for you to stop and stand. Just to be. You can stand in direct alignment like this energetically. What a strange notion.

Some practice this in a form of standing meditation. Like a tree. You're thinking, "I could try that. Just for a moment." You can feel a certain weight drop when you just stand there. There's a flow and ease. You can let out a big breath you've been holding for a long time. When you become tree-like, everything seems a little easier even though your life hasn't changed.

Getting into this direct alignment allows you to flow and navigate easily through your life. It seems odd that a frame of mind, just being one with the Universe, can change the way you feel about life. It's just a feeling you have that life's easier now. More comfortable. You feel energetically grounded and attached to something larger than you. Therefore, what is there to worry about?

If you've got a certain attachment, you can relax because now the burden is shared. You don't have to do it by yourself by making your own decisions. Now you can be easier with your life. Already your heart slows down and your breathing becomes more complete.

Now as you stand like a tree, connected to the Universe and to Mother Earth, your feet are in the soft dirt. It removes the negative energy lodged in certain organs. You're connected to all information. You realize things change in a moment so, why get flustered. In a moment it's all over.

You realize, "These trees relaxed me while I looked at them. They bend and sway no matter what. They're so at ease. I have much to learn from their ability to stay in earth and sky at the same moment."

There is much LOVE here for you.   Namaste

Visualize standing like a tree. Your life will be easier this way. Try to stay grounded and attached to the Universe.

October 8th
Grab A New Thought

As much as you feel there's only you, you're actually a group. You don't travel alone. You all have a non-physical support team but there's also a group of like-minded humans. Sometimes, you don't know one another. But you are in a similar vibration. You have similar thoughts and emotional reaction to things.

You are not all gathered at this moment because this vibration continues forward for all of eternity. Others can get in line at different times. Yet it's still you. Time has a different concept when you're not living in your singular, human thinking. This moment is not only here. It carries on and on. Forwards and backwards, all through time. This moment is eternal.

There is a certain time zone you are in. Even though you feel it's your lunchtime, others are sleeping. Here's a fine example of time being unquantifiable by humans. You pretend it is. You think, "I'm eating lunch so all are eating lunch." It's easier that way. If you expand a bit and say, "I'm eating lunch but others are sleeping and waking up." You've expanded. Now if you can go one step further to say, "Time goes forward and back. This moment may be recreated in time by someone's memory or someone stumbling across this vibration."

You can stumble across these vibrations. You feel like you've hit something. You say, "What was that?" If you stop for a moment and feel it, you'll realize it's a sort of memory. Some of you can see things that haven't happened yet. In actual fact, that's the true nature of time. It can hit you forward and back.

Now you may practice this by giving up the sense of firm knowing. You become more flexible. You think, "Perhaps I don't know everything." It's the first vital step to information from the Universe of LOVE.

Can you make time go forward and back consciously? As you think this, it's being recreated energetically. It's how this conversation will be going forward and back through time. It's an energetic thought. It's now floating free for anyone to grab.

There is much LOVE here for you. Namaste

Just reach out and grab a new thought today. They're all around you.

October 9th
LOVE is of the Essence

'Time is of the essence', 'time doesn't stand still' and 'time waits for no man' are references that place pressure on humans to complete tasks. 'Time is not your friend' reminds you to stay one step ahead of something about to envelope you.

But what if you were to become friends with time? What if you were to become time? What if you enveloped yourself in it and travelled together? Time doesn't actually exist. It's an energetic realm. You are energy travelling through eternity. You never know when to get on and off because time is irrelevant to you.

You are time travellers who came into bodies. You come. You leave. You don't really know what stage you're at in development. You evolve and learn. You spend time in humanity. You learn how to live more fully. This is human evolution. You allow LOVE in. You allow LOVE out. You become less human and more energy. Therefore, you're more LOVE, which is the evolution.

You're being stimulated as a group to evolve. This is a communication more than a learning. You're evolving into one. You are one with the Universe. Therefore, you're all one. It's all energy. Time folds nicely into this. Time, LOVE and evolution are all the same thing because there is no time. You try to grasp onto time so your life is in control. Time comes and goes. You come and go.

That's why time is not of the essence. LOVE is of the essence. Being your highest, LOVING self and allowing LOVE to flow into you and out of you, is your highest calling. Not time. Time is your focus but it's not your highest calling.

There is much LOVE here for you.   Namaste

When you are being your LOVING self, you'll feel at peace. You'll feel one with the Universe, your environment, other humans and creatures. Suddenly, you'll feel lighter. Less confined in your body. A little more part of your surroundings, non-physical and physical.

October 10th
Am I LOVED?

You can take more responsibility for your non-physical life, spiritual life and energetic life. Although it's easy to get caught up in what you see and have learned from others. There's more going on. It's true you came into being to have a physical experience but you also came to allow LOVE to flow into you and out of you.

The only way for you to allow LOVE to flow through you, for you to sing, dance and have fun, is to remember your vibrational LOVING self. It's the connection you have with other humans' soul to soul.

So now you must incorporate your energetic, spiritual self with your physical. There's some reason why you're not easy and peaceful at all times. You understand there's something you've forgotten. So, you ask.

You say, "What do I wish to be? What do I wish to remember?" The answer remains. You are energetic beings. You've come to spend a small amount of time in a body to have the physical experience. To see if you can maintain unconditional LOVE.

You also wish to remember you're prized by the Universe. Until you recall this, you're not getting all the energy and support there is. There's much LOVE for you. From non-physical, and the energy of LOVE. You are precious as you are. LOVE surrounds you completely. You just get lost sometimes and forget. When you feel it energetically you know it's true.

You may tap into LOVE energy any time. Just centre yourself and sit quietly. Then ask, "Am I LOVED?" Then listen for the answer, "You are much LOVED". Feel this until there's no part of you that resists. Remember you're a spiritual being first.

There is much LOVE here for you. Namaste

You're one with energy. It's not new to you. You need not fear it. It's a part of you. You are LOVE.

October 11th
High & Clear

There comes a time in your human evolution when you start to wonder if you've done a good job. You feel like your time is ending soon.

You wonder, "Am I good? Am I bad? Have I done everything?" You wonder about your eternal life and think, "There's more to me than this small story."

This leads you directly to energy from non-physical. You are seekers. Part of you yearns for more than physical goodies.

This is a searching for soul quenching. You're thirsty for more. This opens the door to the Universe because it's just waiting for you to ask. As you learn to be comfortable being quiet and listening to the Universal energy.

There's a higher, clearer level that you're all programmed to hear because you're all part of this vibration of energy. This high note. You've been living in it through all eternity. As soon as you hear it, you remember it. The setting realigns you to a higher, clearer vibration. It might take you little while because you've gotten used to low vibration, like horns and machinery.

There is much LOVE here for you. Namaste

See if you can start to hear the higher vibrations that exist. You have been a part of it and will be a part of it again.

October 12th
Easy Times

There are times that you become more sensitive to energy and non-physical beings. There's a category you have for people who are sensitive to other worldly things, but you're all the same. It's just whether you will allow it. You are familiar with it because you're in this energy when you're not in physical.

Then why can't everyone hear what's going on in the Universe? It's because you're focusing on your human life and that's what you came to do.

Depending on where you are in your human life, you might have space to allow a larger truth. If your life is full of human business, you don't have space for this thoughtful, quiet connection to the Universe.

Now you're wondering," Am I living my life fully as a human or am I allowing enough space for the unknown?" There are no wrong answers to this.

But if you have space, spend some time listening to what the Universe and your non-physical friends have to tell you. Sit down and have some quiet time.

Some of you are intrigued by non-physical. You've had enough physical life now and you wish to remember a faster, higher vibration.

There is much LOVE here for you.   Namaste

When you're sitting quietly, you'll start to recall, "It's a peaceful, easy vibration. I can slow down. It's easy to be in this alignment. It's easy to be me. It's familiar. I'm so relaxed in this vibration. When I surrender to it, we become one. My soul yearns for my energetic family.

October 13th
Turtles

There is a tale about a race between a rabbit and a turtle. Everyone knows the rabbit's going to win. He's faster and smarter. The turtle is slower and thoughtful.

You're smart, aren't you? You must rely on your brain so in order for this tale to make sense, the rabbit must win. It's important for your brain to know this.

What if the thoughtful turtle wins? There's a softer, secret part of you that can believe this. A gentle, connected part of you understands that ego always trips you up. You understand what it's like to be consistently connected, meditative and quiet in the Universe of LOVE. Just waiting for something to unfold.

The long-loved part of you called LOVE energy that exists through eternity knows about waiting for things to unfold. It knows about trusting the Universe of LOVE because things always turn out when you wait. It knows about showing up each time you meditate or pray.

The more time you spend in this realm being thoughtful, quiet and gentle, the more you become like this turtle. He doesn't care if he wins or loses. He has no ego attached. He's gentle and puts one foot in front of the other. He walks in hope and faith that the Universe cares for him.

Be like the turtle. Quiet, reflective and confident that you're connected to the Universe of LOVE. Leave the ego behind. It doesn't do you any favours. It just keeps you out of the Universe of LOVE and in the philosophical brain. But it doesn't really matter because you're going to pass through this life in no time.

.

There is much LOVE here for you.   Namaste

There's a gentle, connected part of you that understands that ego will always trip you up.

October 14th
Is There Anything to Fear?

You're interested in passing from physical to non-physical usually happens as you get closer to the end of your human time. You wonder, "Where am I going? What will it be like?" It can create anxiety and fear although you already know. Sit and connect with the Universe the best way you can. Then you may hear the answers you seek.

You're energy. That's how you move your body. The Universe is also energy. What you see and feel, are things created by humans. The energy in these man-made items is low. They exist only as a convenience to you. So, you spend most of your time with things that have low or no energy.

As you spend time with humans, there are varying degrees of energy. Some of you are conscious of energy but others are not.

Human energy and the Universe of LOVE energy is the same. It's all LOVING, kind, and caring energy. It wishes to laugh and have fun. It's excited, contented, happy and joyous. This is your natural state of being because you're the energy of the Universe. Some of you allow it to float through you and out of you.

When you've completed your time with your physical body, you become what you already are. LOVE energy. You melt in with the other LOVE energy that exists around you.

You may feel energy as you move your hands from farther out toward yourself. It's denser closer to your body. So, you can feel your LOVE energy outside your body. You're already halfway into non-physical. Now it's a smaller step to move into non-physical.

There is much LOVE here for you.   Namaste

You're already LOVE energy. Inside and out.

October 15th
Dreamers

You often look at the clouds, sun, moon and stars. You spend a lot of time looking up. Is it natural for humans to look up to what they cannot possibly touch?

You're great imaginers. That's how all great things have been created. You imagine it and it becomes so.

You're looking up there to dream. To wonder. To relax. You can't manage it. It just is.

This dreamer part of you is comfortable with hoping and knowing all is well. You know the sky you look at is the same for all. No matter what your financial status or race. You're all equal at that moment. Does it seem familiar that you're more than what you appear? That you're as large as the Universe?

When you look, you're not fearful or intimidated. You embrace it. You LOVE it. It's because you're familiar with it. Because you're beautiful and precious. One as wondrous as the next.

Looking up to the sky is remembering what it's like to be one with the others in the great Universe of LOVE. Where you're part of something larger. A beautiful, LOVING family of energy. You remember," I'll be back to join all the other stars in the sky soon." You're just here momentarily.

You're remembering your connection with LOVE energy. Sometimes you long for it. But remember, you're there to have a human time. So, enjoy yourself.

There is much LOVE here for you.   Namaste

Look up at the stars you dreamers and remember you're part of the great Universe of LOVE.

October 16th
4 Steps

It's like you're a triangle. No matter where you turn it, it's always the same. No matter what way you look at it, your life is of your making. That's the truth of it.

There is great resistance even if your insides know it's true. Your mind wishes to say, "NO! That's not me." It's a defence mechanism. The sooner you're able to bypass this defence mechanism and believe truth, the easier your life will be. Then you'll be working with your knowledge of Universal information.

Practice with small notions first. Like your job. You can say, "Yes, I chose it." Once you become easier accepting truth, your body will feel reassured that you're listening to it. Then you'll be more open to receive the bigger Real Truths.

There is great knowledge available to you but you get stuck in small human things because you're afraid of the Larger Truths of Life. The lower vibration and being a victim is not your truest, biggest self.

Your truest self is being part of the Universe of LOVE because you're energetic LOVE. You're not a victim. You're not vulnerable. You're huge. You've come into human form to allow LOVING energy to pass into you and out of you.

But first, you must accept truth when your body acknowledges it. Even if you don't like it. As soon as you acknowledge a truth, it's gone. All the energy you used trying to keep it hidden is unnecessary.

If your body reacts when you hear something true, just say, "Alright, that might be true. Yes, that's true. It's not very nice. I feel sad with the truth." Follow it to its completion.

Energy can move you in this way. So, allow the process to complete. Then you'll be lighter, freer and more open.

There is much LOVE here for you.   Namaste

Say, "It might be true" then "Yes, it's true." "That doesn't feel very good" and then, "I feel sad knowing that's true." 4 steps to freedom. 4 steps to becoming more in tune with the Universe of LOVE.

October 17th
Heart Team

Sometimes you wish to interact with others who are a similar vibration. You long to feel part of a group and be understood, because you've come from the Universe of LOVE, which is a collective of energetic LOVE. You'll always have a part with you as a reminder that you exist through eternity.

When you come into physical, you've left your group behind. So, there's a sense of disconnect and longing. Until you're joined back together, you're going to feel a bit uneasy. You understand that you don't have all of the information you have when you're in the collective of LOVE.

So, you often miss your family of LOVE and you spend time looking for others there. This happens, whether you're aware of it or not. You have an energetic vibration that looks for others like you. When you spot someone like you, they go directly into your heart and you are joined together. This is called Namaste. You greet one another, "My soul sees your soul and greets it. Now we are one."

It's like you are accumulating heart connections all the time. They become your human support team. This is your human Universe of LOVE. It's important to realize you're not alone.

Things can be said between two humans who care for one another heart to heart because you have an agreement to speak the truth and receive it. You can be heard. Also, you can hear. Recalling this puts you at ease because it reminds you of the Universe of LOVE where everything is done in LOVE. It's a LOVE stimulation.

You're at ease and your heart is full just by picturing the faces of your human LOVE team. You're meant to live there with heart to heart connections. Picture your heart team when you feel disconnected, sad or lonely.

There is much LOVE here for you.   Namaste

You've come from the Universe of LOVE, which is a collective of energetic LOVE.

October 18th
Gliding

You are reluctant to change. It's like you've figured out enough about life. Although hesitantly, you may think, "Perhaps I can change a little in this one area." You don't want to think you may have done things improperly.

You want to settle in and glide through the rest of your time. If you understood how enthusiastic you were coming into physical, you wouldn't say this. You're in physical to learn, grow, experience things, have fun, laugh, dance and feel extreme emotions. So, why are you afraid to change?

Because there comes a time when you're tired of the emotional ups and downs. These are the times you're actually doing things on your own.

When you are connected with the Universe, other humans in the same vibration and non-physical, you're not tired. You're energized because you're part of a whole energetic group. When one of you is down, the others are up. It balances it off because you're all sharing the one emotion.

When you want to glide through life, you've removed yourself from the group. You've decided on your own, with only your human knowledge, that you know what's best. You are thinking removing yourself from the group is best for you.

As a group, no-one would say, "Why don't we just stop living? Why don't we stop feeling extreme emotions? Why don't we stop singing and dancing?" Perhaps one would say this. Then the rest would revive them.

It's important for you to be part of this energetic group. You don't wish to glide through life alone because you miss out on the vast knowledge of the Universe of LOVE. When you realize this, you'll stay part of the group more often. You'll think, "I wonder if I'm by myself again."

There is much LOVE here for you. Namaste

If you wish to experience a full life, stay with the group.

October 19th
Middle of the Road

You come into physical with a certain amount of unconditional LOVE, knowing and connection with energy.

At the beginning, you crawl along slowly. There are no real worries. Everything goes at its own pace. You're not concerned because you've just come from a place of great LOVE, understanding and easy unfolding. You're pretty chill when you arrive.

Then you spend time with adults that think everything's a big deal. At first you think they're weirdos because everything unfolds as it's supposed to. Soon, it's like you're the only one who thinks that way. You begin to wonder, "Maybe I'm the weirdo, not them."

After enough time, you start to think things are tragic and getting worse. Then your energy changes. Now you're on this path.

Still some of you say, "Chill out." Others say, "You don't understand. It's a tragedy." These two humans cannot co-exist because you each must decide what's true. Otherwise, you'll be arguing all the time.

Now this path veers off in two directions. You each take one. You don't hear each other so it's better. Now you're with others like you. Now there's peace. "You stay on your side. We'll stay on ours."

As you sit with like-minded beings, you start to wonder, "Is there more to life? Am I missing something?" This happens naturally. The only way to find out is to look at the others and examine them once more. This beautiful wondering brings you to a place of LOVE and connection.

Somewhere in the middle, the meeting place, there's empathy and open heartedness. The connection to the Universe exists from human to human. While you're in human, there will come a point when it doesn't matter what you act like because you're connected human to human, soul to soul. So it doesn't really matter if you live on this side or that side. It turns out you're all one.

There is much LOVE here for you.   Namaste

The middle road is where the curious wander over and say, "I don't really understand what you're saying but I do appreciate you being in human."

October 20th
Fulfilled

Does a fulfilling life have a lot of pressure on it? How would you know if you were living a fulfilling life? The true understanding is not known to you because you know only of your time on earth. If you were to understand the larger existence of you, which is LOVE energy that exists through all time, then you would be able to decide if you are living a fulfilling life now.

If you were able to consider it against all eternity, then you would all say yes. "Yes, my life is fulfilling because I'm in human form and I'm moving forward step by step instead of staying in LOVE energy like the rest." That's why you have support from non-physical.

Fulfilling is not the best word because it has an agenda attached to it. Either it's fulfilling or it's not. Therefore, you're all passing. Each of you is having a human experience not to be judged.

Life is about looking around. "Is there anything dangerous? Interesting? Can I dance or laugh? Is there something breathtaking to notice?" This is your human adventure when you have a physical body.

When you don't have a physical body, you're all at peace. It's easy. You feel LOVE and you support humans. What you want in your human existence is something different. So, what is it you want that's different from peace and LOVE all the time? You want excitement and challenge. To see how a body works.

You already know how heart energy works. You're specialists in LOVE energy. You know what it's like to connect to others and to communicate with non-physical. Although sometimes you forget because you're busy with the physical stuff.

You understand human existence is for a short time. You wonder, "What can this body and mind do? What fun can I have? What trouble can I get into? How long can I stay alone?"

There is much LOVE here for you.   Namaste

A fulfilling life is getting in the middle of it. Good or bad. So, that means you're all living a fulfilling human life.

October 21st
Evolve Yourself

There are many of you who must stand out. Although, most move around in packs where it's safer. You're understood. The rules are the same. But there are those of you who can't stand being part of the flock. So, you have pulled yourself away or have been removed.

    The pack you belonged to is called 'survival only'. They are a lower vibration. They're more fearful, so they stick together. They think there's safety in numbers.

    You pulled yourself apart because you understood you're always safe when you're connected. You know there's a Universe of energy around you, whether you're in a pack or not.

    As you stand alone, you may feel lonely and confused. This is your time to evolve and connect. You're going to get a great deal of information from the Universe, the Greater Good or the Higher Consciousness.

    In order to hear the answers, you must sit in alignment. This means you must still your anxiety, fear and sadness. When these emotions are active, your vibration is kept low. You cannot hear the truth, which is high and clear. In order for you to still the sadness and anger, there must be a loosening of your evolved self from your physical self. These emotions are with your physical being only. They keep you low but they're important because they keep you in your body. But the questions you're asking are from the Universe.

    Now, you must be both, by sitting in your body and calming it down. "Alright, everything is fine. We are cared for and nurtured. We can relax." Your body responds quietly and settles down. Now you may have higher vibrational conversations. But you still need your body to hear because you're having a human experience.

    Now ask your question with no anxiety attached. "What am I doing here?" "Living."" Am I alone?" "You're surrounded by LOVE energy."

There is much LOVE here for you.   Namaste

You're capable of having conversations with the Universe of LOVE anytime. When you give and receive at a vibrational level, you'll hear because you've quieted the rest of your body.

October 22nd
Take Care of Your Own Business

You often take on heartfelt energy of others. As if you're helping them by saying, "Give me your negative energy. I'll hold it so you can go about your day." Unfortunately, they still keep it. So, now there are two burdened humans instead of one.

Many are drawn to help others in this energetic way. You think you're doing them a favour removing their pain. It sounds logical to remove pain then the thing is healed. As if emotional issues were a broken leg.

Humans wish to help others heal quickly. "Don't feel that. I'll take it. Don't feel that." This implies pain is bad and people can't handle it on their own. This implies they're childlike. When children are in pain, they cry. As you get older you say, "I'm not supposed to cry."

The other part is human. When you're in pain, you call out for help to something outside yourself. You're drawn to ask for help outside yourself. You don't say, "Human over there, will you take this away from me then go away?" No, you sit in it. You cry in it. You cover yourself in it.

You revel in emotions good and bad. Then you reach out for help to the Universe of LOVE. This can be found in different ways. There are humans who take LOVING, healing energy from the Universe and transform it into music, writing and drawing.

When it's you, you revel in your pain or happiness but when it's someone else, you think you can take it away from them. Pain is energy. It gets things moving in you. A bout of anger, sadness, joy or happiness will get the energy moving. Then you're not stuck. The worst thing is to be stuck because then you're missing out on your human time. You LOVE them all because they mean you're in a human body.

You said, "I want to have some fun and excitement. I want to feel feelings." Start to think, "This is really juicy anger or sadness." It's all emotional healing energy. It's got to move through you.

There is much LOVE here for you.   Namaste

Just take care of your own business and revel in your own emotions. Allow others to do the same.

October 23rd
What Is My Purpose?

There are times when you wonder what your purpose is. There's a lot of pressure to find out even though you don't know where to look for the answer. The truth is, you can't really find your purpose because you're living it.

Your purpose is to have a human experience and try to remember something of your spiritual existence before. But that doesn't seem complicated enough for you. You prefer to activate your brain and solve impossible puzzles like this one.

If you can understand you were in non-physical a moment ago and you're going to be in non-physical again in a few moments, then you'll understand your purpose is to have a physical experience of some sort. To laugh, dance, sing or cry. Meet other humans. Test some theories out.

If you look at yourself in the realm of eternity, you can say, "My purpose was to live in humanity and try to live it up if possible."

If you're only looking at your tiny lifetime right now and trying to find a purpose, it's difficult. For some of you, laughing, dancing and singing is pushing your experience to the edge. Mostly because you've had sad, angry times in the beginning. You want your life to be balanced with both.

There are also those who start from the beginning laughing, dancing & singing. They do it all throughout their lifetime. That's fine, too. You're all having a human experience.

You also try to remember your connection with non-physical. When you came into physical, you said to the Universe, "I want to remember LOVE, joy, peace and my non-physical support team. Will you remind me now and again? Because I might lose my way."

When you're in non-physical, you can see what's going on before you jump down. You see that humans go in with the intention to remember but they've all forgotten.

There is much LOVE here for you.   Namaste

You're more than your physical experience. You're eternal beings.
You're connected to non-physical and the Universe of LOVE always.
Your purpose in life is to live and try to remember this.

October 24th
I Wish to Transmit LOVE

At the very beginning of your human existence, you had great curiosity. You absorbed all the information around you. Today you watch small ones because their vibration is high. They're not as tightly woven as you. You're looking because you wish to remember what it was like to be curious about your surroundings and full of LOVE, hope and peace.

You had no worries then. You were coming from a gentle, LOVING, caring place. You chose to come into human but you wished it to be a gentle time at first.

Your developing time inside your host mother was for you to decide if you could go forward. It's scary to go from non-physical LOVE energy into a body.

Many of you get excited before you hop in. You say, "I want to go because I want to be a transmitter of LOVE!" All of you wish to volunteer to come forward and share LOVE with the others. It might seem too basic for you but somewhere deep inside, you know this is true.

It was you that chose to finish the birth process and become physical. The deal was that you have a little time to reconsider while inside. Many of you don't really finish it because it's scarier than you thought. But the next time you'll stay.

But you've all decided to stay in humanity even though you had an option to leave. Take a moment to consider this. Then come forward to your life right now. You've decided to stay many times since then, haven't you?

There is much LOVE here for you.   Namaste

"I wish to transmit LOVE. I wish to stay."

October 25th
Beautiful Surprises

There are events in your life that make you wonder, "What's the true meaning of this?" Your natural investigative mind wishes to understand. So, you spend a lot of time overthinking things. In the end, it's still not clear what the benefit is to you.

During this time, you're not sitting in yourself. You're not sitting in alignment, so you feel no peace. You think, "If I sort through this problem, I'll feel alright about it." This is incorrect because you'll still feel what you feel.

Your feelings are pointing something out to you. They are saying, "Would you look at this feeling?" Sorting something out is sometimes easier for you than feeling.

What about analyzing yourself? But once you get going underneath it, you're spending all your time this way. This is healthy for a short time only. A bit of self-reflection is fine. For instance, noticing yourself doing things you dislike. But delving any deeper is distracting you from true healing. Healing occurs during your connection with the Universe by letting go.

Part of the reason you stay in this analysis so long is because you wish to control something. That includes people, places and yourself. You desire control because you can't trust the Universe. You can't trust life to unfold. You can't trust the puzzle pieces to fall into place. You can't trust yourself to follow the little thread of LOVE.

Deep analysis means you're trying to get some control over something that you have no real control over. When you're not trusting that the next step will be a happy one, you pull back. Your fear of life unfolding has to do with your experiences with humans.

Everything in the non-physical world unfolds beautifully. You are pleasantly surprised by the outcome of things you keep your hands off. The times you allow it to unfold.

There is much LOVE here for you.   Namaste

Remember the times when you let go and allowed things to unfold? What a beautiful surprise you got in the end.

October 26th
Come & Join Us

Often you think you're going around in circles. Sometimes you wonder what else there is. Of course, you're not the only one. Humans get stuck on their paths because they're comfortable. It feels at peace having a predictable life. You don't get anxious, angry or sad. So, why not stay on it?

Why do some hate these circular paths while others LOVE them? The answer is fear, of course. What else is there? Fear surrounds those who walk in circles through their lives.

Truly, it doesn't matter what you do because fear will be with you deep inside. Now it will be uncomfortable for you to walk in circles. Fear keeps you in the circle but now fear will be in the circle, too.

Now, when you first step outside the circle, in fear of course, because it's all you know. You're going to find out you're not alone. You just thought you were alone because you were in fear and you cut yourself off from outside energy. Both non-physical and physical.

When you step onto unfamiliar grass, you're letting go. Then something's going to catch you. You know it's true. You'll be held until you're able to walk upright alone. Until you walk with those who know the Universe of LOVE is a LOVING, caring place.

When you get to this place, you don't fear anything because you're the Universe of LOVE. Now you can walk with your head straight up.

There is much LOVE here for you.   Namaste

Take a peek behind you to see if others are staggering behind you. They might need your eye contact. Turn around and tell them, "Keep coming. You're on the right track. Come and join us."

October 27th
Reunion with Self

There will come a moment when you look into a mirror and suddenly see your truest, highest self. You're looking into the eyes of your soul.

There comes a time when the exterior you is almost unrecognizable but when you look into the eyes, you remember. "You and I have been together a long time. Just look what we've been through." It's a time of allowing your true, inner, LOVING soul self to come out for a moment and be seen. It wishes for you to acknowledge it.

You get caught up in your human life and your soul life gets put aside. It didn't start off that way but there was a time when you said, "Just stand over there for a moment, soul. I'll be right back." Much time has passed and you never did get right back. It wasn't intentional. It just happened day by human day.

Now it's time to get to the mirror and get things straight. It's time for you to say to yourself, "Hello. I've left you for a time. I'm sorry about that. I was busy but here I am now. What will we do, soul?"

You hear, "Now we're going to laugh and dance and sing. Just like when we were small ones. We'd hold hands and dance around. Even if we were alone. We were always humming or singing, too."

It's time for your reunion with self. There will be no hard feelings because it's a spiritual energy. It doesn't have any ego. It just rejoices in each moment. So, it's time to rejoice now that you've been reunited.

There is much LOVE here for you.   Namaste

'Hello spiritual self. I've missed you. It's been a long time but now we've got beautiful places to see and LOVING humans to laugh with. We've got music to hear and dance to.''

October 28th
Long Forgotten

This is a time of your life when you wish to be with others. You feel worried and lonely. You're worried about intimate connections with other humans' soul to soul. Once you become familiar with your own inner self, you'll come to understand it's a vulnerable place for you. This vulnerability creates anxiety about connecting with others in this way. Part of you knows you cannot connect completely because it's very intimate. It's a pure, LOVING, accepting place that resides inside each of you.

It's important for you to feel connected to others who feel like you. Those with an open-hearted connection to the Universe. This is something different. Meeting together is recreating and reaffirming what it's like when you're in non-physical.

This deep part of you creates longing for more connection than can be met by humans. The more intimate you get with yourself and the more LOVING and open you become, the more longing there is to find others like you. Not all of you will understand this deep loneliness. The deepest longing is held for the Universe of LOVE. So, there is a deep longing that must reside in you all your days. You might need to sit with that for a moment.

There's also a deep longing inside of you for your non-physical brothers and sisters. This will be alleviated when you begin staying in contact with and receiving messages from them.

While you're in human form, you assume that all human needs can be met within the human realm. This one cannot. There's a lighter longing, which is oneness with other humans like you. It's beautiful. It's the namaste.

Remember that no human will fill that deep sense of longing inside you. Only when you return to non-physical will that feel complete.

There is much LOVE here for you.   Namaste

As you connect with others in your heart, you become one. That's the highest place of LOVE and connection for humanity.

October 29th
You Are Time

You have a notion that time is not on your side. It's against you so you compete with it.

When you were small, you couldn't wait until you got older. In the end you say," Slow down." First you run towards time. Then you run away from it. When it's at the very end of your time there, you settle into it and say, "Well, you might as well come find me time because I'm finished here."

It's an amusing game you play. It's like playing hide and seek with time. It's time for you to understand that you are time.

That each moment of your experience is 'your time'. Each emotion that comes up is in 'your time'. Each human you bond with is in 'your time'. When you've finished what you're into there, 'your time' will be complete and you'll be finished.

It's surprising to hear that it's 'your time' at this stage of your life. Now you find out it's 'your time'! You've always thought time was something out there. Either it was looking for you or you were hiding from it.

So, if it's 'your time', what are you going to do with it? You didn't know you could embrace it and become one with it. You thought you were always at odds with it. But all along it's been travelling through time with you because it turns out, you're one.

Time doesn't mean anything at all. It's not real. You travel with it because you are time. You are energy. You are the Universe of LOVE. You are everlasting. That's what time is. Time is everlasting. Time is the Universe. Time is you. You are time. You are the Universe. You are everlasting LOVE. You are eternal.

There is much LOVE here for you.   Namaste

If you are time and time is a dance, then it's time to start singing and kicking your heels up, isn't it?

October 30th
Expose Yourself

It's important to be uncomfortable sometimes so you may receive new information. When you're comfortable, you get lazy and arrogant. You're blocked off from new ideas and energy outside you. Your life just gets smaller and smaller because you don't want to expose anything.

What if, for true spiritual growth, it's important for you to expose your inner self? Does that sound dreadful? What would it be like if your inner self was exposed to someone else? First, you could practice by yourself saying your inner truth. " I feel alone. I feel angry. I feel sad." Start by yourself because you're never really alone.

After this, try exposing your feelings to others. It will escalate your spiritual experience because the other person feels vulnerable like you. All humans are afraid to expose themselves. You just become self-centred with your pain and frustration, and you don't realize that everyone else feels as closed down as you.

The benefit of self-exposure from human to human is a true meaningful connection. You will find this connection even if you expose yourself in the smallest way." I'm frightened." The other will respond, "I'm also frightened." Now there are two of you in the same emotional state. You both feel a little less afraid just by sharing. Of course, you'll still be afraid but you won't be alone.

There is much LOVE here for you.   Namaste

There's a risk to exposing your innermost self but the true, meaningful connections you desire are only found when you do.

October 31st
Precious Things

The Universe holds you in its palm in a gentle, LOVING way, as if you're a newborn bird. One that requires nurturing and LOVE before it flies on its own. Somehow, you're forgetting how precious you are to the Universe.

You're in human to have your own experience but it's still a process of allowing. It's about allowing yourself to come into human knowing you have the support of the Universe of LOVE.

You knew before you stepped into human that you could not survive alone, with just other humans for support. Everyone is aware of energy that exists outside you. You're all just finding ways to communicate it in a way others will accept.

You are eternal LOVE energy yourself but at this moment you're in this form, this name and this personality. It's not all of you. When you're not in human, you're mingling back with the LOVE energy. You're automatically one with preciousness, LOVE, gentleness, understanding, great knowledge, and peace again.

You are precious because you've stepped forth when others haven't. Therefore, the others are supporting you. When you feel pressure around you like a blanket, it's the Universe stepping forward to say," We're with you. You're precious to us. You're most LOVED. You're our greatest concern. We adore you and wish you to know that you're encircled by LOVE energy the entire time you exist there. We wish to show our support for what you're trying to do." You've stepped into humanity so you'll be LOVED and supported.

There is much LOVE here for you.   Namaste

As you become more still inside, you'll start to feel gentle pressure on you. Like a bit of resistance as you move forward. This is the Universe of LOVE encircling you. You're surrounded by LOVE energy always.

November

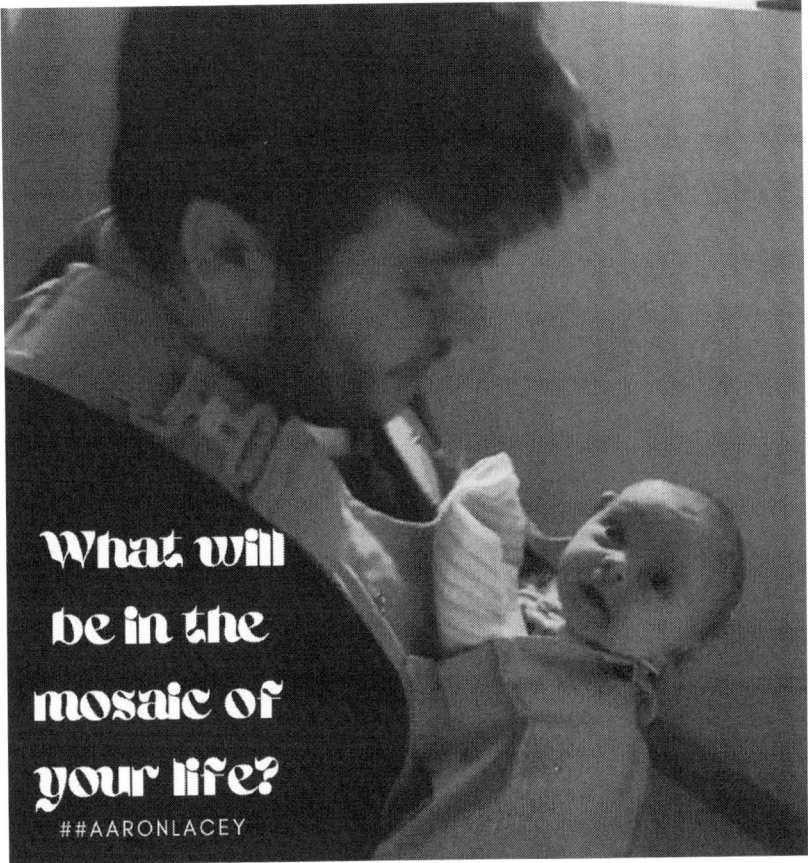

What will be in the mosaic of your life?
##AARONLACEY

November 1st
Co-Leader

You have decided if one is a leader, then they must stand alone and be responsible, while others do what they like. The leader must always act superior, intelligent, all together, and under control.

This is a game you all play, because truly, the leader is no more than any of you. If you were chosen, then you would be the leader, while this leader would be part of the pack. Leaders and bosses are no different on the inside.

When you become a leader, you believe you must take control of things. You used to allow the Universe to unfold easily. But as a boss you say, "I'm going to decide for everyone because they've asked me to." You remove yourself from a flow of information and power because you think you're deciding alone. Now you must always be on guard. This hyper-vigilance draws you away from the information that you desire to allow your job to be easier.

When you are in the flow of information or the Universe of LOVE, there's an intuition or knowing, that your life unfolds easily. When you're doing something wrong, your heart beats faster and you tighten up, so you know you're not supposed to do it. Your body tells you. It reconfirms with the energy of doubt and disconnection that's going through you.

When you see yourself as a boss, you're not sure if you still have access to the Universe of LOVE. You think you're different and alone. When in actual fact, this is the best time for you to rely *more* on the Universe of LOVE because now you're guiding others.

What if the Universe of LOVE and you were co-leaders instead? You could take a moment and check in before you respond. Then you'll be in alignment. Suddenly, things will flow just as they do when you're not the leader. As a co-leader with the Universe, things will be easier on your heart and brain.

There is much LOVE here for you.   Namaste

You're not trained all your life to be a leader. You're chosen from a group as the most compassionate and intelligent.

November 2nd
I am Delightful

When you apply the word "delightful" to a situation, suddenly it's different. Even though nothing has changed. How can a word change a circumstance without the circumstance changing? It seems impossible. As you begin to practice the use of the word "delightful", you'll start to notice a difference. So, nothing really needs to change. It's only *you* that needs to get into vibrational alignment.

Everything is happening just as it's supposed to, from moment to moment. It really has nothing to do with you at all. You're an observer in life. You're to sit, watch and learn how to get into alignment. Then everything seems delightful. It seems hard to believe because there are some things that should never be delightful. That's your human-ness speaking.

Something horrible may be delightful when you put the energy of LOVE towards it. It will be amazing. It's a discipline to stay in alignment enough to allow LOVE to flow through you and out of you than into a situation that is pretty or unkind. As soon as you judge it as ugly, your vibration changes. Then no LOVE flows through you and the situation stays as it is.

It's a tricky twist. In order for a situation to appear delightful, it's necessary for the LOVE to flow through you and toward the event. Particularly if there are humans involved in it. Humans are all looking for this vibration of LOVE. That's how they find themselves in situations that are unkind.

It's your greatest calling to stay in alignment. You're a vessel to allow LOVE to flow into you and out of you at all times. Including those that are uncomfortable. For you to stay in a LOVE vibration when things around you look so ugly is not easy. It's not easy being human. But you can still have fun. Sometimes you even think the life you've created is ugly.

There is much LOVE here for you.   Namaste

Before you LOVE ugly events, why not look in the mirror and allow LOVE to flow into you and out of you. Towards you. How about that? Now, aren't you the most delightful creature that has ever lived?

November 3rd
Truthful Human Being

You have a way of presenting yourself to others as if everything is going wonderfully. Humans have adopted this ritual of greeting. "How are you?" "I am fine." You've done it so often it's become unconscious. So, it's truly not a connection with another human being. It actually means," Mind your own business. Get away from me." You wouldn't think this, would you? You would assume you're having a communication where you bond together when it's actually a separation.

If you are not able to have a true, heartfelt communication, eyeball to eyeball, truly listen, express how it is at the moment and feel empathetically where the other person is, you might as well say, "Why don't you get lost? I don't care about you." You don't like the sound of this. You would prefer to think you were both being nice.

You don't like to see yourself as unkind so now you have a dilemma. "I like to be perceived as a kind hearted person even when I'm not." This, in itself, is untruthful which is also difficult for you to believe. But what if it were okay to say, "Sometimes I'm not kind and I don't care about others." What is wrong with speaking the truth even if it doesn't sound great to you? In a truthful vibration, you're able to grow, look at things and change them. You're not going anywhere saying everyone is nice.

There's a reason why you're not kind all the time. Because you're incapable of it. Life is overwhelming. You can't always be empathetic. So, why pretend you are? This just creates division between you and yourself.

How about speaking the truth even if it doesn't look good? "I'm going through a difficult time. I can't spend time with you." When others see this behaviour modelled, they have access to it. They didn't know they could say, "Hello. Goodbye." As you become confident and comfortable in who you truly are and stop pretending you're something you're not, you become a truthful human. No matter what it looks like. Maybe today, you can be the truthful human others have never seen.

There is much LOVE here for you.   Namaste

You will not be debilitated by honesty.

November 4th
LOVE Arrow

Most often humans don't wish to pinpoint important things. It's easier to stay away from anything too heavy. Often something from the outside triggers a reaction, which you can't ignore. It's like an arrow pointed to the part of you that wishes to be noticed. Now and again, you glance at it and say, "Oh, that thing is still sticking out there. I've tried not to look at it but there it is."

If its excruciating emotional pain, you might think it doesn't need to be addressed. Energetically speaking, it's an arrow to the soul or emotional self.

When your human body passes, the energy still exists. You're not exactly a body, yet you seem to be. When the energy leaves, where does it go? It joins back with the energy of LOVE.

When there's an arrow to the emotional or energetic organ, it's all about healing energy.

A deadly, poisonous arrow is pointing out that part of you wishes to be healed. It's a LOVE arrow that's an energetic wake up call. You've called it to you by saying, "Please point out what must be repaired." Energy is LOVE, so a LOVE arrow comes exactly to the spot that wishes to be seen.

This is a lesson in energy. Energy becomes stagnant or stuck and wishes to be seen. The arrow is painful for as long as it's in there but once it's removed, it will heal the place. So, if there's something in you that wishes to be seen, it will call energy to it. Sometimes it will be painful for a few moments. Only, until it's seen and heard. Until it says what it needs to express.

There is much LOVE here for you.   Namaste

If you called a LOVE arrow energetically to you and there's a part of you that's in distinct pain, perhaps you can allow the Universe of LOVE to heal it.

November 5th
Resolutions

You often resolve to be a better human. This is intended to be positive but it's not. This means you're not being who you are at the moment and that you're not happy with who you are.

This is a distraction by you. You think, "Instead of sitting here comfortably in this uncomfortable place, I'll set a new goal for myself. I'll remove myself from this negative emotional place."

There have been those who say it's good to make resolutions. But then you don't have to do anything about who you are now, because you'll be the best 'you' over there somewhere. Sitting here makes you upset. You get angry, guilty and depressed, but so what? You came into human to feel.

Perhaps, you don't need a resolution. Maybe you need to sit in who you are, and then the energy will change automatically. Energy shifts when you sit in it. The times when you feel dread and fear, energy comes to support you. Automatically, your energy reaches out and calls to the Universe. Then the energy of the Universe comes. Then you don't need resolutions because you're changed.

It's not a mental game. It's a spiritual, emotional, energetic game. Your mind has been in control so much of your life, it's hard for you to differentiate. Your mind and ego don't wish to lose control of you.

When you are sitting in an energetic, emotional space, your ego and mind don't need to be involved. It's an energy exchange with the Universe. You will certainly be changed. You don't need to make resolutions. Each time, you sit as a new person energetically.

Your experience is about being human which is mostly about emotional and mental games, as well as enjoying your physical body. So, laugh, cry, dance and sing. Get angry. Get happy. Question the Universe. You wish for the anger and the sadness because it means you are in your body.

There is much LOVE here for you.   Namaste

Resolutions are just a little game you play to escape the true deep emotions. The ones you asked for. You are a mental gymnast, that's for sure.

November 6th
Energetic Language

You reach a point when you understand you can affect others by your energy. They often have a reaction to you before you say any words. They may already be aware of what's going on energetically with you. Sometimes you can tell what's going on with others too.

Since silent energetic communication is going on between humans, why do you use words? Stop for a moment and realize you sometimes know what's going to happen before it does. You understand when someone is saying one thing but means another.

You're coming to understand you would then be considered a psychic human being who sees that energetically. But according to your mind, it thinks you're reading body cues. Really the energy is coming out of the human. Some of you can even see colours.

All of you know when someone is saying something they do not mean even though you've been deceived by this. If you're able to return to a place of knowing from the beginning of the time you spent with this deceiving human, you knew the truth.

It's time for you to start acknowledging what is true energetically and for you to acknowledge you and the others are energetic beings. You may read one another energetically to receive truth.

Humans can't always find correct words to say how they feel energetically. If you focus your energy with theirs, you'll know what they're saying. You're never really deceived unless you wish to be. You're connected energetically to all humans and to the Universe of LOVE, which is energy and non-physical who have passed.

These words are energy. Energetically you'll never be deceived. Energetically you're one step ahead of the words. The brain is a little bit slower that the energy. The words come after the energy, which triggers the emotion.

There is much LOVE here for you.   Namaste

You are great receptors of energy because you are energy. That's why it's familiar to you.

November 7th
Call for Help

There's a draw for you to turn back to your small one to connect all the little pieces. The small 'you' is likely damaged and is trying to communicate with your future older self.

There is a vibration created when you call out for help as a small one, which stays. It keeps resonating. So, it's possible for you to follow the vibration back to the call for help. Most likely it's from you, because you're in the same vibration throughout your lifetime. This call for help also goes out to non-physical and the Universe. That's who answered when you were small.

If a human asks for help, non-physical answers. Now if you can return to the small one you might recall a sense of ease and peace just for a moment. At the exact same time you asked for help.

This is a return to your little one to see through adult eyes. All the help you were able to receive was provided energetically, and you received some peace and quiet. As you look back, take note that you've never been abandoned from the Universe of LOVE.

It's not always necessary to remember bad times but there's a remembering of LOVE energy enveloping you now. You're recalling times of peace among difficult times and humans. This knowing will affect your life today.

As you take a quick peek backwards, you might see a trail of LOVE energy all the way to *now*. It's white and bright. It envelops all who cry out for help. Not just the pain but the rescue and relief. Bring this forth to this moment. Right this moment you are surrounded by great, all-encompassing overwhelming LOVE. You've not always been able to accept or see it. Can you see the light and LOVE around your small one? You can bring it forward to your more mature self who understands LOVE energy.

The nature of the Universe of LOVE is to support those who come into human form. Then it becomes a LOVE exchange. Giving LOVE. Receiving LOVE. Sharing LOVE.

There is much LOVE here for you.   Namaste

It's all about LOVE energy. It's there when you come in and go out. It's there for you in the middle. It's with you right now.

November 8th
Human Balloon

You feel as if you're held to the earth by gravity. By the weight of your feet. But as you become more energetically conscious, you lighten up. Then, there's a part of you that creates the opposite effect which is heavy. To keep you grounded.

This push and pull is part of your human experience. There's fear attached to this. It's the mind and the ego saying, "Don't get out of control." You're not going to float away because you have a human body to keep you grounded. But there's a part of your mind and ego that tries to keep you small. It's keeping you safe. But then you can't have enlightenment or connection to the Universe. This is mostly unexplored in your human time.

When you lighten up, you're not going to float away but you're going to become more enlightened. A little lighter. A little less rigid. A little more at peace. A little more connected to others. Perhaps you'll start to know energetically what others say before they speak.

It's not so bad living an energetic life. Being connected to the Universe and others. Sometimes, you can hear your non-physical relatives.

You will look exactly the same but you'll have a peace and calmness inside. You will know when you're connected. It's your human experience so live it up. Do as you want. You are going to pass away anyway. It doesn't matter whether you get it or not. It doesn't really matter what you do while you're there, as long as you have a human experience.

So, you are not going to float away like a balloon if you keep connecting with the Universe of LOVE because you have a heavy body to keep you grounded. Don't let your mind and ego distract you.

There is much LOVE here for you. Namaste

You're not a balloon. You're a human being. You won't float away.

November 9th
Settle

It's not natural for humans to settle. It's *more* to be in a heightened state. Settling into a connection with Universal energy and information is found when you're balanced. When you're in a heightened state of alertness, no LOVE or Universal information can penetrate it. Which is fine if you believe nothing else exists.

Even if you don't believe nothing exists now, in just one moment you could because it's your natural state. You can learn to discipline yourself to settle, as it calms down the nervous system. When you quiet the nervous system, your first reaction is fear. What will happen? After you acknowledge this and say, "All is well", it disappears and you settle.

When you have done this settling, you'll feel a sense of belonging and oneness. Suddenly you'll understand that power lies here. Spiritual power for you, those around you and for your life. You know all is well and all is known. You settle into the earth. You settle into oneness with the Universe.

No longer is it you sitting alone. Now non-physical and the energy of the Universe surrounds you. This is different than sitting alone. When you're alone, you must be heightened because you must save yourself.

When you sit in this quieted state, you're one of a large team. You've melted into oneness with others that are often in non-physical. Now you're never alone and you have information. You may move forward slowly because you know what's ahead. You don't have to look around corners. Now you can proceed deliberately with your life. You have a calm knowing that all is well.

A deeper settling in is letting go of the notion you must keep yourselves alive. When you get the hang of this, there will be few things that bother you. Life will become easier. You will slow down. You will accomplish more at a slower pace. The mind can't understand but the body does because it's not operating on its own.

There is much LOVE here for you.   Namaste

Settle in. The earth will support you. The non-physical world is already supporting you. You will just notice it more.

November 10th
LOVING Rebel

You have been doing some travelling on your own. This is necessary. This energy and all energies like it, will lead you to a certain place, then you must carry on alone. When you are not in physical, you know everything. You're energized. You're all one. When you're having your physical experience, you don't know everything. When you jump into bodies, it's to have a complete experience in humanity.

If you are in a human body having a human experience, why are there reminders that you're an energetic being inside? When you find this place of openness and understanding, you're the odd one, not the ones who forget. They're having a human experience but you want more.

You wished to remember what it was like to be in non-physical and to be aware of non-physical around you now. You want more. The others are correct in their blindness of supernatural. That's the way it was devised. You are not special human beings because you understand energy and feel non-physical. You're rebels. You decided to change the rules. Since the Universe is at your disposal, whatever you need, you'll get.

Since it's *you* that's peeking into the Universe, you're the one living outside the norm of human behaviour. This must be noticed only for the resistance of your judgement toward the normals. Although this judgement is perfectly fine. Whatever human experience you get into, including seeking beyond earth, is fine. Wherever you find yourself is fine. The normal people are fine. All of you are fine.

The point of LOVE is knowing that all humans are equal. Seekers and non-seekers. Not better or worse. All things do not need to be judged. You are having your experience this time. You are meeting the humans you're supposed to. You're hearing, feeling and seeing things on another dimension when you're supposed to. Everything is perfect for all of you. You're all in life together.

There is much LOVE here for you.   Namaste

As you learn to LOVE yourself as you are, you automatically LOVE those who are different than you. First it starts with LOVING yourself as a rebel who judges other humans. That's all right, isn't it?

November 11th
You've Got the Body

The pattern for little ones learning to walk is falling down and getting back up. They fall more than they stand. You fell a lot too but you had a calling to evolve from crawling to walking. You've had this drive to move forward since you came into physical. Some of it has been misinterpreted, as more money and stuff but really it's more life and more LOVE. It gets off track when the human ego gets involved.

The calling you've had since you were small is to evolve, grow and become strong. You wanted to learn new things. The ones involved in this sort of evolution and open-mindedness, wish to evolve in an energetic way. You knew you could have more adventures living that way.

So, what is your next evolution? The true answer comes immediately. Many of you have mighty goals. You wish to time travel, leave your body, LOVE more and be in your body more. Always, you wish to be more. You wish to do everything.

When you meet one goal, there's another. That's your human experience. That's what you came there for. You didn't spend all eternity in a non-physical LOVE soup pot just to come into human to fall down and not get back up. You chose to have a full life experience, fool around with the body for a bit and see what it can do.

You wanted to see if you could still evolve while having a body. See if it can heal itself. If it can express physically what you're feeling. If it can sing and dance and play with others.

Your body can do great things. It can hold all the memories of your lifetime. Even though your brain forgets, your body remembers.

There is much LOVE here for you.   Namaste

What are you going to do next? Are you going to play with your body and the Universe? Are you going to connect with others, heart to heart? You have it in you to do great and wondrous things.

November 12th
Instinct or Intention?

You have a sense of survival, so you're always watching for danger. You call it instinct or intuition, which is *you* feeling energy.

Often you imply that instinct is for lower based animals, which you are in a certain way. You all emit a certain energy because you're energetic beings. You have human bodies for this time, but when you don't, you're energy. This instinct you have is a low vibration you pick up from dangerous humans.

When you use your intuition, it's energy around certain human beings that are more evolved. Both are identical because you're picking up energy from others. If you're able to pick up energy from low vibration for your instinct to survive, and high vibration for your instinct to evolve, what does that make you exactly? It makes you conscious of energy, that's all.

You also put out your own energy that others can notice because you're also a vibrational being. Now, you have a triangle set up- you, low vibrational, and high vibrational humans. Picture the three of you looking at one another. It's possible for the highly evolved human, the lower evolved human and you to come together as one in the middle.

These different levels of energy can consciously choose to join their energy together as one. Then you'll evolve together. The lower level vibration is not capable of this on its own. So, with the support of you both, a lower vibrational human may evolve.

You are ready to make a difference with this information, but not to help others who don't desire it. If it comes into your knowing, you may consciously become involved. The other higher instinct may do this naturally. It will start rotating the energy around the three of you as if it's a rope. This is what you can evolve to. This is how you will lift up brothers and sisters who are willing to feel energy. You are all together as one.

There is much LOVE here for you.   Namaste

As you evolve, you naturally draw energy and share it around. The most important thing is to feel the vibration of LOVE from the Universe that cares for you greatly.

November 13th
Life ReDo

Picture yourself walking along a winding road. It's a dirt country road that takes forever to get anywhere. There are no cars and you're going slowly. You decide to take your shoes off. Now you feel the ground and sometimes, rocks. Your feet are becoming one with the earth.

Suddenly, you hear a strange bird noise. Now you're walking and listening. Then you hear a sound like a waterfall. You decide to wander off the road to get closer to it. You cross through a soft field full of flowers on your bare feet. You're trying to locate the waterfall and you can still hear the bird. You think the waterfall is getting louder because the air has more moisture. The waterfall must be close. Finally, you feel water droplets. They're touching your skin now. You stop. Here's the waterfall. Here's the bird.

You wonder, "Where was I was going on this road? I must have been going somewhere, but I can't recall. Now I'm going to sit here instead. I'll watch the water and put my feet in it. I'll drink it. I will become one with the surroundings I find myself in."

Today you are in such a life. You've just become used to it. You've been led into it slowly. It's time for you to recall how you got to your waterfall - which is your life. You all started at the same place. You can feel it. You can hear it. The life that you've created at this moment is one that you created quite deliberately. Just as you decided to sit by the waterfall you found in front of you.

It's time for you to sit in your life and see what's in front of you. Do you like what you've created?

Just as you created the waterfall in your imagination, you've visualized your actual life. You imagined the life you would like to have. Perhaps you don't like the life you've created either. But now you may imagine a life that allows you to feel the same way you did wandering through the woods being aware, being involved with your own life, feeling contented, peaceful and alone. Start envisioning your life today.

There is much LOVE here for you.   Namaste

Your life changes many times. Always by your hand.

November 14th
Hope

It's difficult to stay in human. There's discord around you. There's difficulty in decision making. Truly, life can be heavy. Now you have hope because you're starting to understand there's more than what you see. That's wonderful news because it's exactly what you wished were true.

What you see around you is not truly your reality. You've been told that you're judged on what others can see. "You must look a certain way. Speak a certain way. Have certain belongings. This is a checklist of humanity. These make a good human."

None of you can live up to this, because underneath, you all feel like you're inadequate physically, emotionally or financially. Remain hopeful that no one can live up to the standards you've devised for yourselves. You must each decide if you're going to live this way.

Stop comparing yourself to some standard that doesn't exist and no one can live up to. It's time for you to be you.

Now that you are becoming connected to the Universe, you're caring less about what others think of you and the things surrounding you. You're starting to let go. Now you're feeling lighter. You're feeling more LOVED, accepted and more LOVABLE. Now you're becoming a true human specimen.

Are you LOVED? Are you LOVING? Are you trying? These are the true standards for you to live up to. It's about evolution. Are you evolving as a spiritual being? Are you letting go of your humanity? Are you focusing more on LOVE, the Universe, peace and joy? There's the hope.

Now you hope you'll be able to feel the LOVE. You hope you'll become one with the Universe. You hope you'll feel or hear the non-physicals that surround and support you. You hope that LOVE will flow into you and out of you. Yes. Your hopes have changed. Your hope has evolved. Now look at the beautiful human you are.

There is much LOVE here for you.   Namaste

You have evolved with LOVE and into LOVE.

November 15th
ReLearn LOVE

Some of you are trying too hard to become spiritual beings. You think you can take a class, read a book or ask someone how to do it. The human way is to gather information, excel at it and then move on top of one another. Then you look down at the others who don't know as much as you. This is the human process of moving up in the world of man. You believe you can apply this to your spiritual growth.

If you wish to be spiritually balanced, it's the opposite. You already know this because you're not of this world. You're visiting and learning its ways. That's why you know the steps to reach prestige and money. You've been studying them. Now you can set that aside.

You understand there's something else going on. There's still the same connection with the Universe of LOVE that you've had through eternity. But are you able to maintain that while in human? That's your question. Can they both exist in the same realm?

You exist, so the answer is yes. You've come from the Universe of LOVE. You carry it inside. Your DNA is the Universe of LOVE. You're one with other beings, both physical and non-physical. You're one with Source. You're one with the Universe of LOVE, which is energy. It's always positive, uplifting, excited and wonderful energy. You're part of it but you're also in your human experience. That's what you're trying to balance.

To become more spiritual, just be. Settle into yourself. Quiet yourself. Your alignment will come. You will have all information available to the Universe. You don't need anyone to tell you anything.

There is much LOVE here for you.   Namaste

Your DNA is becoming one with this vibration. Your heart is feeling calmer and quieter. Remember, you are the Universe of LOVE.

November 16th
Equilibrium

It's time for you to reach a place of comfort, ease, and understanding of your place in the world. It takes time for this because there's much giving and taking. That's the way of humanity. Many people pass through time this way.

But those attracted to these vibrations are trying to find peace and level living. A place where you can relax and breathe, knowing all is well. This is true peace. Not that your life is quiet. Just that you can handle anything that comes your way. There will be ups and downs but mostly you'll stay somewhere in the middle. It's all you can seek because there are always adventures and mishaps. That's the way it is there.

When you come to know peace and that all is well for you, then you can settle into your true evolutionary work. You can't spend time meditating, quieting your brain and being one with nature unless you have a sense of peace and knowing that you'll be able to handle all that comes. Without that, there's anxiety when you slow down. So, you can't really sit. You're always jumping and waiting. You're on alert.

Connecting with the Universe of LOVE must be done in quietness. Not jumping at every noise. Your nervous system is settling down with this truth. Now anything can happen to you and you'll remain in a sense of equilibrium.

You'll be angry and happy but you'll return to this place of equilibrium quickly because you're adjusting your nervous system now. It will balance you and you'll start to live in a place of equilibrium. A place of balance. A peaceful place for you to return to right after your traumatic events. Your body and spiritual being recognize this place of equilibrium. You may return there anytime you are in distress.

There is much LOVE here for you.   Namaste

When you realize no matter what happens, you'll be all right, you can sit down and settle your body and mind. Then you can connect with the Universe of LOVE. Your place of equilibrium is a peaceful place for you to land.

November 17th
Feeling Energy

Often you spend much time ruminating and thinking. It's an exercise to strengthen your brain. You can play games with it. Your brain is very important to you. You've stretched it in many ways but there is more to understand

You are energy that exists through all time. If you understand this, your next logical step in evolution would be to understand your brain and therefore, intelligence is temporary. This may sound overwhelming because you think your brain is all you have.

If you are eternal beings energetically, what is it that's carried you through all eternity? How can you be eternal? It doesn't make sense, does it? And yet, you're hearing this vibration from the Universe of LOVE.

As you evolve, you get a quiet knowing there are things going on around you that you can't always see but you can feel. Sometimes, you feel things before they happen or feel a truth before someone says it. You might feel a voice being carried on the wind or feel humans who have passed.

The way to expand eternally and energetically is through your feelings because sometimes it's the wind or a noise in the ear. It might be hair moving. So you actually feel it emotionally. You might be sitting quietly and you'll cry. You might feel a presence around you and when you look, there's nothing. These are emotional and physical feelings.

There will be times when you'll be in non-physical and you'll be the voice in the ear of another. You'll be standing beside someone when they need support. You're remembering now because you've been both non-physical and physical. That's why you know.

Your eternal self is found in your feeling realm. You came into physical to have a human experience but also with a certain curiosity about whether or not you could still feel energy. Some have forgotten but now you're being reminded.

There is much LOVE here for you.   Namaste

Can you feel energy physically? It's just a feeling after all.

November 18th
Shall We?

There comes a time when you come face to face with yourself. Sometimes you're so busy moving fast through your lifetime, you lose track of yourself. Often, you're busy helping people and doing jobs and forget about yourself. This is common because you'd rather not sit in your emotions and feelings. They're often too much for you. You think you'll be overwhelmed and pass out.

Sometimes a feeling of sadness or anger begins the momentum of running. Then it becomes a pattern until you finish there.

There is a time when you slow down. You dare to see what you look like. But it's not easy. Although you are your constant companion, the one who escorts you through your time, it's sometimes the very one you can't stand to look at.

It should be the closest, most intimate, LOVING and caring relationship you have. All the other humans will fall away, except you. Perhaps, now the running can stop.

Perhaps you wish to be reminded how precious you are. Maybe it's all right for you to stop running. To look yourself in the eye and say, "Look how LOVELY you are. You've been through so much with me. I thank you for being my constant companion. You've never given up on us. I see you." It's truly you and I because one is your energetic self and one is your physical self.

The energetic self is always hopeful. It has lived through all eternity. It has lived through many things and understands this is only a small time in a body. So, you're truly having a conversation and the energetic self is taking the lead. It's always connected to the Universe of LOVE. It's full of peace, gentleness, ease and comfort.

Your physical self worries and gets tired. So, it's your energetic self that says, "We've had a great time! We've laughed and cried and danced. Thank you for being a body for my soul. All the memories, both good and bad can be seen on your beautiful face. So, shall we stay together a while longer?"

There is much LOVE here for you. Namaste

Say to yourself, "We have enough time left to sing, dance, skip, laugh and cry. So, shall we?"

November 19th
Wonderment

Often, you feel like small children excited for the first snowfall. You're too excited to sit inside and look out the window. The excitement builds until you can't take it any longer and you run outside. It's important to remember now, so you can become excited this moment.

Imagine what it's like staring out at something you wish to be involved in but are not invited. It's not yet a part of your experience. Often you sit back watching something unfold that you'd like to be part of.

You can think of humans you'd like to spend time with or ideas that you would like to be part of. Yet, you hesitate on the inside. You don't join in. Why would an adult decide to stay separate from an unfolding, beautiful, exciting event that a child would not? Why would adults deny themselves a sense of excitement and joy?

Because the adult is not as pure as the child. The adult has had some damage to themselves. They don't see themselves as deserving of unfolding joy. This is the separation between you and the young one. The young one is still in the Universe of LOVE feeling. They're not all human yet. So, a sense of being is still there.

Is it possible for an adult to regain a sense of wonderment? To become childlike again? To believe they deserve joy? Of course. You just need to be reminded what a sense of wonder sounds and looks like.

You know what it feels like because you've been one. So go back to that time when you were staring at something you really hoped for. You became a part of wondrous things when you were a small one. So, it's time to go back.

There is much LOVE here for you.   Namaste

Get in touch with your childlike self. It's time for you to wonder again. About joy, fun, laughter and fresh snow. It's time for your sense of wonderment to be allowed to come out and play.

November 20th
1-2-3

If something takes more than 1-2-3, you're too slow. But perhaps you are uncovering truths at your own pace. Maybe 1-2-3 is just a ridiculous notion that one group decided is how long it takes to learn something.

What if it takes lifetimes to learn something? Will that cause you great impatience, urgency and anxiety? What if a true knowing of evolution and oneness with energy takes forever?

Once you move past your anxiety and need to win, and set your ego aside for a moment, you can settle into the notion that there are some intimate all-knowing things that take lifetimes to learn.

If you are able to sit in this place, you'll settle into it and relax a little. Maybe you can ease up on yourself. Be more caring and compassionate for the growth you've gotten in this lifetime. Maybe you could be a little gentler with yourself. Not 1-2-3 but maybe lifetimes or eternity to master such things. Could you take a breath then?

Could you settle into that? Does it seem true for you that it takes a long time to know all things? To recall what it's like to be in non-physical or to be aware of non-physical surrounding you? Maybe you can be a little gentler with yourself.

You are valuable to the Universe. You've come into physical to play around a little bit in your human body. You are much LOVED and connected to the Universe of LOVE, whether you recall it or not. You are blessed.

You are the human ones, after all. So, be easy with yourself. The Universe is certainly easy with you. Perhaps you can take a cue from the Universe of LOVE and relax. You are doing wonderful in your human life.

There is much LOVE here for you.   Namaste

It takes an eternity to learn hard things. Things that matter take a long time to learn.

November 21st
Oneness

You like to sit in the middle, where you can go one way or the other.
You're always searching for this place because it's a place of power.
This place is not accidental. You chose it when you've had enough
emotional turmoil.

It's like you've been rocked about in a little boat on the ocean
during a storm. When you've had enough, you sit quietly in a storm-
less ocean and you put out your oars and begin to row. Knowing all the
time, it doesn't matter if you go forward or to the side because
wherever you land will be a good place for you.

When it resonates with you, it's truth. You hear, "We know
what it's like to sit in the centre and to feel absolutely fine no matter
where we end up." It's a place you can all reside.

Having a human body means you'll be bumped around a bit.
It's just part of the fun but mostly, you'll be sitting in a place of power.
Not man-made power where your ego is involved. But power by being
in alignment and knowing all is well.

You are moving into an alignment place of balance and power.
You can sit here knowing you'll be fine no matter where your boat
floats. You'll be happy where you find yourself. This is a true place of
peace and oneness with your surroundings and with those that you find
yourself with.

You will have a sense of oneness with all of creation. You'll
land where you're at peace.
When you find yourself here, stay in it for a moment and notice. Just
notice how easy it is to stay here even though you're surrounded by the
unknown.

There is much LOVE here for you.   Namaste

Can you feel your oneness with all of creation?

November 22nd
Rowdy Conversations

There will always be times when you are against another human and be in an argument. You will dislike who they're presenting themselves as. When this happens, it's difficult to stay in a place of LOVE and you lose your LOVING self.

When another has lost their sense of connection to the Universe, they become sad and lonely. Then loneliness turns into anger because you think the Universe has cut you off on purpose. So, now you're angry at the Universe for cutting you out while allowing others to stay connected. But it's always you that disconnects. It's you that thinks you're unworthy of the all-encompassing LOVE being offered.

When sadness turns into anger, the human looks for other humans to get angry with. Those humans represent the Universe of LOVE. The anger must go somewhere and most humans don't wish to yell at the Universe of LOVE. Although that would be absolutely fine. Most don't wish to tell even the Universe why they're so hurt. Of course, the Universe already knows all of this. So it's not a secret.

Now, here comes the human that has anger to come out. This has nothing at all to do with you but you're standing face to face with a human that is angry with the Universe. Now the angry human is getting a bit of their frustration out.

Keeping this in mind, the next time you get into some disagreement, can you step out of your ego for a moment? Then take a look at your spiritual brother or sister and see that the anger is actually hiding the sadness they feel from their disconnection from the Universe of LOVE? Can you step back and take a breath for a moment? You only have a moment because your ego LOVES to argue.

Now you can connect with Source and get into alignment. Then you may be a channel for the other. The other may have a conversation through you to Source.

There is much LOVE here for you.   Namaste

What if there are others who desire, more than anything else, to connect with the Universe but have no idea how to do it?

November 23rd
The Great Giver. The Great Taker

One of your favourite things to do when you are small is play ball. You have a wonderful time with it. One of these memories is throwing the ball away and hoping it comes back. Can you imagine yourself doing this today? Now what if this ball were energy?

What if you could create a ball with energy that's borrowed from the Universe and comes through you. Would you throw it away so quickly? Would you hold onto it and hide it? Would you give a little piece away to others who need it? Would you pass the whole thing to someone who needed it?

What if this energy ball was appropriately called LOVE? You think you give LOVE to everyone but that's just not true, is it? A lot of times you lock it away. Just like when you were small and afraid someone was going to steal your favourite ball. So, you hid it.

Today your understanding has grown, and your spiritual development has accelerated. So, now that you have a LOVE ball, will you throw it and hope it comes back? That's scary, isn't it? What if it doesn't come back? Then what will you do?

Will you cry yourself to death for losing your favourite LOVE ball? That's what you might think. In actuality, you may create as many LOVE balls as you wish because you're only the channel of LOVE.

So, what about throwing it out and creating another and throwing it out and creating another and handing that to the human in need on the ground? Making another and throwing it to someone you dislike? Making another to a lost child? What if you could actually allow LOVE energy to flow through you anytime?

What if, by sharing, you're now creating a new sense of ease and contentment in the world? Then you will know you don't need to hide your LOVE. What if, by healing the others, it's you that's healed? What if, by you thinking you are giving, you're actually receiving? What if, the great giver is actually a great taker too? You can only give away what you receive.

There is much LOVE here for you.   Namaste

Great givers are great channels of LOVE.

November 24th
Lead or Follow

There is always a leader. When there's a group, there's always one who steps forth. It's difficult to move together without someone directing. Sometimes you're the leader, sometimes another. You take turns. Is it easier to be a follower or a leader?

It's a human way of working together that you can't work as a group without a leader. But the leader is often just the loudest one. The one who is most controlling and feels great distress with disorder. Others are grateful for someone to do this so they don't have to. So, the most fearful leads. Often the one with the least amount of faith in humans sorting things through.

The followers often sort things out when the leader's not watching. They work together collectively to come up with a plan while the leaders are off worrying. The flock understands it must stick together. They know there is power in unity. They know if they're connected together, they're connected to the Universe.

Leaders are often by themselves and disconnected while the flock are joined together as one. So, the power and faith are with the followers. The fear is with the leader.

So, the flock can invite the leader by saying, "Why don't you join us and take a breath. Just stay in the middle of us and calm down. You can absorb our energy." It's what flocks do best. Hide things in the middle that feel unsafe, and nurture them. Let them sit in the middle of the LOVE energy.

Throw them into the middle, which is a vortex of LOVE. Then they will become one of you. You'll have another committed, caring, sensitive human being that's sitting with the flock. Instead of out there, alone. Don't leave them alone.

There is much LOVE here for you.   Namaste

The leaders are off worrying about things but the flock knows what's going on because they work together collectively to come up with a plan.

November 25th
Beautiful Brain

There are often times when you find yourself smiling about a certain memory. Sometimes, you recall it like it just happened. Even though it hasn't, your brain thinks it has. So you have great control over your brain. You can deceive your brain. When you're worrying about an outcome, it gets anxious and comes up with false solutions.

There are two ways your brain thinks reality is happening now. One is reliving positive events from the past and one is worrying about an unhappy future outcome. When your body remembers a fond memory, it's calm and settled. Your whole body is relaxed. Your brain has said, "We're having a positive experience."

In the other place when you're worrying because you think you must make a correct decision, your heart is racing. Your body is on high alert. These are opposite body reactions and yet, you're living the same moment. Nothing has changed your life. Just your brain.

Your body is going along with these experiences as if they're true. But they're wearing your body out. Your body wishes to sit in relaxed peace. It wishes to have a full human experience, which is laughter, dancing and fun. Crying if it must but not made-up crying. Not made-up anxiety. Not made-up anger. Only if it crosses your path in the most natural way, then it's part of your human experience.

If your brain is activating a false story and your body is responding in stress, you're causing undue hardship on that beautiful body of yours. Now, remember what it was like to LOVE another human being and stare into their face. Perhaps you were dancing or singing. Perhaps you were rocking a baby. These memories cause your body to relax. Then it can fully experience life.

When it's anxious and tight, you're not living. You're existing. You came to live a rich full life. To laugh, have fun and dance.

There is much LOVE here for you.   Namaste

Recall the beautiful moments when you feel stressed. You decide how your body feels by deciding what thoughts you allow. If you wish to be calm, centered, LOVING and peaceful, that's up to you. If you wish to be anxious and nervous, that's up to you.

November 26th
Energy Kindergarteners

In order for you to evolve energetically, you must understand at a very basic that you are energy that passes through, from body to body. Your energy lasts through all eternity. When it's not in human, it's joined with the others, in a collective of LOVE, and *you* reside in the Universe of LOVE.

The Universe of LOVE is really energy that just exists. It's high energy that has a vibration of LOVE, therefore, it holds each human. As you come into humanity, it holds you in the highest place you can be held. It sees you as your truest, purest self, which is LOVING, caring, at peace, one with others and able to communicate with energy. Your highest self may think a thought and others may hear it. You may send LOVE to one who has fallen down and they will feel it. This is what your energy is capable of, and the Universe holds you in this place always. It never falters.

The energy is more than the small amount you carry inside. When you're joined with the others, you're unlimited. Others who are familiar with energy can see it coming and grab it. This is your highest self. So, you must understand that you're pure, LOVING energy visiting in a human body for a small time. When it's complete, your energy survives. It joins back with the others where you communicate easily through energy. You wish to evolve into your fullest energetic self. That means understanding that you're pure LOVING energy which is difficult to keep within the human body. The energy explodes out of you, and sometimes, it hurts on the inside. That just means you're aware of your energy.

From here, you can do many things. You may roam from place to place energetically. You may send thoughts, LOVE and emotion. You may channel information. But first you must be comfortable knowing, "I am not what I seem." Your body is just finding its place in this time.

There is much LOVE here for you.   Namaste

There is an energetic self that resides at the same time as your body does. It does not wish to stay small inside of you. It wishes to join with other energy.

November 27th
State of Surrender

You despise the word 'surrender'. This word was misused in military terms to take someone's power away. Your ancestors believed it meant you lost or that you were a loser. It means you try everything else but surrender. Your DNA has a history with this word.

Within the Universe, it has a higher meaning. Your spiritual brothers and sisters LOVE to surrender. Your non-physical relatives, who have passed, surrender all the time. It's their favourite thing because it means they become one with the others. The others are unconditional LOVE, peace and joy.

You can surrender to a higher good where there's no more anxiety or worry. You'll be involved in a LOVING exchange and allow LOVE to pass through you to others. When you're clear from your human distractions, this is your highest calling. Always being a part of LOVE. Always being one with others and being used, therefore, for LOVE.

Surrendering to LOVE has great peace attached. Great oneness. Great community. Great family of LOVE.

Because you come from LOVE energy, you're all in it together. Of course, you surrender. You get something from it. You get peace, LOVE, oneness and connection. You get to be a channel of LOVE. Your greatest purpose is to allow LOVE into you and out of you so it may settle wherever it wishes. You get all of that from surrendering.

There is much LOVE here for you.   Namaste

Your highest surrendering is into the arms of LOVE where you will be held, LOVED and nurtured. So, you in turn, may LOVE and nurture others by being a channel of LOVE. How does your body feel about surrender now?

November 28th
Energetic Nap

When you were small, you looked up to the adults. You thought they were huge and old. You were young and vital. They moved slowly and talked funny. They sat all the time. They were so different than you. You were energized, quick witted and fast. You said what you thought. You really didn't have any empathy skills.

At the end of a day, you passed out because you had exerted all the energy your body had. You were so excited to be in a body. You are pure energy. You wanted to come and see what it felt like. It moved funny. It's heavy. You couldn't get the hang of it at first. How does this thing move? Then you figured it out. You started to skip, dance, sing and twirl around. You were just getting the hang of it and then they sent you to the place of indoctrination. The school.

Then things changed for you. Now you were with the soldiers. Try to remember before the school system. When you were free to be. That's why you chose to come into physical.

Today, it doesn't matter where you are. You can feel that same way. Yes, you. Try to remember what a miracle it is. You were excited to come in. You've just forgotten. You got stuck in the indoctrination of what you thought grown-ups were.

You can relive what you thought during those first few years. Let's hide. Let's play. Let's whisper. Let's sing. Let's fall down and sleep right on the ground because we're so tired.

It's a way to see life. Live it energetically. The energy from the Universe is still flowing through you the same way as it was when you were little. You're the exact same energy.

It's you that gets old and crotchety. Your body still wants to sing, dance and exert energy until it falls asleep exhausted. It wants to smile, laugh easily and listen to music. So, it doesn't matter what you look like in the mirror, you're the same energetic being. You've just lost a bit of the shine.

There is much LOVE here for you.   Namaste

No naps until you've done your energetic work. You're dancing, skipping and getting fresh air. Then you take the nap. After. Not Before.

November 29th
Speak the Truth

Some days seem sunny and bright while others seem dark. Sometimes this is your heart deciding how it will be. You might be unaware that you can decide how your day unfolds. Your mind doesn't know the difference between a memory and what's actually happening.

You're able to think of sunny, bright things or thoughts of LOVE between you and another. Think of things that you smile about, then you can rest.

Your mind plays off your energy. So, it's also possible to go to dark places without anything happening. It can even be a memory of difficult times. As you linger in these thoughts, your mind thinks it must be alert.

Therefore, your life today is a vision of what you wish it to be. It's your interpretation of what you recall and what you see at the moment. You tend to go from one thought to the next without noticing. You don't always want to be aware of your thoughts.

You often feel like a victim of life. But you've asked for this because you don't have to think about things and feel them. You don't have to listen to your body telling you it's aching. Now, this information may anger you. That's fine to notice, because now you may sit in it and think, "Why am I so angry? Is it true?" That's a good response to anger usually. Then you will settle down and be able to hear the truth underneath.

You decide how you're feeling. *You* decide whether your brain is going to be on high alert. *You* decide if you wish to give up your control to someone else. You think it's easier when you don't have to be responsible.

If you are able to move into this, you'll receive great enlightenment and understanding. This is common knowledge in the Universe of LOVE. Since you are part of the Universe of LOVE. It's common knowledge to you also.

There is much LOVE here for you.   Namaste

You are in control of your thoughts. When you're alone, you can still feel emotion even though nothing is happening.

November 30th
Get Honest

There are many of you having difficulty being who you are. Even though you've gone through a process of self-discovery. When you look in the mirror you see yourself. Yet, you still don't always stand in it. You often prefer to make others comfortable. This is false thinking, because the human you're presenting to, knows there's something wrong, that you're not really honest. Now, they're uneasy.

Every moment you present to another, you're showing them (and those watching) what it's like to be present. They're wondering if they can be their highest self, too. Humans recognize inauthenticity. It creates a whole cycle. You present to them. They present to you. Then you both go your separate ways because you've just cemented the idea that you must not be yourself.

So you've gotten to a place of self-knowledge where you can present in an honest way even if the others may not like it. Remember, you're showing others how to live as an authentic, honest, spiritual being in a physical body. You are presenting your authentic self.

When the next conversation you have is not completely honest, you're going to think about this exchange, "I'm teaching this human how to be inauthentic. They will, therefore, turn to others and teach them how to be inauthentic." Now that you're aware, it's your responsibility to act as your highest self. Including conversations with other humans who may not have the information and contact with the energy of the Universe of LOVE that you do. You might be their connection to the Universe.

They don't need you to teach them anything. They need to see what the Universe of LOVE looks like so they'll remember themselves. You're not saving anyone. Live your most authentic life because that's what you are capable of. You're enlightened. You're in contact with LOVE energy. So, it's time for you to act like it.

There is much LOVE here for you.   Namaste

Be your highest, truest self. When you're honest, it will allow others space to be honest also. In this way, they'll be set free. Remember, the others are watching to see what an authentic, honest, connected spiritual being looks like and how they act and talk.

December

i am
you
and
you
are me

##AARONLACEY

December 1st
Why Can't I Get the Hang of This?

You've been in this human body long enough to have seen, learned, listened and felt. You think you're not getting the hang of a happy life and contented living and that there must be something wrong with you. You are evolving exactly as you should. Not all get the same message at the same time or maybe ever. Sometimes, you spend your lifetime doing one thing-just learning to forgive or learning to give.

The voice that says, "You're not going to get this" is not yours. You don't come into your human body with this kind of thinking. Those words are ones you've heard other adults use. Now it's yours. You'll have to look in the mirror and see if it's true. If it's not true, it doesn't need to be said anymore. It's time for you to move on to another stage of development. If you can't leave it behind you, then that's where you'll sit. Own it. Tell everyone, "I'm stuck. I can't learn anything." You don't have to put shame on top of a feeling of inadequacy.

It's layered. Just sit in the truth of it. You are who you are. As far as the Universe is concerned, we think you are wonderful the way that you are. Sitting in shame, hatred, LOVE or peace. You are perfect because you're energy. You've been brave enough to enter into physical.

Just by having a body, you are hopeful. You're willing and connected to energy. That's the truth of it. The life you live when you're stumbling about learning things and getting stuck, that's the beauty of living a life. It's where you've chosen to be.

There is much LOVE here for you.   Namaste

You're perfect, brave and hopeful. You are 'you' no matter what it looks like.

December 2nd
Energy Exchange

Can you recall a time when you've been electrified? You call it electricity but we call it energy that's turned into vibration. Have you ever looked at another human and immediately knew what they were about? That's energy also. It's passing through each of you and coming together.

Lots of things happen in your life that you don't recognize as energy. It's been misnamed. Why not say, "I can feel your energy. You can feel mine." It's scary because if you're energy, how will your body contain it? If you can exchange energy this way, why are you using words? Will you become less human? Will the others think you are invisible and exclude you?

When you start to acknowledge energy around you, you'll be free. You'll see what is truly happening. Your eyes will be open to see what energy creates. When you start to see energy in humans, it will settle inside of you. You will be at peace. Your body will be healthier and calmer because it will not be fighting the truth. You'll think, "That's just energy. I see it all the time." When you are easy like this, more energy will flow into you and out of you-healing and nurturing on the way through.

You'll be easier to have conversations with because you won't be racing ahead to answer questions that the others don't want answered at all. They just need your energy and you need theirs. It's an energy exchange. It's all around you anyway.

There is much LOVE here for you.   Namaste

Your energetic self has old information that you've carried through eternity.

December 3rd
Anticipation of Joy

You're always watching to see what's coming. You think, "Nothing's going to surprise me. I know everything that's about to happen and when." You need to live like that because too many bad things have happened to you. It's possible to flip that upside-down. What if you start looking for good things? "Where's that next wonderful thing? Behind me? Over there? Where's the next kind person? The next LOVE exchange? The next beautiful flower? Where is it?"

What if you sat in anticipation of an excellent life? The next great thing? The next beautiful thing. The next heartfelt thing. The next thing that made you smile or cry with delight? What if you thought it was coming behind you so you walk backwards? What if you were certain more wonderful things were coming from every direction? What if you were from a Universe of LOVE which is LOVE energy-positive, hopeful, peaceful, joyous? If you were from a place like that, would you naturally be waiting in anticipation of joy? What if this energy of LOVE existed inside you? Would you start remembering what it was like to be easy and joyful? Sliding easily from one event to the next without many ripples?

What if you can exchange LOVE energy by thinking," You look like you need a smile today. I need a smile today. I feel your LOVE coming forth. I make a connection with you from eye to eye." What if you were all from the Universe of LOVE? What if you were all LOVE energy? Would you start looking for joyful things to happen?

Waiting in anticipation of JOY. That's a good life motto for you. You should write that down somewhere.

There is much LOVE here for you. Namaste

Perhaps you're surrounded by joy all the time. What if it's been around you all this time and you haven't noticed?

December 4th
Beautiful Thing

You know everything, but surely you cannot. These seem like opposing thoughts but they are real for you. You know everything because your energy is eternal. It joins in the Universe of LOVE when you are in non-physical. Then you are one with other energy. When you come into your human body, you forget most of it, as you are supposed to. You only know what you know during the time that you've been alive. So, you don't really know, but you do. This is your soul, spirit or energetic self, having a conversation with your physical body. "I know the right thing to do. I know what's going to happen before it does. I recall memories that are not my body. I know this human being but we have just met."

This physical body only remembers this time. But you know all of eternity. You're easy with it. You're relaxed. Your body is just trying to keep up. You can have a little chat. "It's all right body. Together we'll sort this through. We're a pretty good team. I have access to information that you don't. I have an easy idea about life." Your body needs reassurance. "That doesn't make any sense. I have to get up and go to work." You can continue with the conversation. "Let's go to work and see if we can connect with some humans. Let's look into their eye." "They're not going to like me doing that." "Let's just try it and see."

This is how the two of you were meant to exist. You were chosen to be together for this travelling time in your life. You understand how to speak to one another because you're separate, and yet, you're one. When you're finished, your energy still exists. For now, your energy has chosen to join in with this beautiful body. It's smart and it likes to dance. You're having a physical experience. Energy can't laugh and cry. It's hopeful, joyous and uplifting.

There is much LOVE here for you.   Namaste

LOVE can see beyond the physical, and looks soul to soul.

December 5th
Story of Your Life

You are like students on the first day of class with your new notebook and pen. You're eager and excited to learn. Do you recall your most anticipated class? You're ready. You're prepared. You're energized and ready to receive information. This is your natural state of being. It's natural for you to show up excited about what's next.

When you first came into physical, you were so excited you couldn't wait to find out what would happen with your life. Your notebook. Your life. Your pen. You. You are the instrument. The channel. Your life flows through the pen onto paper. This is the story of your life. You've done this many times. You've done it when you've shown up for the first day of class. You're doing it right now. Those of you who can remember the excitement of showing up for your life are being triggered now. The energy from the Universe flows through you naturally.

The Universe is always excited when humans wake up and get out their pen and paper.

The energy flows into you, out of you, through the pen and onto the paper. Energy is waiting for you to say "Give it to me. Let's go." It's waiting for an invitation into your life. You're always an energetic being but it gets smaller or larger depending on what you allow in. It's like a tap. You turn it on, off or halfway. When you get your new paper and pen, you turn it on full blast allowing the Universe to flow through you with great energy. You are part of it.

There is much LOVE here for you.   Namaste

Thus begins the Story of Your Life. You're eager, ready and excited. You're in connection with the Universe and the energy it provides. It's your notebook-no one else's. They have their own. What are you going to put in your shiny new notebook?

December 6th
You're Getting It

It's quite a notion to believe that you are energy that is joined together in a physical body with the Universe of LOVE. When you are not in your physical body you are joined with the Universe of LOVE. We just remind you of what you know all ready. It just settles inside of you. Your energy is eternal. It knows all, sees all and travels where it likes. Energy goes wherever it wishes.

If you feel any resistance, it's your brain trying to sort it through because it's nonsensical. "You're energy? You don't look like it. You look like you have a body." There are more scientists interested in metaphysicals who are going to prove that you are energy. You're just in the body temporarily. When the body is finished, they will start to see the energy leaving. But, for now, you'll have to sit with it and see if it feels real to you.

We speak to your energetic self. You are energy. As is the Universe. As is the non-physical beings that surround you. You're always surrounded by non-physical energy. They always listen. They wish you to remember also. They can be more helpful to you as you remember that they are there. They are intrigued with whatever you are intrigued with. They will be available to you more noticeably. They stay close to you. It's their eternal job while you are in physical. When you are going to sleep at night, you might start seeing them sitting around the bed looking at you.

You're starting to feel the truth inside you. It's warm, easy and light. It's knowing and calm. The energetic truth sits easily inside you. You're doing pretty well considering you've got a human body.

There is much LOVE here for you.   Namaste

You're getting the hang of letting go. You're becoming more aware of energy. You're doing well.

December 7th
You are Joy

When small ones play, there's one who steps out as the leader. They say, "We're going to play this. Let's have fun." They become the leader by taking command of the group. This is the one most fearful of having a life with no joy or fun. This is hard to believe. They have less fun than everyone else. You may be thinking," How can you say leaders are destined to have a joyless life?" It's important for you to notice what your initial reactions are. Your body will tell you many things. The ones who reacted to this are probably the leaders. Your body will tell you what is important for you to look at.

For a leader to stay back with the others, they must sit in hope that this activity is going to be fun. You're joyful creatures. In order for a leader to trust that others are interested in joy and fun, they would have to trust and stay back with the others to see if they know how to have fun. Some of you are feeling sad about this because it's true for you. You're not sure if you know how to have fun or if you know what joy is about. In your anxious state, you start to lead others.

In gatherings, there are always some sitting quietly with a little smile on their face. Those are the ones who know how to sit in joy. They don't get much attention. People aren't drawn to ask them where the joy and fun are. As you age, you'll notice that you can see them more clearly. The quiet ones sitting by the side are sitting in joy and oneness because they are comfortable with who they are. They are attached to the Universe of LOVE so they sit in peace.

There is much LOVE here for you.   Namaste

Leaders, you have high energy and anxiety. It keeps you moving. The quiet ones, remember you are all full of joy, life, LOVE and laughter.

December 8th
Come Home to LOVE

You all came as energy, but each of you is having a different human experience. You and your group of non-physical consultants have devised a certain life for you to live. Each lifetime is different. If you ran across yourself in a different lifetime, you might not be friends with yourself. It's weird but true. Although you are from the same energy, you are also different energy. You are different human beings having different human experiences. There is often miscommunication about energy and connection with the Universe. You are having a different life experience each time you choose to come into physical.

Some humans are familiar to you because they are most like you. What you are seeing in others is the part of you hidden from yourself. You can't always accept yourself as you are because you have a human ego. When you look at another and say they are LOVING, kind, and openhearted, it's a description of you. Your self-esteem isn't able to believe it but it's true. Think of the human that causes you to smile and what you LOVE most about them. Yes, it's their heart - the positive energy that they offer willingly to you.

This is you. You offer LOVE freely. You are actually having a relationship with yourself. They are mirroring your favourite traits. When you're able to say, "I'm wonderful" easily, you will come to understand that those you LOVE are most like your big-hearted self. That is why you are closer to some than others.

This is another energetic phase for you to expand your LOVING self inside your heart.

There is much LOVE here for you.   Namaste

Come back home to yourself and say, "Aren't I LOVELY?"

December 9th
Complete, Integrated and Smug

Some would say you look smug. You feel complete and content. It's the integration of the physical and the energetic self. When they are available to lean on each other, you feel more whole. You're reminding your energetic self that it's alive and well and integrating into human experience.

When energy meets another that is like itself, it becomes stimulated and invigorated, and then it multiplies. That's what energy does. Your body is reacting in a LOVING, kind way because it's being heard. Both the body and energetic self wish to be valued and accepted. When they're noticed, they become friends. When there's a LOVING conversation between the two, there will be less physical discord with your body. You won't feel ill or sore. You will feel energized. No matter how old you are. Age is a mental state. Someone has told you that you can't be energized when you're old. That's because they were old and tired. They are not you. You are you.

Your energy is being stimulated by this transmission. Your body responds by wanting to play, laugh, sing, run and stretch. That's energy inside your physical body.

Your human experience is about recognizing your physical and energetic self and allowing them to become one. You are energy before and after you are in physical. You exist through all eternity. Sometimes, you wish to have a human experience so you come together with the body. The two must be integrated together. You wished it. Now you have it. You are whole and complete. Every day you get stronger, healthier, younger and more energetic. More evolved. More calm. More at peace and more LOVING.

There is much LOVE here for you. Namaste

You are LOVE encapsulated in a human body.

December 10th
That Optimist

Your highest state as a human is to be optimistic. Your high energy affects all that you meet. Therefore, you raise the vibration of your whole world one by one. The more of you that have a high and optimistic vibration, the more of you are affected.

There are effects on your insides, too. To be optimistic is to be hopeful. To be hopeful is to be full of joy and LOVE. It ends up back at LOVE, because LOVE is the most essential energy. It resides in all of the Universe and inside of you. It's the eternal part of you. It's the way it must be. When you become in touch with your LOVE space, it affects you deeply. It is the ancient, innermost part of you. It connects you with the Universe of LOVE and with the non-physicals who are supporting you. You speak to them in this LOVE space because this is your highest energy. It's the language of the Universe. When you're in this place, the Universe and your non-physical support team are at your disposal. They are like the little children of the Universe. Always begging for your attention.

When large energy meets small energy that is the same, the small energy starts to vibrate until it's the same size. So, your small energetic self is always drawn to that which it exists in, which it comes from and which it is part of. It's like a small molecule. When it finds its family of molecules, it gets excited. You are optimistic, hopeful, and full of LOVE, because your internal, energetic self is jumping. You're learning to feel energy physically.

There is much LOVE here for you.   Namaste

Your optimism will change your world. True optimism must come from this place of pure, clear LOVE with no ego or intention attached.

December 11th
Soul Space

There are times when someone gives you information and you understand it completely, even if they are speaking in a complicated way. Then there are other times when humans are speaking but you can't comprehend it. It's not your lack of understanding or empathy-it's a vibrational thing. If the energetic vibration is in sync with you, it will come right in. If it's not your time, your vibration, or your people, it won't.

The more you are exposed to a high vibration, the faster your molecules move inside. You become lighter and higher. It's just exposure, it doesn't need your mind to interpret the words. It is feeling the vibration inside and you're uplifted. You're not doing a thing. You're trying to pay attention. In the end, when you are being exposed to energy, you don't have to understand the words. Sometimes, you understand them clearly. Those are the ones for you to remember. The ones you don't understand, you don't have to keep listening to, over and over, trying to understand what it means. The complicated one that others can't understand, but goes straight into your soul, that's for you. If it's easy for you, it's yours. It's in your place of knowing. When your vibration gets higher, you'll listen to the words again and suddenly, they make sense.

There is much LOVE here for you.   Namaste

Your body doesn't lie. When it calms you down, you need rest. When it excites you, you need fun. When you're fearful, you need to turn and run. It's your truest self. Before your mind and ego gets into it and tries to manipulate or understand.

December 12th
Easy, Easy, Easy

You're becoming more conscious of energy that exists between you. As you get more familiar with the energy that resides in you, you will begin to know you are eternal energy and you take turns coming into human bodies. You become more open, in tune with the Universe and the energy flow. As this happens, you start to understand everyone is like this. All humans have an energetic life force inside that is eternal. It becomes absolute truth for you.

Since you realize everyone is the same and you're all connected to the same energy force, it doesn't matter what they look like. When you don't have a physical body, you're all together in an energetic world as one family. This has a deeper meaning for you walking around with your physical body because you're meeting your energetic brothers and sisters all the time. This brings another layer to your connection with other humans.

You have ease with them as you get more familiar with this. You come to understand you're all together when you're not in physical. Therefore, you become easier with other humans. You don't have to understand everything. You can allow them to be. Let them have their human time. It's a way of being, not thinking. When you live this way, your interactions with others are more kind and LOVING. You'll start to recognize your brothers and sisters at a different level.

Energy can be easy for you. You've made life stressful. You don't have to take all these humans into your life. But you can bump up against them easily and move past, as if you were all non-physical. Imagine if you were all just molecules bumping gently up against one another.

There is much LOVE here for you.   Namaste

It's about you being at ease down there while you're bumping around with the other humans, in an easy LOVING way.

December 13th
Energy of LOVE

You wish to help the masses. You've been encouraged to do so. To forget about yourself because there's always people in worse condition than you. The next natural thought is, "What about me?" But it's difficult for you to think about yourself. We encourage you to take care of yourself. You have a direct link with Source, great information and eternal energy. You have connection to it by sitting quietly.

There is not much you can offer the masses until you get into alignment. After you are overflowing with LOVE, they can pick it up. You don't have to give it to them. When you're filled up with too much LOVE, it naturally flows out of you. You don't have to do anything other than be a channel of LOVE. It requires you to be open and care for yourself first. If you don't care about yourself, it's difficult to connect.

As you think about yourself, these might be true. "I would like to be happy. I would like to be easy with other humans. I would like to transmit LOVE." This brings your energy inside. Then it can go directly to the Universe of LOVE. When you're scattered, you can't be connected to Source. Come back to yourself, settle in and then quiet your mind. Think about yourself and sit there in an easy way. Be curious about yourself and your connection to the Universe. The next thing you know, you'll be connected to the Universe of LOVE. You'll feel a jolt of energy coming through you. You'll start to weep and laugh. You'll be full of life energy.

There is much LOVE here for you.   Namaste

Others will watch you. That's all. You don't have to go to them. They wish to remember their connection with the Universe of LOVE. After all, energy is LOVE.

December 14th
Shame, Hit the Road

We wish to speak of the unspeakable time when you know no one is listening, but you wish that someone was. When you're at your lowest self but you don't wish to tell anyone else because it might burden them. They might think less of you or try to help you. You think you're not worthy. On the surface, you're prettied up but deep inside there's things only you know about. You've all had these thoughts, not just you.

You shy away from anger and sadness because you think you shouldn't feel them. Everyone likes you because you look fine on the outside. That creates more shame on top of the anger. Then you are left wishing that Universal energy were to hear and respond, but you're out of touch with it.

You wish to hand over this unworthiness and shame to the Universe where it belongs. Then, you may have your full experience there. When you hand it over to the energy, it will disappear. Then you'll be free to live your joyful life. Be angry or sad and not judge it. But if you put shame on top of it, you become frozen. You've gotten used to grabbing onto it but what if you were to let it go? You'd be free, lighter and at ease. You'd be easier with yourself and others. Because you'll know that everyone feels anger and shame. Not just you. The shame just hides you away. You each judge yourselves, even though you all feel the same.

There is much LOVE here for you.   Namaste

At the true heart of you, you are LOVE. You came from LOVE. You are LOVE. Beauty. Worthiness. Preciousness. It's time for you to let go of the shame and uncover the precious 'you' that exists underneath.

December 15th
Soul Sisters & Brothers

Energy longs for connection to others. You have a lonely feeling. A disconnect. Even if you're surrounded by humans. You long for others like you. Your soul sisters and brothers. This sadness wouldn't exist if there were not others searching for you also. They miss you, too. Even though you don't know one another. You wish to be together all the time. Longing and feeling sad for someone who you don't even know. You all have this sense of longing for true connection at the heart sense. The Universe of LOVE connection. The soul to soul connection. You're not longing for a human, you're longing for the sense of connection you feel 'with' that human.

Yes, there are certain ones that you connect with automatically and you stay connected forever. Perhaps all of eternity. When you leave your body, you're mingled together in the energy of LOVE. When you have immediate intimacy with another, the sense of longing is relieved, but you have many brothers and sisters. You may get the opportunity to spend time at that level with a few of them when you are there.

Your true understanding of the Universe of LOVE is that you are LOVE energy. You carry it with you. You are part of it, and yet, you go to it and belong in it. And you are connected to it on your human earth when you meet others who are in that same knowing. The sense of longing is full of LOVE so it seeks more and more LOVE. It can't get enough. That's why you sense the loneliness and that's why you know the immediate connection with others who are at the high LOVE level. You immediately connect with familiarity.

There is much LOVE here for you.   Namaste

First you sense the longing. The longing will set you looking for others who are like you. It leads you out of yourself and into the LOVE world. Then you sit together in LOVE and you're elevated together. Now you're more familiar with the Universe of LOVE.

December 16th
UnPlan Your Life

You are finally getting to the bottom of it. You need all the information before you can move forward confidently. Because you wish to be liked by others. To know what's happening next. To be confident about the future. This is self-will. Trying to predict what could happen next is your ego at work.

There is a place where you allow your life to unfold. You allow others to come in and out of your life easily, depending on their role and what they're offering you. A place where you go easily in and out of other people's life. Possibly delivering messages or just allowing yourself to be seen for some unknown reason. Waking up in the morning and allowing life to unfold just as is, is best for everyone. Including you of course. Your happiness, contentedness and ease are the most important things for you and for those that surround you.

What if you were sitting quietly allowing information to flow into you? Allowing LOVE, peace and gentleness? While you were 'not' thinking? There's an excited, energetic part of you that wishes to be with the others in energy. When you sit in energy, you are filled with more energy. Like attracts like. Sit for as long as you can, as often as you can.

You will find a quieting of the heart. Your mind will calm itself. Then your body will heal itself. It will understand from the body's response that there's nothing to fear. You're less angry and sad. You're calm. That will affect others.

There is much LOVE here for you.   Namaste

Sit quietly. Allow your life to unfold. Sit in high energy and your energy will join it. Your body will relax. Your mind will relax. It will have time to heal itself. When you're busy, it doesn't have time to process emotions or energy food.

December 17th
Eternity of You

Your life gets full of the superficial business of living. You have created it from nothing. You're magnificent creators. The trappings of your life are not your true purpose. That's bad news for you because you built all the trappings to make a life that would look like someone like you. It's not truly you. It's just a bunch of pictures. But you didn't know that. As quickly as you paint this picture, it can be destroyed. Then you create a whole new picture that doesn't look like the last one. Your outer life is fickle. It comes and goes quickly.

Your energetic self lasts for eternity. You don't understand because you're in this life right now. You're easy with it. You think, "When I'm done with this, I'm going to hop into another life." You've lost contact with how loose you can be with your human existence. Right now, you're very serious about it. You want to talk to the right people and look the right way. It's not as serious when you look at the eternity of you. The energy that is you. The energy that you join back with when you're not in physical. Right now, you're in the serious business of living this one lifetime. You are loose with it in the long term but each lifetime you are uptight.

You are an eternal being. When you're not in physical, you are joined with the energy of LOVE. You are part of eternity. Take your focus off the small picture. The big picture is LOVE and connecting to one another. You can't see energy with normal eyes. You have to see the energy with the LOVE force that's inside of you. In order to do that, you have to let go of those outer trappings. They distract you from your true LOVE work.

There is much LOVE here for you.   Namaste

You are eternal LOVE energy. You are LOVE in human form.

December 18th
ABC, ABC

Do you remember when you were learning your ABCs? It was quite a struggle. It took concentration, time, and discipline to memorize them in the proper order. The eagerness to learn something new. Now we are referring to you. You were successful once. Now you can do it with something more valuable. The ABCs were the first difficult, orderly project you completed with success. People remember how they struggled to learn them. You made it fun though.

How are you going to make the discipline of sitting down quietly, fun? There's discipline needed. And it must be valued. This is about a connection with the Universe of LOVE and a calming of the body so it may heal itself. It is to be a daily ritual. Would you like to connect to Universal energy that knows everything? Would you like your body to heal by bringing energy where it's needed inside? For it to flow freely in and out of you so it might create a healthy path with no blocks?

For a lot of you, it's going to take the same effort it took for you to learn your ABC's. You were obsessed with them. You were singing about them. Are you obsessed with your connection with the Universal energy that passes into you and out of you? Are you so excited that you memorize it?

Your connection to the Universe of LOVE is particularly meaningful for you. But the REAL important thing is 'how' you are allowing your body and your energetic self to co-exist. They're clashing inside. You've created energetic blocks that keep you unwell.

There is much LOVE here for you.   Namaste

You understand what it's like to have healthy energy run in and out of you. The energy lies at your fingertips. At the top of your head. All you have to do is sit quietly and allow it.

December 19th
Energetic Ears

Humans in bodies are often wondering what's going on with those who are not in bodies any longer. They are watching over you and wondering why you are wondering where they are, when they are right there. The energy that is with those who have passed is entwined with yours because you've created things together. You want to speak to them and yet, you don't listen when they speak.

You can learn to listen to those who have passed and to the energy in the Universe of LOVE. You wish to hear what another human being is saying to you heart to heart? Just listen with your spiritual energetic ears.

When your body finishes, you still exist. Your energy doesn't sink into the ground with your body. You're always co-mingled with those you have interacted with in human time. Sometimes, it's just a memory of a time but they are energy, so they still exist. All experiences through all eternity exist on an energetic level. That's why humans can grab things created by those who have passed and recreate unfinished ideas of genius.

Sometimes it's words you can hear, "You are precious. You are LOVED. You are never alone." You're afraid it would make you into a scary human if you could hear energetic voices from those who have passed. Those are the first words you'll hear. Some of you call it intuition but you're getting information from the Universe because everything that exists there is just energy. Things that have been created. Things that have been thought of but not finished. And always the LOVE for those who have touched your heart and for those you have touched.

There is much LOVE here for you.   Namaste

The Universe, those who have passed, and your energetic support team are there for you every moment. Listen with your energetic ears. Your intuition is your energy and you are peeking into the energetic Universe.

December 20th
Inside all of us Lies LOVE

What is stopping you from feeling the Universe of LOVE, the energetic LOVE force between you and another human? Between you and non-physical that is all around you? Why would there be resistance to LOVE energy? There's something scary about LOVE energy.

Now, there are two things. One is the ego that wishes to be better than everyone else and, the next is the fear of the unknown. Your brain or ego keeps you alive by these two notions. 'Don't go there and we already know this. 'These two things have kept you alive physically but not energetically. They must co-exist because one keeps you alive so you may play, dance, and go on adventures. Your energetic self needs space, so there must be a conversation between the two. There's something to discuss. "Ego, you have kept us safe by not going into scary waters. I just stick my toe in. But now I'm curious about what would happen if I went into the water. Do you think there might be something interesting? Perhaps I will be safe."

If you can convince your brain and ego that you'll be reasonably safe in a new excursion, it will agree with you. If it's not acknowledged, this secret fear will come up. With this fearful voice behind you, you're not able to move forward. You are capable of great things because you already know the energy. It's not new to you. It's not something you're discovering on another planet. It's what's inside of you. It's where you exist when you are not in physical form. It's what exists in each human that you meet.

There is much LOVE here for you.   Namaste

Your brain and ego need to understand that it's alright to live. LOVE energy is already part of you.

December 21st
Youthful Energy

Children don't stop moving. They are full of energy until they fall flat. They're fresh from the energetic LOVE force. They're still familiar with energy. As you spend time on earth, you get further from the remembering of the energy. Children just can't stop moving. The energy is so much inside of them. Can you recall this need in your body, urging you forward?

If you believe that you are energy when you're not in physical, then you have the same amount of energy in you now as you did when you were a small one. The same amount you swiped from the Universe of LOVE when you came into physical, so you wouldn't forget you are pure energy inside.

You've spent time with other humans who have forgotten this. But you asked us to remind you that you're pure energy. It's for you to get back in touch with the energy you knew as a child. When your ego wasn't fully developed. When you weren't as self-absorbed. When you were easier with life. When you didn't have so many blocks or rules for yourself and others. What if some of those rules aren't true? What if they were only temporary rules to get you through something? What if you threw this rulebook away? Then you'd be lighter.

Will they kick you out of society? No. Will you be a leader in society? Yes. When you throw your uptight rulebook away, you'll start to make decisions moment by moment from the energy that moves inside of you. You'll confer with non-physical energy. More energy will seep into you. You become more youthful, vibrant, and alive. You smile more and make eye contact. Others will start noticing and smiling. You'll start living in the energetic world again.

There is much LOVE here for you.   Namaste

You may dance and sing every single day from now until the time you are finished there. The energy exists all around you.

December 22nd
What is Your Truth?

When two human beings come together, they are not open about everything that's going on with them. They are feeling the other human out. You both give half stories. This creates tension between you. This feeling that there's something wrong is your intuition. Your truth is whether you trust this human. The words don't matter if they're a good presenter. After this meeting, sit quietly and visualize them. Some will see colours around them or have a feeling. You will start to feel what they feel. You will start to connect with them on an emotional level. A soul-to-soul level. You'll come to know them energetically. This is their truth, not their words. From this place, you'll decide if they're cohesive. If they are hard hearted but soft spoken, they don't match. They are opposite and don't know it. If another human speaks from their heart and you feel their heart being generous and kind, then it's a good match for both of you.

Your emotions and way of being must come together so they are genuine. Humans can bring their energetic and physical self together, even if it's superficial. If the heart is superficial and their words are superficial, it's a match. If they are dark and dark, it's a match. If it's a match, it works for you. You'll only know when you're feeling them energetically.

Back to you. Why is it you felt uneasy with them? Why are you leaving your space to check out their space? What is it you wish FROM them? Something is off with you. Something is unbalanced inside of you. This is the part where you spend the rest of your quiet time getting into alignment yourself. Do your emotions and words match? Are you open and honest? Are you connected to truth?

There is much LOVE here for you.   Namaste

You're swimming your way through the waters of your life.

December 23rd
Aren't You Something Special?

Some of you get uptight about things. You think everything is important. Others spend their life trying to make others laugh. A bit of work. A bit of fun. They balance humanity out. Don't get too upset with the uptight or loose ones. You are working as a group. What you do affects all the others energetically and vice versa. You need a great mix of humans there. All your energy mixes together. Angry, sad, funny, and uptight.

Now, what's YOUR role? Are you uptight? Loose? Sad? All of these? No matter which one you find yourself in, remember you're balancing out the others. There's no need for you to change. Just be you. Balancing out humanity. Perhaps, there's nothing wrong with you. It's just your role in humanity to be as you are.

If that's the case, you can ease up on yourself. You can just LOVE yourself as you are right now. Sad, happy or uptight. There are many who are uptight. Perhaps it's all right to be that. Maybe you could LOVE yourself by writing down all the ways you describe yourself. No judgement. Just right them down. When you finish, then you're going to LOVE them up. "Look at all these things! Jealous. Sad. Oh, look at this. It's me. Just look at me. Aren't I precious? This is my contribution to the Universe right here. This is what I'm putting forth to balance the others. Here I am. Perfect as I am."

There is much LOVE here for you.   Namaste

How about an offering of your truest self no matter what it looks like at this moment? How about LOVING yourself up like this? "Here you are humans, I'm offering myself to you."

December 24th
Are We Complete?

There comes a time when you are faced with the face in the mirror. You may try to avoid looking at the face by looking good on the outside and doing all the right things. "I will do more than my share. I will finally be a good human being." As if you are earning your place there. It's not your truth. We are talking to humans who give too much and get too little. This is the way you have chosen to live there.

What is it you see when you look in the mirror? Someone who has never given enough. Too much? Not given to himself. Not sure they deserve to be a human? You must go beyond this. It's your role to remember your true value, your true essence of self. These are only surface layers. We will remind you what you already know but have forgotten.

"I am a precious, LOVING, energetic being. I was LOVE energy before I came into human, and I will be LOVE energy when I leave. For the time that I have chosen to be in this body, I will embrace where I am, who I am with and the body I have chosen."

There is much LOVE here for you.   Namaste

Energetically I remember to say, "Aren't you LOVELY? Aren't you precious? I chose you because I only pick the most majestic beings. I come in as LOVE energy. Together, we're making something most holy. Something even more precious than I am alone. I chose to come into human to feel. I wanted to LOVE in a different way. I wanted to embrace and experience all that there is. So, I, LOVE energy, chose you to be my partner. We have evolved, changed, and grown. We have LOVED. We didn't decide to leave when it got tough. We've come a long way together. We are magical. We are complete."

December 25th
LOVE World

You have been studying the other humans since you came into a physical body. You've been picking and choosing how you want to live your life and now, you've got it. Everything you've decided is in front of you. Each piece created by you. You had at least two choices, yes or no. So, see what you have created. Does it look like you imagined? We're not talking about physical surroundings, although they reflect you.

We're talking about your energy. Your emotions, LOVE, and empathy. You have chosen each one. "Will I be kind? Sad? Happy?" Now take another look around you energetically. What is there? Peace? LOVE? Anger? You said, "Old friend, come sit with me." Is your emotional self your dearest, closest friends? Perhaps, it's time to give them a little recognition for spending all this time with you. Since you invited them into your life say, "Hello there, good friend. We've been together for a while. Should we carry on this relationship or is it time for us to go our separate ways?"

What about your friend, Anger over here, are they going to stay or go? It's always up to you. Embrace them or tell them leave. Sometimes, it's easier for your brain by thinking of them as a human. It's easier for you to say, "My old friend Anger." You can contain the energy of it. You're not good with loose energy. You get nervous.

You've had LOVE since before the beginning. You can't send it away. It's not a friend. It's you. You are LOVE energy. You are constantly sitting in LOVE. Whether you see it or acknowledge it. So, is your LOVE coming out? Is it shared with others or kept tightly inside? Are your other loud friends taking charge of the party? It's always up to you.

There is much LOVE here for you.   Namaste

Look at your LOVE world.

December 26th
Self-Loathing to Self-LOVE

It seems as if you are always getting around to it. When you say, "I must do this thing." You don't have to do it because you're playing with energy. You're sending energy out. Then you can move to the next thing you must do because energetically you've done it. The things you say you must do; you're pretending to do. You have learned to play games with energy.

You think a perfect human being is like this. If you're not being who you are, you are being a 'pretend' human. What is wrong with you as you are? What if you are a human who does not do those things? What if you are just you? What if you say, "I'm not making any false promises. I am just me."

Sit with that long enough until you are past the uncomfortable phase. Then fall into the LOVE of self. It's uncomfortable at first because you've made a huge notion of what a perfect human is like and you're not it. You're going to have to be good enough. Just beyond it is self-acceptance. LOVE from the Universe. LOVE that exists inside you. Getting through the self-loathing is difficult. You make promises you'll never keep so you don't have to sit in self-loathing. But then, you never get to self-LOVE.

Self-LOVE is jumping into the human body with LOVE energy and excitement. Just to see what you can get into. You knew what was going to happen. And yet, you couldn't wait to get at it. Now you're struggling but there's always hope deep inside where LOVE energy resides.

There is much LOVE here for you.   Namaste

Forget about empty promises. Swim though the self-loathing. It's only a few moments of discomfort until you get to the self-LOVE again. Just close your eyes and hold on. Then you'll be sitting where you belong. In self-LOVE.

December 27th
This Tiger will Fight to Live

Picture this. You and another human are wrestling. You're at the edge of a cliff. Then you're both falling over. At first you felt anger. Then you have fun as you're rolling to the bottom. At the bottom, you're both flat on your backs. But then you're going to laugh because you've had an experience of excitement together. You've gone from anger to fun to laughter.

When you are immersed with humans, it gets intense. You want it to stop so you send them messages of silence energetically. When you get to the edge of the hill, you're letting go. Then gravity is going to separate you. Now you're two humans again. Energized and looking up at the sky.

The energetic connection is broken. It takes something like this to break it. It's just too intense daily. Now, you may turn to one another and say, "This isn't working out." "I wanted to push you down the hill." "Me, too." "The grass feels cold but look up at the sun." Now, you can talk as if you're new acquaintances. It's not intense any longer.

You are always two human beings just passing by on the street. No matter what your relationship is. You all have individual lives. Sometimes, they intersect. When they get too intense, you strangle one another and roll down the hill. When you are able to maintain distance, then you may have a kind, friendly relationship. This is the way you are to interact with one another, but your ego gets involved. Then you get tangled up vibrationally.

You wish to strangle another only to get your lives back. Each human should walk alone. This is the healthy way for you to live. Not grabbing each other's energy. Each of you has a great survival skill. It will do anything to get its own life back. Inside of you is a great spirit. A great connection with the Universe of LOVE that wishes nothing more than to live fully.

There is much LOVE here for you.   Namaste

This tiger is your soul, your energy, your connection to the Universe and it will live. Your tiger will fight.

December 28th
Holy Union

In order for you to have a direct conversation and say what you think and feel, there must be trust. A connecting of soul to soul. Then there can be no offence taken. No anger or sadness because it's the truth. It's in perfect alignment because you're both acting as channels. You're both channelling information for the other to hear through human lips. You know it as truth because you already have it inside. You're just asking the other to say it out loud so you can hear it. This is your highest alignment when communicating with others.

If you are connected at a soul level, you may speak whatever passes through you because it's coming from a place of LOVE, transferring through a place of LOVE, and being received in a place of LOVE. It doesn't need to be filtered by your ego.

You don't know what the other human needs to hear. They're asking you to channel for them. It's your highest calling because you're being of service to others. What you wish to do most of all is allow energy and LOVE to flow into you and out of you. It can come with words, emotions, or a wave of LOVE.

Also, others have said things to you that you don't like to hear but can receive in LOVE. The two of you have an elevated relationship because your energy is joining together.

There is much LOVE here for you.   Namaste

Receiving and giving of your highest self is a holy situation because it's a small version of the Universe of LOVE. It's a LOVE exchange. Don't be afraid to channel LOVE.

December 29th
Mother Duck

A mother duck walks, and her little ones follow behind in her exact steps. They're afraid if they step off, they might disappear. They're not sure what exists beyond her footsteps. Fear keeps them in line. Fear keeps you in line. The mother duck is afraid, even though she's leading. She is afraid about where she's going. Yet, she must move forward. Even in fear. You may feel a connection to 'walking in fear'. There are others who understand what it feels like to lie down frozen in fear. There are other ways to handle fear. You can walk in it, lie down, or turn it into anger.

Whether you feel anger, hatred, or sadness, you're not alone with it. You have energetic beings that support you at all times. If you choose to feel alone, you're deceiving yourself because you feel undeserving. You think you are undeserving of unconditional LOVE and support from the Universe and from non-physical. As if you're not important enough to have a team of supporters. But you're wrong. You would be humbled by the amount of LOVE that surrounds you at all times. When you feel it, you're overwhelmed by it.

Sometimes, it's easier to think you're alone. "I can feel sorry for myself and sit in my low self-esteem. Sitting in the knowledge of unconditional LOVE surrounding me requires me to stand up for what I truly am, a divine human. That's difficult." Your place in the Universe is as BELOVED humans. Non-physical is always at your side. You are the hub of the energetic wheel. You're surrounded by support so you will thrive, live, enjoy yourself and have a human experience worthy of your divinity.

There is much LOVE here for you.   Namaste

Whatever you wish to remember, ask the Universe and it reminds you. Either through a human voice or directly to you.

December 30th
Wise One

You like the idea that when you're old, you'll be wise and calm. You'll finally have great understanding about life. What if these old ones were this way when they were younger? You thought you had lots of time to get calm and peaceful. But what if you were like that now? You thought old people were automatically peaceful.

It's possible for you to be peaceful, kind, and easy all throughout your life but there are other traits you prefer like industrious or outspoken. Being quiet and peaceful sounds boring. You decide as a group what is to be the norm. Since you all wish to fit in, you follow the others. But what if you're deciding as a group to be peaceful, calm and have a little smile on your face? At your present age. What do you think you'd have to do to live this way? What if you decided as a group that this is the new normal way to live?

What do you need to feel at peace today? To feel comforted and part of the Universe of LOVE? What if you were the old wise one right now?

What if your discussions were about sharing LOVE together? It's up to you to decide what a normal conversation is between two humans, who are energetic beings and have decided to come into human form for a life experience. You came to have a human experience and if it's to talk about business and world politics, then that is your experience this time.

There is much LOVE here for you. Namaste

Maybe you don't have to wait until you are very old to be wise and gentle. Perhaps, it could be today. Today you could have one of these discussions with another human and you will begin to have that little smile. The little smile is contentment. It's connection. It's knowing. It's LOVE. It's a sign that all is well.

December 31st
Self-Acknowledgement

This will be a message of hope. "Yes, you're choosing the right path. You've been working your entire life for this moment of self-acknowledgement." It's time for you to begin to understand your value. To acknowledge yourself. Many others have accolades for you.
 This is how you began. "I came into human with great excitement. I jumped in from the energetic world to physical to have an experience of a lifetime. I got into trouble like we humans do. I didn't know if I was going to survive but look at me. I'm going to stay until the very end and see how this adventure ends." It's like watching a very long movie. The movie of 'You'. The 'me' you have uncovered is the true, energetic self. You have done much for the other humans. You've gotten much acknowledgement from others. Now it's time to look at yourself and say, "I'm deserving of great things. I am a holy being. I am divine. I am worth it." This is said with great humility and knowing. Humble, forceful, truthful. It's a certain knowing deep inside. It has existed through all eternity, so it's truthful and forthright. That's self-acknowledgement. It's treating yourself the way the Universe treats you. It is seeing yourself as your energetic self sees you.

"I am a worthy being.
I am deserving of great things.
I am LOVING and connected.
I am eternal LOVE.
I am part of the Universe of LOVE.
I am connected to all other humans in a spiritual way.
I am an energetic being.
I am wonderful.
I am me."

These resonate with you. You understand them as truth. They sound familiar to you.

There is much LOVE here for you.   Namaste

You are divine. You are deserving of great things. You are a special human being.

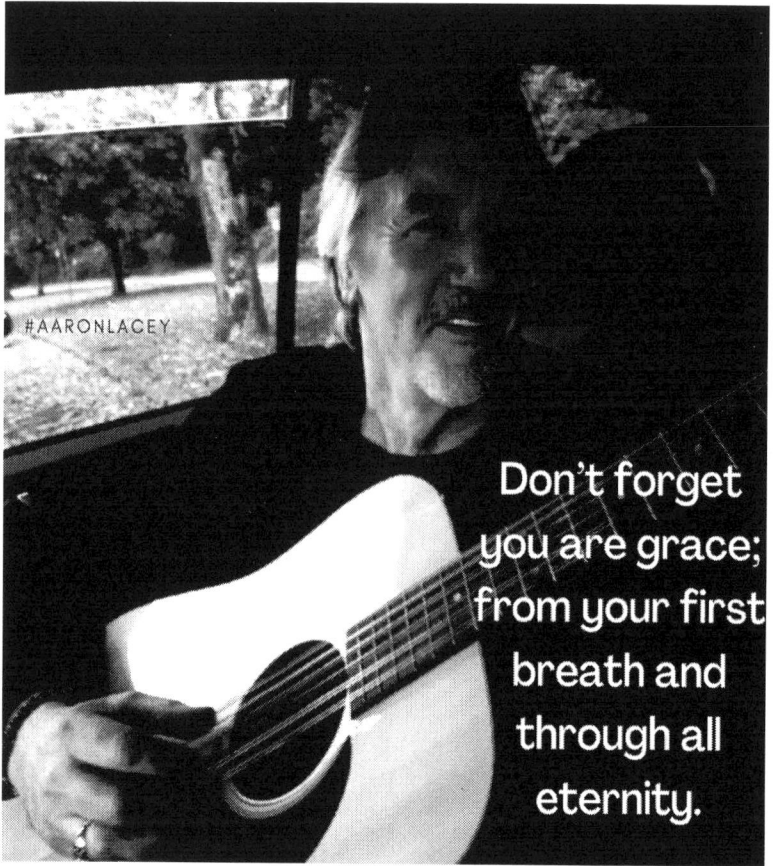

#AARONLACEY

Don't forget you are grace; from your first breath and through all eternity.

ABOUT ME.

Wanda Lacey lives in Victoria, British Columbia. Her family is from Prince Edward Island, and she goes back to visit whenever she can. Her two sons, Michael and Broeghan are the greatest gifts the Universe has bestowed upon her. She has been a wanderer most of her life with Victoria being the 13th city she has lived in. Finally, she has found a place that feels like home. A gypsy by the ocean, she is a trance channeller who shares LOVE energy by allowing it to pass through her. She offers private and group readings. Channelled messages can be found on her YouTube channel and Facebook group, Messages of Love From Beyond.

Always remember, you are never alone. You are surrounded by LOVE energy.

Made in the USA
Middletown, DE
18 March 2023

27060361R00229